CIVILITY

BOSTON UNIVERSITY STUDIES IN PHILOSOPHY AND RELIGION

General Editor: Leroy S. Rouner

Volume Twenty-One

Civility

Edited by
Leroy S. Rouner

UNIVERSITY OF NOTRE DAME PRESS
Notre Dame, Indiana

"Making Peace" by Denise Levertov from *Breathing the Water.*
Copyright © 1987 by Denise Levertov.
Reprinted by permission of New Directions Publishing Corp.

Library of Congress Cataloging-in-Publication Data

Civility / edited by Leroy S. Rouner.
    p.   cm. — (Boston University studies in philosophy and
religion ; vol. 21)
    Includes bibliographical references and index.
    ISBN 0-268-02250-0 (cloth : alk. paper)
    ISBN 0-268-02256-9 (paper : alk. paper)
    1. Civil society.   2. Courtesy.   I. Rouner, Leroy S.   II. Series.
JC377.C58   2000
177'.1—dc21   99-059811
                                                                    CIP

∞ *The paper used in this publication meets the minimum requirements*
of the American National Standard for Information Sciences—Permanence of Paper
for Printed Library Materials, ANSI Z39.48-1984

Manufactured in the United States of America

FOR WENDY DONIGER

Worthy successor to the great Mircea Eliade, she is a student of world cultures in past and present and a lover of their stories. Her work is a model of wide-ranging scholarship and thoughtful interpretation. She has helped us all to a better understanding of the human adventure and the transcendental resources which guide us.

Contents

Contents

PART III: CIVILITY IN VARIOUS CULTURES

Preface

Boston University Studies in Philosophy and Religion is a joint project of the Boston University Institute for Philosophy and Religion and the University of Notre Dame Press. The essays in each annual volume are edited from the previous year's lecture program and invited papers of the Boston University Institute. The Director of the Institute, who is also the General Editor of these Studies, chooses a theme and invites participants to lecture at Boston University in the course of the academic year. The Editor then selects and edits the essays to be included in the volume. Dr. Barbara Darling-Smith, Assistant Director of the Institute, regularly copyedits the essays. In preparation is Volume 22, *If I Should Die*.

The Boston University Institute for Philosophy and Religion was begun informally in 1970 under the leadership of Professor Peter Bertocci of the Department of Philosophy, with the cooperation of Dean Walter Muelder of the School of Theology, Professor James Purvis, Chair of the Department of Religion, and Professor Marx Wartofsky, Chair of the Department of Philosophy. Professor Bertocci was concerned to institutionalize one of the most creative features of Boston personalism, its interdisciplinary approach to fundamental issues of human life. When Professor Leroy S. Rouner became Director in 1975, and the Institute became a formal part of the Boston University Graduate School, every effort was made to continue that vision of an ecumenical and interdisciplinary forum.

Within the University the Institute is committed to open interchange on fundamental issues in philosophy and religious study which transcend the narrow specializations of academic curricula. We seek to counter those trends in higher education which emphasize technical expertise in a "multi-versity" and gradually transform undergraduate liberal arts education into preprofessional training.

Our programs are open to the general public and are often broadcast on WBUR-FM, Boston University's National Public Radio station. Outside the University we seek to recover the public tradition of philosophical discourse which was a lively part of American intellectual life in the early years of this century before the professionalization of both philosophy and religious reflection made these two disciplines virtually unavailable even to an educated public. We note, for example, that much of William James's work was presented originally as public lectures, and we are grateful to James's present-day successors for the significant public papers which we have been honored to publish. This commitment to a public tradition in American intellectual life has important stylistic implications. At a time when too much academic writing is incomprehensible, or irrelevant, or both, our goal is to present readable essays by acknowledged authorities on critical human issues.

Acknowledgments

Jim Langford concluded his long and highly successful tenure as Director of the University of Notre Dame Press at the end of August, 1999, and we take this occasion to salute him for turning a modest press into a publishing house of international distinction. The Institute for Philosophy and Religion at Boston University is proud of its association with the University of Notre Dame Press, and grateful to Jim for his friendship, his shrewd editorial eye, and his willingness to take chances on uncertain ventures.

When I first thought of publishing our annual lecture series I approached several major university presses. They all had elaborate reasons for not taking us on. (My favorite one was the Ivy League editor who insisted that collected essays could make a coherent volume only if they read as though "they came from a single hand." That was not my idea of good editing.) In the meantime Tom McCarthy, then Chair of the Philosophy Department at Boston University, told Jim about us; Alan Olson, then the Institute's Program Director, talked with Jim at a meeting of the American Academy of Religion; and eventually I went out to South Bend to talk with Jim myself. He had his own ideas about what a university press ought to be doing, and he thought a series of this sort could be successful. He was then rebuilding the Press, and this venture went counter to the common wisdom in publishing, so it was a brave gamble. That was twenty-one volumes ago. I have not had the courage to ask whether we have made much money for them, but I know this: for the past twenty years and more, Jim and I have worked together to produce some pretty good books on some very important topics, and that was made possible by his courage in taking us on. For that we are more grateful than we can say.

Barbara Darling-Smith, Assistant Director of the Institute, continues to be the person who makes our program work. During the year she runs the office, greets guests, instructs our work-study students, contacts lecturer/authors, rides herd on the budget, and does other graceful and kindly things which have never made their way into a job description. During the late spring and early summer—in addition to all this—she does manuscript preparation for our annual volume. This is not simply copyediting; it is also gentle nudging of schedule-impaired authors, genial negotiations with our friend Ann Rice at Notre Dame Press about publication dates, and some dark and definitive deliberations which are best kept in-house.

We would not have a book were it not for the generosity of our authors. Those outside Boston University are not adequately paid, and my Boston University colleagues are not paid at all, so there is no good economic reason why this venture should work. But the old liberal argument that everything finally comes down to economics is given the lie by these gracious participants in a venture which holds little reward except the satisfaction of knowing that they have made a careful public statement on an important issue about which they cared deeply. So once again we have occasion to thank them for their generosity and their fine work.

Contributors

LAWRENCE CAHOONE is Associate Professor of Philosophy at Boston University and a frequent contributor to these volumes. He did his first degree at Clark University in psychology and philosophy, and his Ph.D. at the State University of New York at Stony Brook. He is a member of Phi Beta Kappa, has won the Boston University Undergraduate Philosophy Association Excellence in Teaching Award on several occasions, as well as the Kayden National University Press Award for his first book, *The Dilemmas of Modernity* (1988). He has since written *The Ends of Philosophy* (1995) and edited *Modernism to Postmodernism: An Anthology* (1996).

DANIEL O. DAHLSTROM did his Ph.D. at St. Louis University. He has had numerous awards for study in Tübingen and Cologne, Germany, and taught at the University of Santa Clara, the Katholieke Universiteit Leuven, Belgium, and the Catholic University of America, before coming to Boston University in 1996 as Professor of Philosophy. He is the author of some sixty-five papers in both German and English, thirty book reviews, several translations, and *Das logische Vorurteil: Untersuchungenn zur Wahrheitstheorie des fruhen Heidegger* (1994).

EDWIN J. DELATTRE is Professor of Education, Professor of Philosophy, and Dean of the School of Education at Boston University. He was Professor of Philosophy at the University of Toledo from 1968 to 1976, director of the National Humanities Faculty from 1976 to 1980, and President of St. John's College in Annapolis and Santa Fe from 1980 to 1986. He is the author of two books—*Education and the Public Trust* (1988) and *Character and Cops: Ethics in Policing* (1982)—and numerous articles. He is also an adjunct scholar of the American Enterprise Institute for Public Policy Research.

CARRIE DOEHRING is Assistant Professor of Pastoral Psychology at Boston University. She is also a licensed psychologist and supervisor at Boston University's Danielsen Institute. She has been a Presbyterian minister for twenty-one years, serving fifteen of those years in parish ministry. She is the author of *Internal Desecration: Traumatization and Representations of God* (1993) and *Taking Care: Monitoring Power Dynamics and Relational Boundaries in Pastoral Care and Counseling* (1995). Her areas of research interest are feminist pastoral theology and problems of social identity and oppression.

ADAM McCLELLAN graduated from Macalester College in St. Paul, Minnesota, in 1993. He wrote his senior thesis on the place of honesty in the rhetoric of Vaclav Havel. The thesis earned him a B.A. degree, *cum laude*, in Communication Studies. He then turned to the role of religion in social ethics, and he will receive a master's degree in Theological Studies from the Boston University School of Theology in January 2000. He is the first Institute Seminar student to have his term paper published in our series.

ROBERT B. PIPPIN is the Raymond W. and Martha Hilpert Gruner Distinguished Service Professor in the Committee on Social Thought, the Department of Philosophy, and the College at the University of Chicago. He has won numerous honors, awards, and prizes, and currently serves as Chair of the Committee on Social Thought. He is the author of six books on such varied topics as Kant's theory of form, Marcuse's critical theory, Hegel's idealism, and—most recently—Henry James and the modern moral life.

HENRY ROSEMONT, JR., is George B. and Willma Reeves Distinguished Professor of the Liberal Arts at St. Mary's College of Maryland; Senior Consulting Professor at Fudan University; and Professional Lecturer at the School of Advanced International

Studies of Johns Hopkins University. Professor Rosemont is the author of *A Chinese Mirror* and the forthcoming *A Confucian Alternative*. He has edited and/or translated seven other works, the most recent of which is a translation, *The Analects of Confucius*, with Roger T. Ames.

LEROY S. ROUNER taught at the United Theological College, Bangalore, India (1961–1966), before becoming Professor of Philosophy, Religion, and Philosophical Theology and Director of the Institute for Philosophy and Religion at Boston University. He studied at Harvard College, Union Theological Seminary (New York), and Columbia University. He has edited eighteen volumes in the Boston University Studies in Philosophy and Religion series and contributed to many of them. He has also edited *Philosophy, Religion, and the Coming World Civilization: Essays in Honor of William Ernest Hocking*. He is the author of *Within Human Experience: The Philosophy of William Ernest Hocking; The Long Way Home* (a memoir); and *To Be At Home: Christianity, Civil Religion, and World Community*.

JAMES SCHMIDT earned his Ph.D. in Political Science at the Massachusetts Institute of Technology, and has been Professor of Political Science and Sociology at Boston University since 1996. He is the author of numerous articles and review essays. He has been the Director of National Endowment for the Humanities Summer Seminars for College Teachers on numerous occasions. He is the editor of *What Is Enlightenment? Eighteenth Century Answers and Twentieth Century Questions* (1996) and author of *Maurice Merleau Ponty: Between Phenomenology and Structuralism*, which is soon to be translated into Chinese.

ADAM B. SELIGMAN did his Ph.D. in Sociology and Social Anthropology in 1987 at the Hebrew University of Jerusalem. He was a Visiting Scholar at the New School for Social Research and an Associate Professor at the University of Colorado-Boulder before coming to Boston University in 1996 as Associate Professor in the Department of Religion, and Research Associate at the Institute for the Study of Economic Culture. He has coauthored and edited several books and is the author of *The Idea of Civil Society* (1992), *Interworldly Individualism: Community and Its Institutionalization* (1994), and *The Problem of Trust* (1997).

NINIAN SMART is J. F. Rowny Professor of Comparative Religions, *Emeritus*, at the University of California, Santa Barbara. He has written both technical and popular books in the philosophy of religion, Indian philosophy, the history of religions, methodology, religious dialogue, religious education, and politics. Educated at Oxford, he founded the first major department of religious studies in England at Lancaster University. He was editorial consultant for the thirteen-part television series in Great Britain on the world's religions called *The Long Search*. His many books include *The Long Search*; *Religion and the Western Mind*; *Beyond Ideology*; and *Worldviews*.

VIRGINIA STRAUS graduated from Stanford University, where she did a B.A. in English Literature. She later earned an M.A. in American Studies from the University of London. During the 1970s she served as a public policy specialist in Washington, D.C., where she was Managing Editor of *The Legislative Digest*, a weekly congressional publication. She moved to Boston to serve for seven years as Co-Director of the Pioneer Institute. Since 1993 she has been Executive Director of the Boston Research Center for the 21st Century.

STEPHEN TOULMIN was educated at King's College in Cambridge, where he received the Ph.D. in Moral Sciences. He is now the Henry R. Luce Professor at the University of Southern California. Among his many books are *Knowing and Acting* (1976), *The Return to Cosmology* (1982), and *Human Understanding*. Volume 19 of this series was dedicated to him as a "critic of the modern nation-state, champion of ethical accountability throughout the human community," and one whose lectures in these volumes have "discomfited the mighty and celebrated the power of moral influence."

ALAN WOLFE studied at Temple University, Vanderbilt, and the University of Pennsylvania, where he received his Ph.D. in Political Science. He has taught at Rutgers, the State University of New York, the City University of New York, the New School for Social Research, and Boston University, where, until recently, he has been University Professor and Professor of Sociology and Political Science. He is author of some dozen books, most recently *One Nation after All: What Middle-Class Americans Really Think about God, Country, Family, Racism, Welfare, Immigration, Homosexuality, Work, the Right, the Left, and Each Other* (1998).

DAVID B. WONG has been Chairman of the Department of Philosophy and is currently Harry Austryn Wolfson Professor of Philosophy at Brandeis University. He graduated *summa cum laude* from Macalester College in 1971, with Special Honors in Philosophy, and did his Ph.D. at Princeton in 1977. He is the author of some thirty articles and reviews, and the book *Moral Relativity* (1984). He has an anthology of Chinese and Western ethics which he has co-edited with Kwong-loi Shun, currently under review by Cambridge University Press. He is also working on a study of ethical theory, tentatively titled *Pluralistic Relativism*.

Introduction

LEROY S. ROUNER

GOING TO GRAMMY'S house was always a big event in our family, and we went there a lot. My wife's mother was a wealthy widow who lived in a large stone house which her architect-husband had designed and built on some hundred acres in Westchester County, New York. Grammy was a warm and wonderful woman, a poet with a lively sense of humor. To know her was to love her; she didn't have a pretentious bone in her body, although—in that setting—she was something of a Grande Dame, in spite of herself.

Our boys were ten, eight, and six when I first remember instructing them about manners at Grammy's house. Grammy had a cook/butler, and a schedule. Tea was at 4:30, drinks at 6:30, and dinner at 7:00. Be there. We "dressed" for dinner, which didn't mean black tie. You could come to tea in your shorts and T-shirt, but you had to look like a grown-up for dinner: coats and ties for the gents; long skirts for the ladies. At 6:20 I had the boys all shined up and waiting in the living room while Grammy was still upstairs getting dressed, and I said to them, "When Grammy comes in the room, you need to stand up."

They were not averse to instruction, but little boys that age are incurably philosophical, so they wanted to know why they should do that and why that was such a big deal. First I said that it was good manners, and a way of honoring her. I added that Grammy would like that. And then, after reflection, I said, "It is a generous thing to do. It is a kindness."

Not all would agree that good manners are directly connected to the deeper issues of civility. Some, indeed, argue the opposite. For Marxists the social graces of wealthy Westchesterites only paper over economic lives of class exploitation. Freudians, on the other hand,

1

suspect that they paper over inner neuroses of "quiet desperation," and there is at least enough truth in both accusations to keep the argument going. Among our authors, however, there is a common interest in the deeper motivations for civil behavior (including ordinary good manners) in what most agree is our increasingly uncivil society. This is a difficult issue to understand because it belongs to a nebulous area of common life which lies between individual rights and common law.

John Silber focused on that issue in a commencement address several years ago at Boston University. His theme was "Obedience to the Unenforceable" and his argument was that our culture presents us with three kinds of responsibilities. There are some things, decreed by law, which we all have to do, like obey traffic signals. And there are some areas of life in which you can do whatever you want, and are responsible only to yourself, like deciding to live in Missouri, or become a writer. Between these two is an area of what Silber called "the Unenforceable," those things which cannot be required of us or refused to us, but which make or break our social, political, and cultural community. This is where any specific culture lives or dies. It lies not in the recognition of common laws, or in the exercise of common freedoms. It is that "unenforceable" middle ground of generous, creative behavior where a culture does its crucial work, and where a distinctive community becomes itself. On this reading, *civility*—always closely linked to *political community*—is almost identified with *culture*. This middle area of our common life is volatile and vulnerable to attacks from both the right and the left. The left seeks to extend the reach of autonomous freedoms in "free speech" claims, for example, while the right seeks to extend the reach of law in limiting unbridled "free speech." But attempts to free this middle ground from the reach of law, or to override it with the reach of law, are benighted, because they would destroy the creativity of our common social, political, and cultural life. At the far end of autonomous freedom lies chaos; at the far end of "the rule of law" lies totalitarianism. So "civility" is not just good manners at Grammy's house, or good citizenship in the *polis*. It may even be the central, unenforceable bond which makes community possible in our pluralistic world.

We regularly set some of our lecturers to the task of defining the topic, and that is the business of Part One. Since civility is much debated, our Part Two deals with some aspects of that debate, including Dan Dahlstrom's response to Robert Pippin's essay, and Larry Cahoone's response to Alan Wolfe's. And we almost always deal with our topics as interreligious and cross-cultural matters, and that is the work of Part Three.

Part One introduces James Schmidt's question, "Is Civility a Virtue?" which will dog us throughout the book. Schmidt begins quaintly by examining the "Rules of Civility and Decent Behaviour in Company and in Conversation" that the fourteen-year old George Washington copied from a book of manners. The book came to Schmidt's attention when the President of Hamilton College gave a copy to each member of the entering Class of 2002 in the good hope that it might inspire them "to treat everyone with kindness, decency, respect and graciousness." Grammy would approve, and so would Schmidt, because this is a universal norm, valid for everyone, everywhere. Schmidt's difficulty is that there are relatively few generalizations of this sort. Using some of Washington's illustrations of bad behavior he notes that "we could easily imagine a society functioning quite happily in which individuals jostled their feet under the table, unfolded their napkins with little or no regard for what others were doing, and left their hats on their heads as they passed one another in the street. Would we want to say that a society of this sort, though 'uncivil' by Washington's standards, was in any sense 'immoral'?"

This point establishes at least a bit of common ground in our discussion, and that is simply that different cultures, and changing cultures, have different "manners," and that what is gracious in Westchester may be only odd—or perhaps even offensive—elsewhere. Schmidt's major concern, however, is the role of civility in civil society. He takes us through a careful examination of ways in which the identification of civil society with political society has been broken, especially in Hegel and Tocqueville. Today, he notes, it is still easier to define civility by what it is not, rather than by what it is. Stephen Carter and Edward Shils are exceptions, and they define civility largely in terms of sacrifice and restraint. Schmidt is dubious, however, especially when the claims of civility are balanced over against those of social justice. He concedes that civility may be a virtue, but then minimizes his concession with the comment that "it is probably not a virtue that will be of much help in deciding the political questions that ultimately matter."

Larry Cahoone is not interested in manners. He is interested in the responsibilities of citizens. For him, *civility* characterizes the appropriate action of citizens in a civil society. But does this differ from *political society*? Schmidt had noted that Hegel and Toqueville had both made this a major distinction: Hegel between a *state* which governed and *civil society* which dealt with the market and its values; and Toqueville between a political society and a civil society dealing with relations of citizens among themselves. Cahoone also retraces the Hegel/Toqueville discussions, but turns to Michael Oakeshott to frame a view of civil society as a community of "partners in a place whose aim is living." For Cahoone, this means a neighborhood. It is the only form of association which can balance liberty and membership.

So civil society is local, and not primarily political. If you can't care about your immediate neighbors, you can't really care about the larger world. The relation of civil society and culture is dialectical. "Civil life cannot mean without culture, and a culture of citizens must be civil." Cultural consensus—or what Silber called the "unenforceable" center of our common life—will occasionally be violated, and some of these violations must be tolerated on the grounds of the civil liberties of members. To the suggestion that these restraints put us on a slippery slope toward tyranny, Cahoone replies that *"life* is a slippery slope" and that the tolerated violations can be decided through culturally informed negotiations.

Adam Seligman reflects on civility by contrasting confidence and trust. Confidence results from a certain amount of control in a situation. Confidence is what you have when you know what to expect, and is regularly accompanied by formal or informal sanctions. One has confidence, for example, that a certified plumber will do his job properly, and if he doesn't you can refuse to pay, complain to the Better Business Bureau, and tell your friends not to hire him. Confidence can also be built on familiarity such as sharing a common background, interest in common activities, and the like. Trust, however, "is what you need when you do not and cannot have confidence or predict behavior and outcomes." If you leave the baby with the plumber while you go out to a meeting, that is trust, not confidence.

Crucial to his analysis of trust is the notion of system limits, the limits of our ability to predict the behavior of another person. In traditional societies organized around kinship bonds, there are very high levels of confidence based on familiarity and sanctions. But modernity, Seligman notes, is just the opposite of this, because it is life among strangers. And because we must work with strangers in the various systems which make up our social order, we must rely on trust. "Trust becomes necessary in the face of the free, autonomous, and hence unknowable individual." Civility now replaces kinship bonds and traditional expectations as the means of mediating among strangers based on a shared belief in promise keeping. As long as there is a strong sense of individuality and responsibility, as there was in classical modernity, these systems work. Today, however, the individual has taken on many different roles, thus de-stabilizing each of them and leading to an increasing need for "systems experts"—lawyers and social workers—and for public regulation ("speech codes," housing association regulations, smoking laws) in place of the civility which previously undergirded trust. "What this may mean for the concrete organization of society may well remain an open question. It will, however, herald an end to trust as a form of sociability and interaction, making life that much more nasty, short, and brutish."

Adam McClellan thinks we have paid too much attention to the superficialities of courtesy and manners in trying to get to the heart of civility. He is also skeptical about rediscovering the "true meaning" of the term in the Middle Ages, or the eighteenth century, or wherever, largely because notions of civility are tied to a particular civil society which is always geographically limited. Like Schmidt, McClellan is persuaded that principles of civility will have force only insofar as they are universal, and he proceeds to redefine the term. Civility, he argues, is a disposition or mood of individuals and societies when three criteria are met. First one must acknowledge the full humanity of both oneself and the other. Secondly, one must recognize his or her interdependence with the other. And, finally, one must desire to make common cause with the other.

Lest "full humanity" be sentimentalized, McClellan is quick to point out that there is good news and bad news. The good news is that we all have a fundamental worth and dignity. The bad news is "human sinfulness" and the recognition that we are "fundamentally flawed." Not only are we finite in our judgments and understanding; we are also selfish. McClellan's caution echoes Reinhold Niebuhr's advice that in dealing with one another we should be "wise as serpents and gentle as doves." The second criterion—"recognition of interdependence with the other"—regards individual relationships in terms of a larger community. Thirdly, we must want to make common cause with the other. McClellan admits that there are vestiges of self-interest in all of these, but the weight of his definition falls on the side of the community. Unlike Stephen Carter—whose book on *Civility* does not fare particularly well at the hands of our authors—McClellan doesn't think of civility as particularly sacrificial, but only as the way we need to live if we are to have what Cahoone called the kind of "neighborhood" we all want.

Stephen Toulmin thinks that the dogmatists are the real barbarians at the gate, and he establishes his point with a careful examination of the way dogmatism has corrupted civility in the Western world from classical Greece to the present. It wasn't so bad in Greece, where a dogma was what "appeared to be so" and was therefore an "opinion" or "judgment" fit to be taught. Surprisingly enough, it wasn't so bad in the medieval Western Church, either. "Before 1500, debates about theology and philosophy left room for a variety of views." Before the Council of Trent and the Protestant Reformation, "doctrines" and "dogmas" were pretty much the same, and all these views were pretty much revisable or reformulable.

After that, things started to go downhill, and the unlikely culprit was Samuel Morse's telegraph. "From then on messages could be exchanged among the authorities of Church or State some hundreds of miles apart in minutes, not days or weeks. . . . The seeds of centralization, sown at the time of the Counter-Reformation, turned into the effective power over Church teaching exerted nowadays by Cardinal Ratzinger and his colleagues." Toulmin is persuaded that "the bitterest lesson of our century is that it is possible to make an ideological issue of just about any difference between our own community and another, suspect group: between Us and Them." We suffer from "the narcissism of minor differences" such as Jonathan Swift explored in his fable about the battle of Big-Enders against Little-Enders, folk who open their hard-boiled eggs at the wide end versus those benighted souls who corrupt the community by opening theirs at the pointed end. Or, as McGeorge Bundy noted during his years as Dean of the Faculty of Arts and Sciences at Harvard, the reason that academic debates are so bitter is that the stakes are so small. Survival, Toulmin believes, lies with the Skeptics who refuse to allow any doctrine to be set beyond challenge, and "who recognize that the very act of turning a legitimate belief into an unquestionable axiom is too often the prelude to belligerence."

Part Two takes up the debate about civility in earnest, beginning with Robert Pippin's essay on "The Ethical Status of Civility." Here he picks up on James Schmidt's question about whether or not civility is a virtue. Schmidt, you will recall, thought it might be, but not a weighty one. Pippin doesn't think it is a virtue, but he knows it is important, and tries to find a way of relating those two ideas. He starts with the point Schmidt made earlier, that there are forms of behavior which may fray the fabric of society but which are not "a sanctionable violation of human rights" or the sort of thing that there ought to be a law against. Are there "forms of incivility that are not illegal or immoral but, in some sense yet to be identified, still wrongs"? At issue here is whether something can be unethical without being immoral. Pippin notes the point which Seligman made earlier about modern society being a society of strangers, but observes that these strangers "aspire in their trade and professional associations, universities, civic clubs, corporations, and charities to a kind of distinctive ethical relation with one another, a civility, a relation we also hope will hold society-wide. . . ."

Pippin offers three critical points. First of all, civility has a distinct ethical status in that it is more than being polite, and different from being morally righteous in general. Secondly, it is of fundamental importance in a modern civil society "because the end of modern civil societies, our highest good, is a free life, and civility is of vital importance in the collective pursuit of a free life." Thirdly, civility needs to be compatible with an extremely competitive, ethnically diverse, rapidly transforming consumer culture. Whereas McClellan understands civility as the commitment of individuals to the community, Pippin understands it as "the enactment in daily rituals of our equal status as free agents." But what makes incivility "wrong"? For Pippin the issue is recognition. A civil society of free individuals works only insofar as each recognizes the other as such: "being a free individual somehow just consists in being regarded as one." Civility makes possible a civil order, which is the only way of leading a free life.

In response, Dan Dahlstrom moves quickly to the issue of whether civility can be an ethical category without being a moral one. He agrees that civility means a kind of "appropriateness" in social behavior—thus anticipating arguments from Chinese culture which David Wong and Henry Rosemont will explore in Part Three. But Dahlstrom bears down on the idea that civility can be a normative or ethical notion without being moral or legal. Pippin has argued that being civil is not a "moral duty." Dahlstrom agrees that civility is more than politeness, and less than a legal sanction. "At the same time, however, there seems to be something highly counterintuitive about the claim that civility is not a matter of morals. The lack of civility among some Boston drivers and European soccer fans is a moral outrage!" Dahlstrom gives Pippin credit for the view that civility is "morally important in some way" but points out that the two senses of morality operative here are never clarified.

Alan Wolfe's "Are We Losing Our Virtue?: The Case Of Civility" proclaims good news on the civility front. While others presuppose a decline in civility in America, Wolfe argues, on the basis of recent sociological research, that a "decline" in ill-mannered speech really reflects an increase in people's honesty and willingness to speak their minds. Wolfe does not deny that America has suffered what he calls a "virtue deficit" if one speaks of old-fashioned ideas about chastity, self-control, honesty or loyalty. "But what so many writers see as a sign of our decadence could be interpreted as good news, even perhaps, cause for a certain celebration."

Wolfe's "good news" is that, while Americans are no longer turning to the Bible, their parents, or great works of literature to find out what is right and proper, they must now turn to themselves. "And when they do that, they discover that being virtuous does not consist in finding the right rule and adapting it to one's circumstances but instead involves figuring out what the right rule ought to be. The missing ingredient in accounts of virtue lost is that Americans have been forced by the circumstances in which they live to be *creative* when it comes to knowing how to live." In other words, what seems to other social critics to be relativism, narcissism, and the hedonism of "anything is okay just so long as it doesn't hurt anyone else" is, in fact, a new creativity in shaping an ethic. Unbound from tradition, Americans are rethinking and reshaping their understanding of virtue.

Larry Cahoone is not persuaded. He summarizes the three points Wolfe made in response to those social critics who argue that we have suffered a decline in civility. First, Wolfe notes, "it is never completely clear what virtue is." Secondly, "goods can be in conflict." And finally, "there will always be some conflict between the ideal and reality. . . . People understand why it is sometimes necessary not to practice what we preach." Cahoone notes that here civility is trumped by realism, and by greater freedom, that is, a different good. But Cahoone is not convinced by Wolfe's implication that "incivility is or can be a good thing *per se*." There may be occasions when civility must give way to another good, but that is to honor it in the breach. Cahoone goes on to argue that Wolfe's moral freedom, or moral democracy, cannot mean that coercion will be absent from moral life, since "the people" construct moral rules. The majority will impose them, and minorities and individuals will feel bound by them. His major point is that there can be no "free morality" devoid of either authority or tradition. He implies that "a morality" means having an authoritative tradition. Shifting meanings and individualistic interpretations do not "a morality" make.

Ed Delattre turns to the question of civility as a form of tolerance and asks how much is too much. Alan Wolfe's view of a people now reconstructing their moral values clearly makes Delattre nervous. He is persuaded that we have done altogether too much reconstructing of our values and have thus poisoned our own wells, especially in his field, which is education. He begins with the current celebration of diversity and the obligation to be nonjudgmental in our thinking about others and our conduct toward them. Using Massachusetts as his test case, he shows how this thinking has been incorporated into education law, regulation, policy, and practice. Using the law requiring "sensitivity to impediments to learning" he fears preemptively destructive pity, and uses deaf children as an example of occasions when "sensitivity" has simply meant a lowering of expectations for children who are bright and perfectly capable, given well-trained teachers who are expert in American Sign Language. "Bias review committees" are another source of the problem, and he quotes an actual case where the word "ruthless" was removed from a test question in history in reference to Joseph Stalin because "that might offend the emotional sensibilities of socialist students."

Delattre's concern is therefore with the misuses of civility. "Where civility declines into indiscriminate, nonjudgmental tolerance, indiscriminate tolerance becomes wholesale indulgence, and education becomes a seedbed of incompetence, deception, and flattery." Rather than say that we think something is wrong, we more often hear, "I am not comfortable with that position." And when a criticism is based on ignorance we often fear to say so because of those who will be offended. Delattre notes the infamous recent instance when a public official said he would have to be "niggardly" in the distribution of scarce funds and was maligned by colleagues for making a racial slur. The official agreed to resign, even when it was made clear that the word is Scandinavian in origin and has nothing to do with race or racial epithets. The great misuse of civility has been the promotion of "sentimental relativism," and as long as that pervades our institutions "we must expect cynicism within them, and opposition to intellectual and moral seriousness, self-knowledge, and wisdom."

Carrie Doehring is another critic of the misuses of civility, this time within family life. Her essay on "Civility in the Family" begins with the realistic observation that there is always stress and conflict in families. She notes that civility can be a creative way of dealing with these tensions. Her primary focus, however, is on that "cold" politeness based on disrespect which is destructive to family life. Doehring is a social constructivist who believes that many aspects of personal identity are socially constructed from one moment to the next by individual, family, community, and cultural systems of meaning. All meaning therefore takes place in a particular context, and civility is often used in these situations to support the dominant culture in ways that are oppressive.

The test case for her thesis is Mike Leigh's film "Secrets and Lies." She gives an extended analysis of the main characters in the film, illustrating the uses and misuses of civility in the move toward honesty with one another. She concludes with observations about the role of religion, and ways in which religion can encourage repressive forms of civility. Here she takes issue with Stephen Carter's book on civility in which he defines civility as a form of sacrifice without making a distinction between "chosen sacrifices and sacrifices that are forced upon people." Like Stephen Toulmin's skepticism in the face of dogma, Doehring suggests "a hermeneutic of suspicion regarding how religion can be used to support oppressive social systems of meaning." Carter, she fears, "is uncritical of the implicit patriarchy in many cultural and religious teachings about sacrifice."

Part Three begins with Henry Rosemont's essay "On Confucian Civility," and here we revisit Robert Pippin's debate with Dan Dahlstrom about whether civility can be ethically important without being a moral value. Pippin had referred to civility as "appropriate" behavior, and this notion is key in Confucian philosophy. Rosemont begins by making a clear distinction between modern Western and classical Confucian notions of civility. In the modern West we regularly regard "civil society" as that area of common life which lies between the family ("the private sphere") and the state ("the public sphere"). Confucians, he tells us, have nothing to say about civility in this sense. What is important to Confucians is what many of our authors have regarded as the superficialities of manners. McClellan thought "social grease" missed the deeper realities of civility, but Rosemont would argue that little boys standing when Grammy comes in the room are touching on the deepest meaning of civility, which is "to be respectful of the other's humanity." Formal politeness was central to the classical Confucian vision of the ideal society. Concerned less with the meaning of life than the discovery of a vision and discipline in which everyone can find meaning *in* life, politeness is the way the classical texts of Confucianism integrate sociality in aesthetic, moral, and spiritual aspects of life, no less than its political and economic dimensions.

Whereas the Western view of individual selfhood is autonomous, the Confucian view is relational. Rosemont notes that ". . . in order to *be* a friend, neighbor, or lover, for example, I must *have* a friend, neighbor, or lover." Other people are essential to my development as an individual human being, and homely little activities are the stuff of our human interactions, in which we are bound to our elders, our contemporaries, and our descendents. This Confucian notion of civility is comprehensive. It is not only a way of life; it is a conception of transcendent values. Oneness with all of humanity "enables us to form a union with all those who have gone before, and all those who will come after." Rosemont admits that while the early Confucians "were neither citizens, civilians, nor 'civic-minded,' they were always civil, and consequently may have much to teach us about civility."

David Wong continues our Chinese exploration by noting the fragmentation of modern Western democratic life and suggesting a foray into classical Chinese notions of harmony and ritual as a way of addressing that problem. He begins with exploring John Rawls's notion that a pluralistic democracy can function with an "overlapping consensus" in which different religious, political, and ideological groups find certain common ground which all can support. Wong is not sanguine. He thinks that this would, in actual fact, be very hard to achieve. But then, how do we find a center which *will* hold? He points out that this "fragmentation" worry has a mirror image in the Chinese tradition's worry about "harmony" as a constraint on freedom. Wong notes that social values in Chinese culture were to come from the person of the ruler. This trickle-down morality would affect the ministers and subsequently the hierarchical divisions of Chinese life.

Wong's reflections on these American and Chinese worries leave him searching for the inevitable "judicious balance." Without ties of attachment, loyalty, and human feeling, will the new democratic "communities of choice" (rather than the traditional "found" communities of origin) ever possess enough cohesion and stability to influence and counterbalance the state? In answering his own question, Wong turns to the role of ritual as creative of those ties. Before there is agreement on specific values and doctrines, there are rituals which promote the kind of harmony which makes agreement on values and doctrines possible. Ritual thus allows for unresolved disagreement on specific issues, leaving these conflicts on fundamental values open and ambiguous. This proposal is in keeping with Wong's view that there is an operational relativism in moral matters which is less a collapse of a strong moral position than it is a realistic reflection of a moral concern in search of cultural harmony.

Ninian Smart begins with the important observation that "we have a fairly narrow conception of what counts as a moral issue or a moral rule in Western society." With a provisional bow in the direction of the traditional No-No's, from murder to breaches of etiquette, he raises the question of what counts as a moral virtue, and what does not. Civility includes gentleness, but that is not quite a moral virtue, even though it is a good thing to have. Cheerfulness and a sense of humor are also great human gifts, and much to be desired, but are they virtues? Smart's focus is on "the large role played by politeness and civility to one another," largely because of the democratization of the elite, because the elite have elevated manners. "After certain phases of social revolution, everyone becomes a gentleman or a lady." Courtesy, he says—in a way that would please both Henry Rosemont and Grammy—becomes the way a person gains human dignity.

Smart argues that civil behavior is continuous with ethics and part of education. The Confucian ethos of continuing education through life is important. Self-improvement should have a continuous place in the spiritual life. In addition, Smart notes that the Christian idea of the sacredness of the person who reflects the nature of God "helps us to see how performatively the person may induce proper behavior in others." He admits that Buddhism does not give much sacred significance to individuals, but "in its practical advice emphasizes courtesy and respect for persons."

We conclude with Virginia Straus's exploration of the ways civility is "respect and care for fellow citizens and a capacity to put the common good over private interest." She is principally concerned—as her title indicates—with "International Civility and the Question of

Culture." Here the challenge of those who argue that our conception of civility must become global is met head-on. She is not concerned with "lower forms of civility" which—along with Carrie Doehring—she sees as "the outward show of good manners that acts as a smoke-screen for self-interested behavior." Nor is she interested in the kind of civility—the good manners of personal kindness—that Henry Rosemont and Grammy think of as the foundation of a civil society. Straus is quite specific: her civility is the common interest of citizens in a civil society.

Straus's concern for cultures of peace is based on a conviction that war itself is a cultural invention and that it can be replaced with another set of cultural inventions that will make it possible for humans to live in dynamic peace with other humans and the earth. The last ecological note is critical for her Buddhist notion of civility. It is not enough that we be gracious toward our fellow humans. It is also critical for a civil life—and indeed for human survival—that we learn to be civil in our relations to the earth as well. She concludes with lines from Denise Levertov's poem "Making Peace":

> A line of peace might appear
> If we restructured the sentence our lives are making,
> Revoked its affirmation of profit and power,
> Questioned our needs, allowed
> Long pauses. . . .

So what is civility, after all? Surely it is a good thing—some faintly formal quality of deep culture which bespeaks care for the other, and can even be seen in the graciousness of small boys to their grandmother. Is it really declining? Probably. Is that a bad thing? On balance, yes; but "new occasions teach new duties; time makes ancient good uncouth," and the new morality of our consumer democracies is in the making. So what does that mean?

It means that we should "hold fast to that which is good"; sit loose to the rest; be ready for tomorrow; stand up for Grammy; and, whatever happens, try to be civil.

PART I

What Is Civility?

Is Civility a Virtue?

JAMES SCHMIDT

WASHINGTON'S RULES

At the beginning of the 1998 academic year Eugen Tobin, the president of Hamilton College in Clinton, New York, gave each member of the incoming class a copy of a small book containing the "Rules of Civility and Decent Behavior in Company and in Conversation" that the fourteen-year-old George Washington copied from a seventeenth-century English translation of a sixteenth-century French book of manners. In a note accompanying the book he expressed the hope that Washington's rules would inspire students "to treat everyone with kindness, decency, respect and graciousness." He explained, "Since a liberal arts education is a rehearsal for dealing with differences among human beings, the requisite arts of listening, understanding and negotiating are among the most important intellectual skills and virtues we are called upon to master."[1] There is little to fault in President Tobin's understanding of the attitudes towards others that one would hope to find in those who have taken the principles of liberal education to heart. Yet, with all due respect to the Father of Our Country, at least some of Washington's maxims cannot but strike the modern reader as rather odd.[2]

The list opens auspiciously: "1st. Every Action done in Company, ought to be with Some Sign of Respect, to those that are Present." But on the way to the sublime closing invocation to "Labour to keep alive in your Breast that Little Spark of Ce[les]tial Fire Called Conscience," we run into this bit of prosaic advice about how to conduct oneself around earthly fires: "Spit not in the Fire, nor Stoop low before it neither Put your Hands into the Flames to warm them, nor Set your Feet upon the Fire especially if there be meat before it" (Rule 9). Sometimes the advice Washington gives is straightforward enough—

"3d. Shew Nothing to your Friend that may affright him"—while at other times it is unsettlingly detailed: "13th. Kill no Vermin as Fleas, lice ticks &c in the Sight of Others, if you See any filth or thick Spittle put your foot Dexteriously upon it if it be upon the Cloths of your Companions, Put it off privately, and if it be upon your own Cloths return Thanks to him who puts it off." Washington's rules include a brief discussion of fashionable dress (Rules 51ff.) and of table manners (Rules 90ff.) as well as some advice that participants in undertakings such as the present one might well take to heart: "80th. Be not Tedious in Discourse or in reading unless you find the Company pleased therewith."

The body looms rather large in these rules (which should come as no surprise to readers of Norbert Elias). Every inch of it must be kept under scrutiny, as if it were a province on the brink of rebellion.

> 2d. When in Company, put not your Hands to any Part of the Body, not usual[l]y Discovered.

> 4th. In the Presence of Others Sing not to yourself with a humming Noise, nor Drum with your Fingers or Feet.

> 10th. When you Sit down, Keep your Feet firm and Even, without putting one on the other or Crossing them.

> 11th. Shift not yourself in the Sight of others nor Gnaw your nails.

> 12th. Shake not the head, Feet, or Legs rowl not the Eyes lift not one eyebrow higher than the other wry not the mouth, and bedew no mans face with your Spittle, by appr[oaching too nea]r him [when] you Speak.

> 53d. Run not in the Streets, neither go t[oo s]lowly nor wit[h] Mouth open go not Shaking y[ou]r Arms [kick not the earth with yr feet, go] not upon the Toes, nor in a Dancing [fashion].

Even one's facial expressions must be carefully managed:

> 19th. let your Countenance be pleasant but in Serious Matters Somewhat grave.

> 20th. The Gestures of the Body must be Suited to the discourse you are upon.

22d. Shew not yourself glad at the Misfortune of another though he were your enemy.

23d. When you see a Crime punished, you may be inwardly Pleased; but always shew Pity to the Suffering Offender.

Another group of Washington's maxims are concerned with the demands of a society in which there are superiors and inferiors: one must learn to give the former the deference that is owed them. Rules 26 and 27 provide us with agonizingly detailed descriptions of how to go about removing hats as a sign of respect, Number 28 addresses the problem of when to sit and when to stand, Number 29 negotiates entry through doorways, Number 30 deals with how individuals are to arrange themselves while walking down the street, while Numbers 31 and 32 address the question of who gets which lodgings when traveling. Indeed, even the simple task of unfolding a napkin at a table requires attention to what others are doing:

104th. It belongs to the Chiefest in Company to unfold his Napkin and fall to Meat first, But he ought then to Begin in time & to Dispatch [w]ith Dexterity that the Slowest may have time allowed him.

One can only wonder what impact this advice has had on dining practices among the first-year students at Hamilton College.

That Washington's rules should be distributed to college students at the close of the twentieth century tells us something about the curious career of the notion of civility: it is something which a good many people are inclined to promote, even though they may not be entirely sure what it is that they are promoting. A small part of the flood of books and articles on "civility" and "civil society" has appeared in the last several years. All of these discussions appear to be in general agreement that something called "civility" is a good thing—a "virtue," if you will—and it is a good thing because it brings about the conditions that sustain the existence of "civil society"—which is regarded as a very good thing. As one example among many, consider the "strategy for renewal" of civil society published by the "Council of Civil Society"—a self-described group of "nationally distinguished scholars and leaders" chaired by Jean Bethke Elshtain of the University of Chicago. Among its recommendations are proposals for strengthening the family (by making divorces harder to get), fostering greater piety and charity (through legislation that would permit "faith based organizations, without denying or relinquishing their religious charter, to compete on equal terms with other private groups for government contracts to deliver welfare services to the poor"), and encouraging less consumerism and materialism (by encouraging employers "to recognize the moral dimensions of the decisions they make" and urging citizens to "resist the pressure to acquire more and more material things").[3]

It is hard to say bad things about civility.[4] But it might be worth a try, especially given the elusiveness of the thing that is being praised. Let me begin by briefly considering what it means for something to be a virtue, and then go on to consider how *civility* and *civil society* have been used during those periods in history with a more subtle understanding of the nature of virtues than we seem to have today. After that, I will consider some of the differences between traditional and more recent uses of these terms and conclude by examining what it means to speak—as Edward Shils and Stephen Carter have[5]—of a "virtue of civility."

VIRTUES, PRACTICES, AND SOCIETIES

If pressed for a brief account of what a virtue is, it would be difficult to improve on the definition Aristotle offers in Book II of the *Nicomachean Ethics. Arete* ("virtue," or, more literally, "excellence")

> causes its possessors to be in a good state and to perform their functions well; the virtue of the eyes, e.g., makes the eyes and their functioning excellent, because it makes them see well; and similarly, the virtue of a horse makes the horse excellent, and thereby good at galloping, at carrying its rider and at standing steady in the face of the enemy. If this is true in every case, the virtue of a human being will likewise be the state that makes a human being good and makes him perform his function well.[6]

Aristotle situated his account of the virtues in a more general account of human action which sees it as teleological (seeking to attain certain ends and goals), as subject to reflective correction (that is, we are capable of reflecting on what we are doing and improving it), and as transpiring in concert with others. Thus, in discussing the virtues that allowed Ted Williams to become the last .400 hitter in baseball, we would need to consider his natural ability to follow pitches until they were almost at the plate, the skills he acquired in reckoning where the ball might be going in the split second when he could no longer maintain sight of it, and the happy and contingent historical fact that he was a member of a society in which peculiar talents such as these could be utilized within a complex social practice known as baseball.

For civility to be a virtue, according to this account, it would be necessary to show that it allowed its possessor to perform certain functions well. To the extent that knowledge of when to unfold napkins, how to tip hats, and where to put one's hands fits one for the practice of interacting with others in a society of a certain sort, Washington's rules of civility would seem, unproblematically, to be virtues. But, of course, there is more to the question than that. Virtues, as Alasdair MacIntyre has reminded us, are embedded in specific practices, and the possession of virtues that are specific to certain practices may not be relevant for other practices (just as Michael Jordan's virtues proved massively irrelevant to the practice of baseball, so Ted Williams— while an excellent member of the Red Sox—would probably not have been as effective as a Celtic). It is also quite possible to be excellent in the pursuit of any number of particular practices and nevertheless still be less than excellent as a human being. Moral virtues, in Aristotle's account, are those virtues that enable us to be good human beings. The question that we probably want to see answered about civility is not whether it is a virtue, but what it has to do with *moral* virtue.

One problem with accounts of virtues of the sort I have been giving is that it is not always clear whether one has given a sufficiently generalized account of what it is to be a good human being to escape the risk of defining human excellence in terms of a rather specific set of traits, peculiar to one particular society, but not to others. Thus Washington's "Every Action done in Company, ought to be with Some Sign of Respect, to those that are Present" may very well be a norm that would have to be followed in order to foster interactions between individuals in any conceivable society. If civility meant this, and only this, it might be a moral virtue. Yet we could easily imagine a society functioning quite happily in which individuals jostled their feet under the table, unfolded their napkins with little or no regard for what others were doing, and left their hats on their heads as they passed one another in the street. Would we want to say that a society of this sort, though "uncivil" by Washington's standards, was in any sense "immoral"?

Another problem with the status of civility as a virtue has to do with the breadth of its concerns. Aristotle's virtues tend to have a particular range of applicability. *Courage* involves the management of feelings of confidence and fear in situations of threat and danger. *Temperance* is concerned with the proper enjoyment of bodily pleasures. *Generosity* has to do with the use of money. *Wittiness* is concerned with saying and listening to the right things in the right way, and so on. A glance at Washington's list suggests that *civility* is concerned with so many different things that it is difficult to specify the range of its applicability. It would seem to deal with nothing less than the successful management of social relations with others. There is, however, at least one virtue in Aristotle's account that has the same expansiveness: justice. At the start of Book V Aristotle explains that *justice* is used in two senses. In its most precise usage it denotes a particular virtue concerned with the question of fairness in the distribution of things that are either scarce or which would lose their goodness if everyone had them in equal amounts. But it is also used in a more general sense in which it means "lawfulness"—doing those things the law commands. To be just in this latter sense is to be able to fulfill all the demands which the political community makes on its members. To do this, one must possess all of the virtues which fit one for political life. Justice in this more extensive sense thus means nothing less than the possession of the totality of all the other virtues.

In this light, Washington's *civility* begins to look like a somewhat impoverished version of Aristotle's definition of justice as lawfulness. It includes some, but not all, of the virtues that are needed for successful performance of one's responsibilities as a member of a political community. Yet it seems to have less to do with membership in the political community than with membership in "civilized society," to have less to do with "morality" than with "manners." Since all these terms have rich and intertwined histories, perhaps we can make some headway in understanding the sense in which civility might be a virtue if we look at what it meant in Washington's time for something to be a "civil" society.

CIVILITY AND CIVIL SOCIETY

Samuel Johnson's dictionary of 1755 provides a definition that lies close enough to Washington's day to serve as a point of departure. It begins simply enough: "1. Relating to the community; political; relating to the city or government." But Johnson then proceeds to define *civil* in terms of what it is not, and in the process produces a rather curious list:

> 3. Not in anarchy; not wild; not without rule or government. 4. Not foreign, intestine. 5. Not ecclesiastical. . . . 6. Not natural. . . . 7. Not military. . . . 8. Not criminal. . . . 9. Civilised; not barbarous. 10. Complaisant; civilized; gentle; well bred; elegant of manners; not rude; not brutal; not coarse. 11. Grave; sober; not gay or shewy. 12. Relating to the ancient consular, or imperial government. . . ."

This set of definitions captures one crucial feature of eighteenth-century usages of *civil*: to say that something is "civil" more often than not meant to say that it is not something else. Thus, if we look at the history of usages of the term *civil society*, we find that the term has taken on a variety of different meanings through its juxtaposition to a series of other forms of association.[7]

The term *civil society* itself entered Western political discourse in the translation of Aristotle's *Politics* by the great Florentine civic humanist Leonardo Bruni. Bruni used "societas civilis" to translate Aristotle's *koinonia politike*—a term that he used as a way of explaining what sort of community (or *koinonia*) the *polis* was: it was a *political* community, and Aristotle began the *Politics* with a contrast between the political community or *polis* and the domestic community or *oikos*. This juxtaposition exercised an enormous influence in the history of political thought, and as late as Locke's *Second Treatise* and Rousseau's entry on "Political Economy" in Diderot's *Encyclopedia*, we find civil or political society defined by contrasting it with the household. We can also find a well-established tradition in which civil society is juxtaposed to ecclesiastical forms of association: Augustine spoke of "two cities or societies [*duae civitates hoc est societates*]," the *civitas Dei* and the *civitas terrena* (*Civitate Dei* 12.1), and Aquinas followed suit, juxtaposing the *communitas civilis* to the *communitas*

divina (*Summa Theologiae* 1.2.100.2c). In the seventeenth and eighteenth centuries similar distinctions would be elaborated in Locke's
Letter on Toleration and Kant's *Religion Within the Limits of Reason
Alone*. Civil society was also defined, in modern natural law theories,
by contrasting it with a prepolitical state of nature. Finally, civil (or
"civilized") society could also be defined by contrasting it with those
"rude" societies inhabited by "savages" who lived without laws, con-
veniences, or commerce. Thus, at one or another point in history, the
term *civil society* might have been defined in opposition to domestic,
to ecclesiastical, to natural, or to rude societies.

In all of these juxtapositions, civil society is synonymous with
"political society"—Locke, to cite the most famous example, used the
two terms as equivalents in Chapter VII of the *Second Treatise*: "Of
Political or Civil Society." In thinking about the way that civil society
is to be distinguished from these other societies, one may focus on
those peculiar virtues—designated as "civic" virtues—that distinguish
the free head of the household from other members of the family, that
distinguish the citizen who pursues ends in this world from the Christian who aims at salvation in the next, that distinguish an individual
who has subjected himself to the conditions of a social contract from
the resident of the state of nature, or (finally) that distinguish a civilized and polished individual from a rude barbarian. Given the diversity of modes of life that are defined as "uncivil," it is little wonder
that the particular virtues associated with civic life should be so wide-
ranging or so variable. Thus the rules of civility that Washington
copied out might be understood as defining civil life across a number
of these different dimensions: to be civil is—at one and the same
time—to strive to avoid falling back into a brutish rudeness (so keep
that greasy knife out of the salt), to be sensitive to the joys of worldly
fellowship (so be tedious only among those who won't mind it), to have
left behind the world of women and servants and entered into a domain of men who deserve equal respect (so give that respect to all
those with whom one keeps company), and to have entered into a
society where—unlike the equality of the state of nature—there are
clearly laid out ranks and divisions (so wait for cues from your betters
before unfolding napkins).

The rules of civility that the young Washington copied in 1744
thus give us a glimpse of the sorts of virtues that a citizen of a civil society required in order to perform the role demanded of him. Yet this

list was, even in Washington's own day, likely to have been a dated and garbled one. He had copied it from a 1640 English translation of a list of French Jesuit *Rules of Civility and Decent Behavior* dating from 1595. There was a vast difference between the world of a sixteenth-century French gentleman and that of a member of the gentry in colonial America. As a trivial example, consider the matter of napkins. Brissot der Warville, an eighteenth-century French visitor, recorded with astonishment that

> Virginians do not use napkins, but they wear silk cravats, and instead of carrying white handkerchiefs they blow their noses either with their fingers (I have seen the best-bred Americans do this) or with a silk handkerchief which also serves as a cravat, a napkin, etc.[8]

It is thus possible that the young Washington copied out rules for the use of an item that he would encounter only infrequently. But more is at stake here than simply the absence of napkins in colonial Virginia. In French society at the close of the sixteenth century, it would have been obvious who one's betters were. If such notions may have been more difficult to maintain in colonial America, they would become almost impossible in a postcolonial America, where, as Alexis de Tocqueville—that most famous of all French visitors to the new democracy—would observe, all distinctions of status and rank seemed to melt away into one vast, undifferentiated class of relentlessly active individuals. Whatever rules of civility Washington put together in 1744 would have to be revised in the course of framing those virtues required for free citizens of the most ambitious attempt at republican self-governance since antiquity. The age of democratic revolutions required a rethinking of what constituted appropriately republican forms of civility, and both in France and in the newly independent colonies one finds extended discussions of the sorts of mores and manners appropriate to a free society of equals. Washington himself was forced to ransack antiquity for the proper model of a leader of a republic— he found it in Cincinnatus, the general who saved Rome in its hour of greatest need and then resigned his office to return to his farm. Benjamin Franklin, on the other hand, experimented in his own writings with the construction of a persona that combined the traits of commercial industriousness, scientific inquisitiveness, and democratic simplicity—a persona that would win him fame in Europe as the most illustrious new man from the strange new world.

REDEFINING CIVIL SOCIETY: FAITH, THE FAMILY, AND THE MARKET

Anyone familiar with these eighteenth-century patterns of usage cannot help finding something peculiar about some of the ways in which the terms *civility* and *civil society* are being used in recent discussions. It is as if all the finely wrought distinctions between civil society and other forms of association have been dissolved. The report of the Council on Civil Society, for instance, assures us that the family is "certainly civil society's most important institution"—yet, in Washington's day, civil society referred to that domain of activities that lay *outside* the sphere of domestic life. Likewise, Stephen Carter doubts that "we can reconstruct civility in America without a revival of religion as a force in both our public and private lives"[9]—yet the eighteenth century fought hard to *distinguish* civil society from religious forms of association. And Lawrence Cahoone has told us that "civil society is not primarily political" and to treat it as such is to "engage in an overvaluation of the political"—yet, before the beginning of the nineteenth century, it is impossible to find a thinker who understands civil society as anything other than a political society.[10] Alasdair MacIntyre began *After Virtue* by imagining a situation where, after a collapse of civilization, a new generation began picking up bits and scraps of what had survived from the earlier scientific writings and proceeded to use its terms in ways that bore scant resemblance to earlier patterns of usage. He proposed this as an analogy for what had befallen modern discussions of virtue. It might also serve as a rough approximation of what has happened to discussions of civil society: a term that was once employed to carve out a domain that was political, rather than a domestic or an ecclesiastical society, has now been depoliticized, domesticated, and sacralized.

But why hold eighteenth-century usage as sacrosanct? Though Alan Wolfe may be wrong to claim that Hegel saw the family as "a crucial component of civil society"[11] (Hegel, in fact, emphasizes that the family is not part of civil society, as he understands it), he is on firmer ground when he suggests that "it is certainly useful to inquire into the origins of the term *civil society*, and to be reminded of its context in eighteenth-century Scotland or nineteenth-century Germany, but just about all the terms we use today meant something different when they were introduced." The fact that we are deviating from earlier usages of *civil society* should not, Wolfe goes on to argue, "prevent us from using the term today to describe families, churches, and neighborhood associations—so long as we are clear that we are doing so."[12] Wolfe may be right that it would be pedantic to hold to eighteenth-century usages. But surely part of what might be involved in being "clear" as to how "we" are using the term *civil society* today would involve a consideration of how the meaning of the term has shifted and what the implications of this transformation might be. To do this, we need to examine the transformations in usages of *civil society* that are associated with the names Locke, Hegel, and Tocqueville.

When Leonardo Bruni translated Aristotle's *Politics* in 1438, he used "civilis societas" to render Aristotle's *koinonia politike*. Bruni's translation established a convention that would have a remarkable staying power: *civil society* is a term of art used by political theorists to describe that form of association which is conventionally called a *polis* or a *civitas*. But while the linguistic convention of identifying the *civitas* as a *societas civilis* continues into the eighteenth century, problems begin to arise with the continued use of the term *civitas*. For Bruni, a humanist and rhetorician who twice served as the head of the Florentine chancellery, it was unproblematic that Florence was a *civitas* and, hence, a form of political life rather like ancient Athens. He regularly drew on models provided by ancient authors in the speeches he delivered as part of his duties, and his translation of the *Politics* is filled with terms that he took from Florentine political discourse.[13] The vocabulary of civic republicanism, a vocabulary which Bruni played a major role in crafting, led fifteenth-century Florentines to interpret their political life in a narrative that hearkened back to the Roman Republic and the Athenian *polis*. While it was possible for Bruni and his contemporaries to narrate their political life in these terms, it was difficult for later thinkers to maintain the analogy. Consider that remarkable moment when Jean-Jacques Rousseau invokes the convention Bruni founded to describe what issues from the social contract and then immediately realizes that it doesn't work: "This public person, formed thus by union of all the others formerly took the name *city*, and at present takes the name republic or *body politic*, which is called *state* by its members when it is passive, *sovereign* when it is active, *power* when it is compared to others like itself."[14] He inserts a footnote immediately after the word *city* which reads:

> The true meaning of this word is almost entirely lost on modern men. Most of them mistake a town for a city and a bourgeois for a citizen. They do not know that houses make a town but citizens make a city.

After this momentary nostalgia for a way of speaking that his contemporaries have forgotten, Rousseau proceeds (back in the text itself) to plow through the various different words—"people," "citizens," "subjects"—that are used to refer to those who are associated in the social contract before observing, "But these terms are often confused and mistaken for one another. It is enough to know how to distinguish them when they are used with absolute precision."

This, however, is not enough, and Rousseau—as the footnote suggests—knows it. Modern men don't know how to use political terms inherited from the ancient world because they no longer live in the forms of political community that gave rise to this vocabulary. Try as he will, Rousseau cannot get around the ugly fact that a modern "state" is not what used to be called a "city" and a modern "city" is neither a *civitas* nor a *polis*. The experience of political life has undergone a sea change with the collapse of the small, self-governing city-republics of Renaissance Europe. The category of "civil society" was abstract enough to survive this transformation unscathed—but not the assumption that the *civitas* was the locus of political life. Thus, even those thinkers who continued to insist that a civil society was a political society could question whether the "state" or the "government" was identical with civil society. Consider Locke. In Chapter XIX of the *Second Treatise* he carefully distinguishes between the "dissolution of society" and the "dissolution of government," arguing that it is possible to "dissolve" government while leaving "society"—by which he meant "civil society"—intact. The actions of monarchs such as Charles II or James II, which alter the way in which society is governed, may lead to a "dissolution of government" in which those associated into a civil (and thus still political) society exercise their native right to establish a new government. Citizens may, with good enough cause, end the trusteeship arrangement on which government rests.

But in doing so, they have not dissolved the bonds that unite them into a civil society.

It is only in the early nineteenth century that we begin to find thinkers employing "civil society" to mean something other than "political society." For two markedly different ways of making this distinction, we need to consider the work of Georg Friedrich Wilhelm Hegel and Alexis de Tocqueville. Hegel's *Philosophy of Right* (1820) rigorously distinguished "state" from "civil society" and replaced the Aristotelian dichotomy of household and polity with the trichotomy of family, civil society, and state. In the revised usage that Hegel proposed (and it takes only a glance at the first reviews of the *Philosophy of Right* to remind us of how novel Hegel's proposal was), "civil society" denotes the sphere of market exchanges and the legal and social framework that sustains the market as a domain distinct from both the private sphere of the family and the political sphere of the state. Civil society, Hegel tells us, is the domain of the *"Bürger als bourgeois"*— the citizen in the role of bourgeois: an individual who is concerned with the pursuit of private interests and who pursues these interests in a market where all other individuals are likewise concerned with the pursuit of their own interests.[15] In his drafts for *Democracy in America*, Alexis de Tocqueville outlined a different way of separating political and civil society when he suggested that the book might be organized around a tripartite division between

Political society [*société politique*]—Relations between the federal and state governments and [between] the citizen of the Union and of each state,

Civil society [*société civile*]—Relations of the citizens among themselves, [and]

Religious society [*société religieuse*]—Relations between God and the members of society, and of the religious sects among themselves.[16]

In distinguishing civil society from political society, Tocqueville was following the lead of his teacher François Guizot and his mentor Pierre-Paul Royer-Collard. Like Hegel, both had distinguished between state and civil society, and on the basis of this distinction had argued that it would be impossible for France to return to the form of government that had preceded the massive social transformation which led to the Revolution.[17] In his study of American democracy, Tocqueville pressed their distinction further, separating off political forms of association from what he termed "civil associations." The former were established, in part, to oppose actions by the state and thus to preserve the "independence" of the citizenry. The latter, which addressed the needs of "daily life," aimed at the preservation of "civilization" itself. Without them, the citizens of a democracy would descend into "barbarism."[18] While Tocqueville may have begun *Democracy in America* with the idea of distinguishing "civil society" from both "political society" and "religious society," in executing the book he focused so exclusively on the opposition between political society and civil society that when he came to discuss "religious associations" they became one example, among others, within the broader class of "civil associations."[19]

We are presented, then, with two markedly different ways of distinguishing civil from political society. In the model Hegel offers, the family is conceived as a private sphere that binds its members together through love, civil society is viewed as a sphere in which individuals pursue private interests publicly, and the state is conceived as a domain in which the articulation of shared, public interest is realized. In Tocqueville's model, "civil society" encompasses the sum total of all those nonpolitical forms of association which structure social interactions between its members.

To summarize the path that has led to this result: Down to the end of the seventeenth century, "civil society" was equated with the state and used to denote a political society that was distinguished from domestic, ecclesiastical, natural, and rude forms of association. From the seventeenth to the beginning of the nineteenth century, civil society comes to be distinguished from the state, but is still defined as a political, as opposed to a domestic, ecclesiastical, natural, or rude form of association. Finally, in the first half of the nineteenth century it comes to be distinguished from political society and is now conceived either in terms of the actions of individuals operating within the economic sphere or along the lines of nonpolitical forms of voluntary association including churches. As long as civil society is understood as "political society" the virtues associated with it will be—unproblematically—civic virtues: civility is the virtue of the citizen. But once civil society has been split off from political society, what sort of virtue is associated with "civility"?

WHAT ARE THE VIRTUES OF CIVILITY?

As we move from eighteenth- and nineteenth-century discussions of civility and civil society to those of our own day, at least one thing has remained unchanged: more often than not, civility tends to be defined by being juxtaposed to what it is not. For the Council on Civil Society, the prime example of uncivil behavior is a set of actions that flow from something called the "philosophy of expressive individualism": the view that individuals are "self-originating sources of valid claims, essentially unencumbered, self-owning, and auto-teleological." Against this notion, the Council defends a view of humans as "intrinsically social beings," which "can only live in communities."

> From this perspective, the basic subject of society is the human person, and the basic purpose of government—and all other institutions—is to help foster the conditions for human flourishing. In turn, the essential conditions for human flourishing are the elements of what we are calling democratic civil society, anchored in moral truth.[20]

If the report is somewhat vague about the "moral truth" on which "democratic civil society" rests—we are told that these truths are "in large part biblical and religious" though they have been also "strongly informed by the classical natural law tradition and the ideas of the Enlightenment"[21] (passages such as this remind one that this report was the product of a committee)—it is a bit clearer what the authors of the Report regard as moral falsehoods. They are opposed to experimentation with forms of intimate association that fall outside what the report terms the "culture of marriage" (though the members of the Council are curiously silent as to whether their enthusiasm for the "culture of marriage" is robust enough to lead them to endorse the elimination of laws that prevent members of same-sex unions from partaking of the benefits of this culture), they are critical of those who would seek a limitation on the role of religion in public life, and they view the alleged virtues of the free market with some suspicion, insisting on the need to "relativize economics, recognizing that free markets and cost-benefit analyses are primarily means, not ends."[22] Somewhere, Rousseau is smiling.

The vices that the Council on Civil Society wants to restrain are those uncivil virtues that distinguished Hegel's *Bürger als bourgeois* from Rousseau's *citoyen*. Hegel's civil society was, if nothing else, a playground for "expressive individualism." It offers us a "spectacle of extravagance and want" where that individuality that first dawned "in an inward form in the Christian religion" is given free reign (*Philosophy of Right* §§182, 185). Driven onward in a relentless pursuit of self-interest, Hegel's *bourgeois* comes to realize that he is immersed in a social order that transcends the intentions of any given individual. With this comes the painful recognition that, to achieve one's interest in a market, it is necessary to do something other than simply pursue one's *own* interests: one must instead anticipate the motives and desires of other market actors. In this way, Hegel assures us, the *bourgeois* learns to know, will, and act "in a universal way." As his particularity is "educated up to subjectivity" and purged of his idiosyncrasy, the *bourgeois* begins to take on the semblance of the *citoyen* (*Philosophy of Right* §§187, 189). At least that was how it was supposed to work. That the Council on Civil Society finds it necessary to call upon family ties and religious piety to curb the excesses of bourgeois individualism suggests that something has gone terribly wrong with Hegel's vision.

Civility, as John Hale has observed in his discussion of Renaissance manners, "was about taming."[23] Within the classical republican tradition, civic virtues aim at the taming of individual avarice and the binding of individuals into a political community. But when civil society is no longer understood as a political society, the virtues that are to restrain individual idiosyncrasy can no longer be civic ones. Hence the popularity of family values and religious piety among those seeking to promote what now passes as "civility." Stephen Carter's *Civility* can serve as an example. As evidence for what he describes as a "crisis of civility," Carter points both to various forms of boorish behavior (rude drivers, sullen gas station attendants, and quarreling talking heads on talk shows) and to the "essentially empty rights-talk of our age."[24] Carter's evidence for the latter includes a fired waitress's claim that she had a "right" to pierce her face with as many studs and rings as she wishes and a high-school boy's claim that he has a "right" to wear droopy pants. Significantly, he doesn't include efforts by "family-values conservatives" to pass legislation defending a "right to spank" in his list of examples of "empty rights-talk"—perhaps because what he sees as empty here is the "weird new argument" that parents should refrain from striking their children. "I was spanked as a child," he tells us, "and somehow survived."

> My wife and I certainly took the time to slap our two children's bottoms or hands when they were young, usually for truly dangerous infractions, like running into the street. And our children, like most others whose parents occasionally spank, seem none the worse for the experience.[25]

Faced with such a passage, one pauses at the phrase "*usually* for truly dangerous infractions" and—after unsuccessfully resisting the urge to ask when *else* the Carter children have their "bottoms or hands" slapped—wonders what has become of civility when discussions of the virtue engage in personal confessions of this sort.

In a somewhat less disconcerting example of the "cause and effect of civility" in the family, Carter recalls a passage in Joseph Cardinal Bernardin's memoirs in which Bernardin—shortly before his own death from cancer—recalled how, when he was about five years old, his father prevented him from falling off of a porch, paying no attention to the fact that in saving his son, he had reopened an incision from a recent cancer operation. Carter takes this story as an example of how "civility builds on itself": a father "sacrifices his own comfort, possibly his own health, to console his child" and then the child "remembers the story and tries to act out of the same sense of sacrificial love."[26] But does this story tell us anything about "civility" at all? Are the sacrifices that members of families make for one another appropriate as models for the relationships between members of a civil society? By grounding the norms of civility in "a sacred language" of "sacrificial civility," Carter would seem to have established an impossibly high standard (in theory) that, as it turns out, results in rather empty practical advice. Explaining what we should do when we are faced with a beggar on the street, Carter tells us that "civility by itself cannot provide the proper standard of charitable giving."

> Each of us must decide that for ourselves—in accordance, however, with strong norms of sacrifice for others. But civility, as we

have used the term, does suggest that the one thing we cannot do about the beggar is ignore him. . . . We owe the beggar the same boon of greeting or conversation that we would bestow on anybody else we happen to meet.[27]

A norm of "sacrificial civility" that can run the gamut from risking one's own health to save a child to wishing a beggar a pleasant day is so broad as to be no norm at all.

In a number of essays, the late University of Chicago sociologist Edward Shils has offered a definition of the virtues of civility that—like Carter and the Report of the Council on Civil Society but with considerably more theoretical sophistication—defines civility largely in terms of sacrifice and restraint. Civility, as Shils defines it, involves restraints on "particularistic ends."[28]

> Civility is a belief which affirms the possibility of the common good; it is a belief in the community of contending parties within a morally valid unity of society. It is a belief in the validity or legitimacy of the governmental institutions which lay down rules and resolve conflicts. Civility is a virtue expressed in action on behalf of the whole society, on behalf of the good of all members of the society to which public liberties and representative institutions are integral. Civility is an attitude in individuals which recommends that consensus about the maintenance of the order of society should exist alongside the conflict of interests and ideals.[29]

Threats to civility come from a complex of tendencies—"collectivistic liberalism, emancipationism, anti-patriotism, egalitarianism, populism, scientism, and ecclesiastical abdication"—that Shils collectively denotes with the term "progressivism."[30] All of these tendencies find their origins in the opposition to authority and the imposition of restraints that Shils sees as the hallmark of the Enlightenment's attempt to "elevate the subject into a citizen"[31]—though in other contexts, Shils seems to locate the origins of the attack on civility with romanticism rather than with the Enlightenment.[32] While Shils's historical argument is casual, at best, the general thrust of his argument is clear enough: civility involves "a solicitude for the interest of the whole society, or in other words, a concern for the common good."[33]

We would appear to be back on traditional ground. Civility is the "virtue of the citizen," the individual who is concerned with the common good: it would appear to be the virtues of the *citoyen* rather than those of the *bourgeois*. Shils follows Hegel in distinguishing civil society from both the state and the family, but insists that the virtues associated with civil society cannot be the virtues of the self-interested *bourgeois*. Instead, the virtue of civility must tame the potentially destructive individualism of civil society:

> Substantive civility is the virtue of civil society. It is the readiness to moderate particular, individual or parochial interests and to give precedence to the common good. . . . Whenever two antagonistic advocates arrive at a compromise through recognition of a common interest, they redefine themselves as members of a collectivity, the good of which has precedence over their particular objectives. The good which is accorded precedence by that decision might be no more than the continued existence of the collectivity in which they both participate. The common good is acknowledged wherever a more inclusive collectivity is acknowledged.[34]

Incivility thus involves an assertion of particular interests and ends over those of the community, and it draws its impetus from a skepticism about the ultimate goodness of public good.

The great enemy of political civility is something Shils dubs "ideological politics." Those who engage in ideological politics are motivated by "a coherent, comprehensive set of beliefs which must override every other consideration." Convinced that "they alone have the truth about the right ordering of life," partisans of ideological politics distrust political institutions, distrust politicians, and introduce a "moral separatism" into politics that separates good from evil, left from right, national from unnational, and American from un-American.[35] Civil politics, in contrast, requires an understanding of

> the complexity of virtue, that no virtue stands alone, that every virtuous act costs something in terms of other virtuous acts, that virtues are intertwined with evils, that no theoretical system of a hierarchy of virtues is ever realizable in practice.[36]

Civility—which, Shils assures us, means a good deal more than "good manners in face-to-face relations"[37]—would thus seem to be the virtue of knowing how to compromise between various competing virtues. It is the virtue of knowing when not to be too obsessed with virtue.

JUSTICE OR CIVILITY?

Let us conclude by considering whether the following example might satisfy Shils's requirements for "civil politics." Members of Congress, faced with an issue that has caused considerable animosity and bitterness between the contesting parties, recognize that continued debate of the issue will be unlikely to lead to a resolution and will instead only aggravate differences and prevent other public business from being conducted. They propose the following course of action. A resolution is drawn up which pays lip service to the claims of both sides, but which stipulates that all future petitions and legislation having to do with this issue will be tabled without discussion. A majority of members of Congress, weary of partisanship, adopt the motion. Everyone gives up something, civility is restored, ideology is restrained, and Congress can go back to doing the public's business.

Some will perhaps recognize that the example I have sketched is the infamous "gag rule" enacted by the United State Congress in May 1836 as a way of coping with the increasingly bitter debate over what should be done about slavery. The gag rule was put into effect when South Carolina's Henry Laurens Pickney introduced resolutions stating that 1) Congress had no power to interfere with slavery in the states, 2) it would be "unwise" and "impolitic" for Congress to interfere with slavery in the District of Columbia, and 3) any further measures on the "subject of slavery or the abolition of slavery" would "be laid on the table" and no further action taken. It is worth remembering that this rule represented a compromise between the contesting parties (the second resolution made interference with slavery in the District of Columbia "impolitic" but not, as others in the South Carolina delegation had argued, "unconstitutional") and that it did provide Congress with a means of moving on to considering other business. Perhaps, to that extent, the cause of civility was served—which may be enough to suggest that civility is not the first virtue of political associations, a point that certainly was not lost on John Quincy Adams, who secured his greatness through a long, heroic, and ultimately successful, struggle to break the gag rule.[38]

Arguments in favor of civility of the sort we find in Carter and Shils draw much of their persuasive force from the weakness of the opponents they construct. It is easy to disparage the "empty rights-talk" that concerns itself with baggy pants and nose rings. It is equally easy to favor sober compromise over wild-eyed ideological fantasies. But easy cases make bad norms. That we would be inclined to grant the virtue of civility trumps in cases such as these tells us little about how we distinguish empty rights-talk from more serious claims or how we distinguish reasonable compromises in the name of the public good from timid acquiescence in the face of continuing political evils. For better or worse, the only way to get clear on what rights we have is to look more carefully at what it means to be a bearer of rights, and the only way to evaluate the justness of political compromises is to get clear on what we mean by justice. Civility may well be a virtue. But it is probably not a virtue that will be of much help in deciding the political questions that ultimately matter.[39]

NOTES

1. "George Washington's Rules of Civility & Decent Behaviour Distributed to Freshmen By Hamilton College President as Guide to Student Behavior," PRNewswire, 20 August 1998.

2. For the text of Washington's rules see John Allen Murray, ed., *George Washington's Rules of Civility and Decent Behavior in Company and in Conversation* (New York: Putnam, 1942). For a discussion of Washington's sources, see Moncure Daniel Conway, *George Washington's Rules of Civility Traced to Their Sources and Restored* (London: Chato and Windus, 1890).

3. Council on Civil Society, *A Call to Civil Society: Why Democracy Needs Moral Truths* (New York: Institute for American Values, 1998), p. 18.

4. For one refreshing attempt, see Benjamin DeMott, "Seduced by Civility: Political Manners and the Crisis of Democratic Values," *Nation*, 9 December 1996, pp. 11–19.

5. Edward Shils, *The Virtue of Civility* (Indianapolis: Liberty Fund, 1997); Stephen L. Carter, *Civility: Manners, Morals, and the Etiquette of Democracy* (New York: Basic Books, 1998).

6. Aristotle *Nicomachean Ethics* 2.6.

7.   For a discussion of this point, see my article (from which the next several paragraphs draw rather heavily) "Civil Society and Social Things: Setting the Boundaries of the Social Sciences," *Social Research* 62 (1995): 899–932.

8.   Cited in John Kasson, *Rudeness and Civility: Manners in Nineteenth-Century Urban America* (New York: Hill and Wang, 1990), p. 14.

9.   Carter, *Civility*, p. 73.

10.   Lawrence Cahoone, "Civic Meetings, Cultural Meanings," in *Civility*, ed. Leroy S. Rouner (Notre Dame, Ind.: University of Notre Dame Press, 2000), p. 48.

11.   Alan Wolfe, *Whose Keeper?* (Berkeley: University of California Press, 1989), p. 48.

12.   Alan Wolfe, "Revisiting Predictions of the Decline of Civil Society in *Whose Keeper?*" *The Brookings Review* 15, no. 4 (1997): 9–12.

13.   See my discussion of Bruni in "A Raven with a Halo: The Translation of Aristotle's *Politics*," *History of Political Thought* 7 (1986): 295–319. For a wide-ranging discussion of the ideal of civility—and of the perception of threats to it—in Renaissance Europe, see John Hale, *The Civilization of Europe in the Renaissance* (New York: Touchstone, 1995): pp. 355–463.

14.   Jean-Jacques Rousseau *On the Social Contract* 1.6.

15.   For a discussion see my article, "*Paideia* for the '*Bürger als Bourgeois*': The Concept of 'Civil Society' in Hegel's Political Thought," *History of Political Thought* 2, no. 3 (1982): 469–93.

16.   Manuscript draft for *Democracy in America* cited in James T. Schleifer, *The Making of Tocqueville's* Democracy in America (Chapel Hill: University of North Carolina Press, 1980), p. 7.

17.   For a discussion, see Larry Siedentop, "Two Liberal Traditions," in *The Idea of Freedom: Essays in Honor of Isaiah Berlin*, ed. Alan Ryan (Oxford: Oxford University Press, 1979), pp. 153–74 and Larry Siedentop, *Tocqueville* (Oxford: Oxford University Press, 1994), pp. 20–40.

18.   Alexis de Tocqueville, *Democracy in America*, ed. J. P. Mayer (Garden City, N.J.: Anchor, 1969), pp. 514–15.

19.   Ibid, p. 513.

20.   Council on Civil Society, *A Call to Civil Society*, p. 16.

21.   Ibid., p. 12.

22.   Ibid., p. 15.

23.   Hale, *Civilization of Europe*, p. 368.

24.   Carter, *Civility*, p. 67.

25.   Ibid., p. 239.

26.   Ibid., p. 231.

27.   Ibid., p. 72.

28.   Shils, *Virtue of Civility*, p. 3.

29. Ibid., p. 4.
30. Ibid., p. 5.
31. Ibid., p. 9.
32. Ibid., pp. 45, 83.
33. Ibid., p. 71.
34. Ibid., p. 345.
35. Ibid., pp. 26–28.
36. Ibid., p. 52.
37. Ibid., p. 49.
38. My thanks go to Ken Haynes for suggesting this example. For a discussion, see William Lee Miller's utterly engrossing book, *Arguing About Slavery: The Great Battle in the United States Congress* (New York: Knopf, 1996).
39. While editing this talk for publication, a juxtaposition of articles appeared on page A16 of the *Boston Globe* of June 18, 1999. They can serve as an oddly appropriate postscript. Across the top of the page a headline announces, "America's civic health is on upswing, report says." In the story that follows, William A. Galston, executive director of the National Commission on Civic Renewal, is quoted as reporting that the nation's "civic health"— as measured by such indices as crime rates, confidence in government, and involvement in community affairs—is "rebounding after a 10-year slide." Directly beneath this story is a smaller headline: "Canadian executed in Texas." It reports that the state of Texas executed, by means of lethal injection, Joseph Stanley Faulder, a Canadian citizen convicted of killing a Texas woman during a 1975 burglary. The Canadian government, which abolished the death penalty in 1976, had filed documents protesting the actions of the state of Texas. The two stories suggest rather different notions of what constitutes a "civil society." The National Commission on Civic Renewal appears not to consider the increase, over the last decade, of government executions as a counterindication of "civic health." In contrast, the Canadian government, along with much of the rest of the industrialized world, holds that a state's killing of those it has imprisoned cannot be reconciled with any notion of civilized behavior.

Civic Meetings,
Cultural Meanings
LAWRENCE CAHOONE

WE ARE WITNESSING the end of an era in Anglo-American political theory. Post-World War II political theory was dominated theoretically by a version of liberal republicanism that we may call "neutralist." It held that individual liberty ought to trump all other values, requiring law and government to establish just rules of association without favoring any particular conception of the ends or ultimate goods of human life. It was compatible with the modern view of human interests as primarily economic. The main intraliberal debate was one of distributive justice couched in the language of rights: libertarians or free-marketeers argued that rights (and prosperity) precluded redistribution of wealth; welfare or egalitarian liberals argued that rights (and prosperity) required redistribution. That this neutralism was never put consistently into practice did not detract from its efficacy as one of a small set of key political conceptions of our time.

But, to paraphrase a colloquialism, stuff happens. Domestically, dissatisfaction with excessive individual liberty and welfare statism encouraged a conservative reaction. At the other end of the spectrum, progressive hopes metamorphosed from the familiar politics of class into a politics of what we could, including gender, sexual orientation, and disability with culture, call "somatic-cultural" identity. In the middle, "communitarianism" evolved within political theory, insisting that the dominant Manichaean discourse of Markets and States had, as Alan Wolfe argued, forgotten something, namely, society.[1] Internationally, fundamentalist Islam since 1980 and the post-1989 rise of nationalism in the former Soviet Bloc have shown that reports of nationalism's death had been greatly exaggerated and that for many people, at least occasionally, cultural solidarity and religious identity are higher priorities than liberty and prosperity.

The things liberalism forgot can be placed under two headings: civil society and culture. In 1990s political theory *civil society*, with its associated virtue, *civility*, is the successor to *community*, *republic*, and even *discourse* as a name for the solidarity liberalism neglected.[2] The second heading may seem less obvious. Current nonneutralist or perfectionist liberals, who maintain that liberalism affirms a normative account of "the Good," are in effect promoting a *liberal culture*. Culture is at the center of the domestic politics of identity and the international politics of fundamentalism and nationalism. Liberals have been scrambling to find a place in their philosophy for group rights and somatic-cultural identity that does the least damage to individualism, rational choice, and tolerance. Paraphrasing Gilles Kemple's and Samuel Huntington's name for the contemporary return of religion to political relevance, *la revanche de Dieu*, we seem today to be witnessing *la revanche de la culture*.[3]

These debates intersect where conservatism and liberalism meet. Both claim civil society as their own: liberals emphasize democratic participation and tolerant rules of engagement; conservatives emphasize the inculcation of virtues necessary for citizenship. If all has been quieter on the cultural front, that is because culture separates the two sides more deeply. Despite the fact that liberalism has sometimes been a friend of nationalism, the dominant forms of liberalism have been hostile to culture *per se*. For culture is both the inherited, unreflective customs which John Stuart Mill condemned as "despotic" in order to enhance liberty, and the partisan normative worldviews which John Rawls rejects as "comprehensive doctrines" in order to ensure tolerance.[4] In contrast, conservatism since Edmund Burke has accepted the holistic view that politics cannot be utterly distinct from culture. Liberalism has repeatedly fought holism, insisting instead on what Rawls calls the "free-standing" nature of politics.

I share the stated diagnosis of neutralism. Liberalism is not dead, but its neutralist diet, a political macrobiotics, is not rich enough to sustain life. I also share confidence in the stated treatment programs. Given a regimen of civil exercise and a culturally nonneutral diet, liberal republicanism's prospects are excellent. But the treatment is expensive. Its side effects are too often minimized. And the patient must learn to live with the fact that the two treatment protocols, of civility and culture, are in conflict.

I. CIVIL SOCIETY

Philosophically, the concept of civil society is an Aristotelian inheritance. Aristotle described the city as *the* political community or partnership *(koinonia he politike*, latinized as *societas civilis).*[5] This is not an inevitable conception. As Niklas Luhmann points out, it presumes that human society is what humans make it, and thus is subject to moral legitimation.[6] The *polis* is fundamentally humanistic or anthropocentric, a human circle, which gods, tradition, and the natural world may condition but may not determine.

The ancient Roman *civis* meant citizen, and *civitas* referred to sovereign or quasi-sovereign political units. Roman law distinguished *civil* law, governing conflicts among citizens, especially regarding property disputes, from criminal law, crimes against and punishable by the state. The other antonym of civil was *military*. In medieval times it acquired a further opposite, *ecclesiastical*. So, *civil* referred to the association of citizens, in distinction from the special institutions of government, army, and church. At the same time, *civil* was connected to *civilization*, the acquisition of the manners and habits of civil persons. The antonym of civilized, *barbarous*, meant "foreign," and bore a relation to language; its Greek root meant "stammering," unable to speak *our* language. Thus *civil* functions in two distinct albeit related orders: the status of the *citizen* or *civil society*, and the manners of the *civilized*.

Norbert Elias has shown that the modern meaning of civility had its origins in medieval *courtoisie*, courtesy, the name for the behavior required at court.[7] Courtesy became particularly important during the rise of absolute monarchy in the sixteenth and seventeenth centuries. This standard of behavior, according to Elias, is one of increasing restraint, self-consciousness, "affective neutrality," the heightening of shame and repugnance, and the concealment of a range of bodily functions. This becomes one hallmark of what constitutes "civilization." The warrior nobility was gradually transformed into a courtier nobility. This required more stringent childrearing, resulting in works like Erasmus's famous 1530 book *De civilitate morum puerilium.*[8]

The process was not without dissent or difference. The French versions of *civilité* and *civilisation* became the norm. This led the Germans to denigrate mere *civilisation* as a characteristically French external artificiality, in contrast to their own term, *Kultur*, which referred to the inner formation of spirit. Kant distinguished culture, which is truly moral, from the "mere semblances of morality, e.g., love of honor and outward propriety, [which] constitutes mere civilization."[9] While the rising bourgeoisie and its intellectual representatives came to regard courtly manners, with the Germans, as affected, they adopted their own version of civilized self-control, partly in their need for aristocratic emulation. Despite modern egalitarianism, *civil* has rarely extinguished its connoted opposition to the low manners of the peasantry or workers, the "internal barbarians," if you will.

Back to the other strain of its history, in modernity *civil* also came to designate a new kind of social order. Jürgen Habermas points out that the concept of "civil society" (*bürgerliche Gesellschaft* in German, *societé civile* in French) was connected to the emergence of formerly unseen household economic activities into town life through the burghers—merchants, craftsmen, and officials—of the late Middle Ages and early modern period.[10] The town's independence from legal subservience to the manorial lord was the precondition for the modern experience of a public realm of equal members. In the seventeenth century *civil* came to be understood, especially through the development of social contract theory, as synonymous with social or conventional and opposed to natural, hence aligned with the Greek *nomos* as opposed to *physis*. It is one thing to view the rules of society as based on agreement; it is yet another to conceive social life as a *process of forming agreements*, that is, contracts. The latter would be the revolutionary eighteenth-century idea, which is arguably the beginning of the self-conscious development of modernity in Europe, that is, the notion of a commercial society.

After early formulations by Daniel Defoe and Bernard Mandeville, first Turgot and the French Physiocrats, then the Scottish Enlightenment, most famously Adam Smith, argued that commerce was a self-correcting process. This entailed the morally revolutionary idea that the good society requires not a permanent hierarchy of virtuous elites and restrained citizens, but merely constitutional rules to channel the otherwise uncoordinated self-interest of its members. It nurtured the more general revelation, as Elias recounts it, that "society and the economy have their own laws, which resist the irrational interference of rulers and force . . . [in which] men, for the first time, [come] to think of themselves and their social existence as a process."[11] Karl Polanyi called this "the discovery of society," the breakthrough into the consciousness of the time that Church, nobility, and King were not the emanating centers of the structures of life, that those structures had their own weight.[12]

The modern theoretical history of civil society may be said to begin in this period with Scotsman Adam Ferguson's 1767 *Essay on the History of Civil Society*. Ferguson was, as the historian J. G. A. Pocock remarked, the "most Machiavellian" figure of the Scottish Enlightenment, that is, the closest to the traditional republican model of a society of warrior aristocrats, whose virtues Ferguson sensed in the unrefined martial attitudes of Highland culture.[13] Ferguson's book was well known when, early in the next century, Hegel permanently imprinted *civil society* with his stamp. In his 1821 *Philosophy of Right*, Hegel conceived civil society as *bürgerliche Gesellschaft*, which stood between the private, biological realm of the family and the public, political realm of the state, all three constituting *Sittlichkeit*, the concrete embodiment of ethical life.[14] Civil society included the system of needs, the "administration of law," the "police," and "corporations." I should add that what succeeds civil society as the first "moment" of the state in Hegel's scheme, the constitution, includes as an element "public opinion."[15] Habermas has shown that the development of public opinion, especially of a reading public, was crucial to the rise of modern civil society.[16] But the novelty of Hegel's usage was fully to distinguish civil society from the state, as a distinctive layer of human association, with its own, if largely negative—that is, economic, competitive—moral lessons to teach.

Shortly thereafter, in his masterful 1833 study, *Democracy in America*, Alexis de Tocqueville emphasized the cultivation of voluntary associations among citizens in American democracy, including "not only commercial and industrial [associations] . . . but others of a thousand different types—religious, moral, serious, futile, very general and very limited, immensely large and very minute."[17] He defined "civil" society as such associations among citizens, as opposed to "political" society which concerns the relations of citizens to government. This "art of association" replaced the hierarchical, paternalistic structures that democratic equality has erased, mitigating an otherwise unbearable individualism. While Tocqueville's belief, that democracy and associational life are "congruent" or mutually reinforcing, has been recently challenged by Nancy Rosenblum, his attention to pluralistic voluntary association is a key addition to the concept of civil society.[18]

Despite Tocqueville, it was Hegel's primarily economic notion that, in a simplified form, defined the concept of civil society for the next century and a half. For Hegel's emphasis allowed Marx to purify it of its moral, pedagogical meaning as preparation for true citizenship, rendering it an illusory and oppressive condition. Thus *civil society*, with its rich history, was reduced to a name for the capitalist class and the order it imposed. Some within the Hegelian-Marxist tradition, like Antonio Gramsci, later tried to liberate civil society from Marx's simplification. But it is only recently, spurred by the critique of neutralist liberalism and by the concern to reestablish substate social structures in the former Soviet Bloc, that political theorists have successfully revived the concept in a noneconomistic form.[19]

It is time to suggest a way of capturing what *civil society* can mean for us today. My suggestion will follow the work of Michael Oakeshott. To speak of civil society is to speak of society as *civil*, as partners in a place whose aim is living. It is to regard members and their society as the logically prior and morally independent association for which the state exists, hence to grant society a degree of "autonomy" from state, and its members a degree of freedom and equality with respect to each other.

Civil society is not essentially "economic." The modern economic system is that realm of activities, properties, and their effects that are tightly bound up in the "'logic" of the market. Civil society is a level of public social existence whose shape is not constituted by the economic system, although it is subject to it. Arguably, the market economy was the vehicle through which modern civil society came into the world, through which the state was forced to make room for pluralistic association from below. Nevertheless, it is not itself economic; its rules are not those of the market, and its players are not corporations. Neither is civil society "private." "Privacy" can only mean the *domos* or household, the realm of family and friends. Civil society is public. But it is, Habermas argued, a public of private individuals or households.[20] It is a *network of privacies*.

Morality both underdetermines and exceeds civility. Unlike some versions of morality, civility is tied to a place and its residents. Civil society presupposes morally obligatory rules, but these are only a part of morality. As Lon Fuller argues, we must distinguish the "morality of duty from the "morality of aspiration."[21] Civil morality is, if you will, horizontal, not vertical. More brazenly, it is metabolic or vegetative; its goal is living-with. What I would call the cult of activity stemming from German idealism and the civic republican tradition fails to appreciate the value of place and mere living together that is the basis of civic life. Andrew Arato and Jean Cohen rightly call civil society a "self-limiting" society.[22] Morality as a set of concerns that transcend membership exceeds the *civitas*. The perfectly civil individual can fail morally in the pursuit of the Good.

We must also distinguish civil association from voluntary associations among citizens. The term *civil society* has come in current political theory to serve the salutary function of carving a space between Market and State, yet within the public sphere. In such a space voluntary associations would be included. But religious, recreational, and economic voluntary associations are distinct from the association of citizens qua citizens. Voluntary associations legitimately exclude some citizens, and presuppose interests or aims not intrinsic to civil membership. We may say that civil liberty makes such association possible, and that the plurality of such relations "thickens" civil association, hence the meaning of citizenship. But they remain distinct.

In short, the *civitas* is not a contractual or voluntary association, an economic enterprise, or—with a modal exception to be noted later—an enterprise association of any kind. It is also not an intimate association, a community of belief, a religious cult; nor is it a culture or a political forum. It is, to use Ferdinand Tönnies' famous opposition, neither *Gemeinschaft* nor *Gesellschaft*, association via tradition nor association via contract. Any such reduction makes society uncivil.

Oakeshott specifically defined civil association as an association of *cives* or citizens according to procedural laws, which have no end other than the maintenance of a just association.[23] Government is the agency that adjudicates and applies the laws; politics is the discussion of those rules by citizens. His aim was to deny that civil association is or can be an "enterprise association," which, as managed rather than governed, cannot be free. Extending Oakeshott, I would claim that civil association is the only form of association that can balance liberty and membership. The values most fundamentally embodied by civil association are civility, liberty, membership, and dignity, civility being the rules of association for free members and so the basis of their social dignity.

But two points contra Oakeshott. First, I suggest that civil society is the source of law, and not the other way around. To be sure, civil society is inconceivable without rules. But these rules can be tacit, while positive law cannot. Positive law is largely a formalization of the restraints built into the typical practices and institutions of the civil association. Civil society evolves law out of its "substance," to use a Hegelian figure.

Second and more crucially, the independence of households and individuals in civil society is only quasi-independence and its rules are only quasi-procedural. While it is true that the *civitas* serves no purpose beyond the *civitas*, the maintenance of the *civitas* and its goods is an intrinsic *telos* which may require that citizens engage in joint enterprise. In particular, there is in civil society shared concern for the minimum requirements of the positive dignity of members; each must have "enough," or a minimum decency, not material equality. If this is not so, if I have no more obligation to my neighbor's decent existence than to that of persons on the other side of the globe, then membership is meaningless. That is, following Michael Walzer and American Express: membership has its privileges. Economic redistribution at some level is justified by the sheer fact of membership in civil society.[24] Civil society is the kind of procedural association that under certain conditions must become an enterprise association. If it does not then it is not a civil society.

Furthermore, civil society is primarily local. That is, the most fundamental form of civil society is what in contemporary social terms we would call the *neighborhood*. All other forms of desirable political solidarity are parasitic on the neighborhood. The civil state, whether provincial, regional, or sovereign, is then both a mega-neighborhood, a metaphorical superneighborhood, and a meta-neighborhood, a framework for neighborhoods.

Now, localism is a *bête noire* for many liberals. Christopher Lasch, in his late endorsement of populism, was one of its few recent supporters.[25] For many contemporary liberals locale is virtually synonymous with racism and intolerance. People, they seem to imply, are basically good, but only at a distance. More mildly, some object that local solidarity does not insure intercommunal concern; for example, a public-spirited Brookline may be indifferent to the plight of Roxbury. My claim is the modest one that localism is a necessary, not sufficient, condition for wider concern. A deep and reliable, versus a superficial and spasmodic, nonlocal solidarity can only be achieved by building upon local forms of identification and community. For if Brookline's residents cannot be counted on to care about Brookline, how are we to get them to care about Roxbury? This hypothetical is not so far-fetched, since our social condition is arguably so fragmented that getting fathers to care for their *own* children is no safe bet. Can we establish cosmopolitan empathy by leap-frogging their nearest and dearest and exhorting them to cathect the offspring of distant strangers? I believe not.

Last, following Oakeshott, civil society is not primarily political. Politics is the process of social decision making and decision enacting. In liberal republican societies, that takes the form of discussion among citizens about collective decisions. Such discussion does not constitute the civil bond. The *civitas* is a partnership in living, not talking. Politics and government are rooted in civil society, not the other way around. As Nancy Rosenblum suggests, it is entirely possible for "democratic political culture [to] threaten to colonize personal and social life."[26] To be sure, Oakeshott's distinction of the civil from the political is not consistent with the pre-nineteenth-century meaning of *civil society*.[27] But its usefulness lies in denying that relation to government, even self-government, whether executive or legislative, constitutes civil association.

This priority of the civil for the political and governmental is, to be sure, neither historical nor causal. I do not claim that politics and government evolved from civil society, nor that civil society generates or causes government or politics. Clearly it can be argued that government and politics are necessary conditions of the *civitas*. The priority of civil society is experiential and practical—if you like, phenomenological. The basis of the political experience, and its legitimacy, lie in the civil experience.

This conception of civil society distinguishes the present approach from three fellow travellers in the critique of neutralist liberalism: *civic republicanism*, for which self-rule is the central experience and the ultimate value of political society; *participatory democracy*, which makes the fundamental civil experience political involvement; and *"discourse"* theory, based in the work of Habermas and his followers, which makes talking the fundamental ethical and civil experience.[28] All these understandable attempts to revive liberal republican solidarity in my opinion overshoot the mark; they engage in an overvaluation of the political. This is a mistake philosophically, sociologically, and politically. Philosophically, it inherits the idealist tendency to make activity the human essence, the aristocratic republican contempt for passive, quotidian existence, and the Socratic bias that the unexamined life is not worth living. Sociologically, it makes politics the glue of society, rather than a dimension of social activity. Politically, it mistakes self-rule for the ultimate end of the *civitas*, rather than the necessary means to the goal of living-with. In robust versions these mistakes engage the idolatry of expecting the *civitas* to provide the meaning of, not merely the conditions for, life.

II. CULTURE

Now to culture. There are two modern philosophical answers to the question of the relevance of culture in the *polis*, both forged in the eighteenth century. Montesquieu sought to deflate the moral pretensions of Christendom, especially in its brutal dealings with non-Europeans. To this end he promoted humanity or humaneness, respect for human beings as human beings, culturally naked, as it were. The cosmopolitan humanism of Kant and others pursued the same course, and was eventually built into neutralist liberalism. In the other, subordinate tradition, first Giambatista Vico and then especially Johann Herder asserted that human history is composed of the unfolding cultures of distinctive peoples, and must be studied as such. Samuel Fleischacker, following Ernst Cassirer, makes the point that Vico and Herder operated from a Leibnizian inheritance.[29] Herder's approach is in effect a social application of Leibniz, that each people, like a monad, is unified by an inner principle which uniquely reflects the whole. Each reflection is necessary to the full expression of the human essence as designed by God.

The nineteenth century, being Romantic, went in both directions at once. When it took society as its subject, it became nationalist, hence the sympathy of nineteenth- and early twentieth-century liberalism for national self-determination. But when it took the subject to be the individual, Romanticism produced a passionate attack on culture. Inspired by Humboldt's conception of the individual as an organic whole, John Stuart Mill regarded custom as *the* obstacle to the individual's development of its inner powers. Subsequently, the Marxist view of the cultural "superstructure" as a threat to the development of class consciousness was inherited by progressives and egalitarian liberals. In the mid-twentieth century, first European Fascism, then

American racism resolved whatever ambivalence liberals retained regarding culture. Ethnicity, cultural particularism, and religious identification were seen as primitive, irrationalist, and proto-Fascist. When John Rawls in his recent work insists that "comprehensive doctrines," whether religious, metaphysical, or moral, threaten liberal political discourse, he continues an old liberal animosity toward culture. Of course liberals have engaged in political analysis of high and mass culture, in what is called "cultural politics." But until the recent *revanche*, the cultural dimension of human existence played little positive role in liberal anthropology.

But what is this thing called culture? The anthropologists Kroeber and Kluckhohn produced a list of 164 distinctive meanings that have been ascribed to the term *culture* in its various linguistic cognates.[30] Its Latin root *colere* meant tending, as in agricultural husbandry. Culture came to mean the cultivation of human faculties and manners, a consequence not of nature but of the human effort to control nature through art and science. In Voltaire's 1765 *Philosophy of History* it referred to the higher values of the Enlightened era. The first use of *culture* to mean the complex of customs, beliefs, and political forms that characterize a society was by Gustav Klemm in 1843. The influence of anthropologist E. B. Tylor's 1871 *Primitive Culture* made that sense of the word standard in English. Franz Boas, one of the earliest and most influential ethnographers, teacher of Ruth Benedict and Margaret Mead, was influenced by Adolf Bastian, himself influenced by Herder.[31] Twentieth-century philosophy has not played a major role in this process of definition. With the exception of Ernst Cassirer, recent philosophy has been about as concerned to produce accounts of culture as fish have been to produce accounts of water, unless one says that much of its preoccupation with language, especially in the cases of hermeneutics, structuralism, poststructuralism, and ordinary language philosophy, in effect places knowledge and meaning in the context of culture.[32]

By *culture* I mean humanly created public signs, their meanings, and the activities and experiences involved in creating, experiencing, and interpreting them. Culture is a collection of media: social institutions, practices, and artifacts, art, sport, religion, public discourse, manners, styles of dress, and so forth. Its role is to be the public medium in which the meaning and value of other things obtains and is adjudicated. If society is the horizon of interaction and interdependence, culture is the horizon of meaning. They are then two over-lapping circles. Within them we may distinguish three levels of socio-cultural phenomena. First, there is the complex of economic, social, and governmental institutions and practices, including the means of production, the division of labor, the system of roles and statuses, the patterns of interdependence, and state involvement in all of these. Second, there is the universe of personal interaction, the rules and media of intelligibility and propriety in social intercourse, including language proper. Third, there are symbolic practices, including rituals, metanarratives, artifacts, and symbols, which interpret the meanings of things in terms of public or shared ends.[33] The last serves as the interpretive anchor of the first and second. To appropriate the Kantian phrase, then, culture is the kingdom of ends (whereas what Kant referred to is actually the "kingdom of choosers of ends").[34]

But our trouble is not over, for culture comes in packets, and defining culture is a different job from defining *a* culture. Bhikhu Parekh has offered an admirable metaphor here, saying that a culture is a "grammar of life"; hence, for example, being British means sharing this grammar.[35] I would modify this notion in two ways. Grammar is only part of language; there is also vocabulary. A culture is not only a set of grammatical-procedural rules for how to think, act, and speak; it is also a repertoire of possible interpretive patterns, a hermeneutic vocabulary, from which individuals can select. A culture is, metaphorically speaking, a language and not only a grammar. Further, a culture is a particular kind of language, a thick language with embedded ends. Culture is not merely a how, a grammar, and a what, a vocabulary, but also a why and a whither, a set of ultimate values and ultimately valued things.

Now, as noted, the attempt to reconcile liberal theory with ethno-cultural identity under modern conditions of pluralism is a major topic in current political theory. Iris Young, John Gray, Yael Tamir, Will Kymlicka, Samuel Huntington, Michael Walzer, David Miller, and Bhikhu Parekh, to name a few, all claim, versus neutralism, that culture matters. Some, however, do not go far enough in recognizing the problems culture causes. For example, that culture subtends identity threatens liberal anthropology—in particular, the common liberal notion that moral obligations must rest on choices of rational beings. Some liberals accept that inherited culture constitutes the self, but insist that critical self-consciousness and rational choice remain uncon-

strained. Yael Tamir's "liberal" nationalism insists that national identification is based in individual choice, not "blood and soil."[36] But most
forms of human identity are not chosen, and nationality is no exception. If I am constituted by cultural membership, then membership
cannot be electively discarded or acquired. All societies are significantly if incompletely based in blood and soil, that is, descent and
territory, even where culture fails to valorize, for example, a particular
turf. Similarly, Will Kymlicka says that an individual's self need not
have been "chosen," but must in every element be revisable, capable
of being subjected to critical self-consciousness.[37] This claim is merely
a metaphysical stipulation, and an implausible one. It is fantasy to say
that all aspects of all selves are revisable; some are, and some are not,
even if we are unable to say generally or in advance which are which.

In short, many liberals fear to recognize that culture is sometimes, to use Edward Shils's term, "primordial." Shils distinguished
primordial connection, based in links of descent and territory, and
their occasional concomitants, like language, from personal, sacral,
civic, and rational-legal forms of association.[38] He believed that the
primordial is ubiquitous and irremovable, however much modernity
alters its status. But what precisely is primordiality, that is, what is the
distinctive nature of the call of blood, soil, or language, a call that is so
troubling to liberals, and not without reason? There is nothing "mysti-
cal" about it: genetics aside, what is primordial is the past. The past
for the individual is natality and maturation. The primordial is the
maturational world. This means family first of all, or whatever group
takes the place of family, and the social and cultural world the family
presents as primary. Blood, soil, language, and group matter primor-
dially where they are markers of a maturational world which the many
can never escape—nor do they desire to—and the few can escape
only partially.

This touches on the very complex issue of the relation of a culture to ethnicity, nationality, and race, which lies behind the contemporary discussion of culture in politics. There is a tendency among
some theorists to accept a rather thick notion of ethnicity and nationality, thereby separating culture from each, in order to accept cultural
membership as politically relevant but nonprimordial, so to deny that
the populations of modern pluralistic societies are ethnic or national.
In a sense, an ethnic group is treated as a kind of watered-down race,
hence kept at arm's length. My objection is not based in Romantic

yearnings, but in my opposition to the tendency to load too much into ethnicity.

Race can be put aside, since we can analyze it as genetically produced morphology, which exists because of long periods of genetic isolation in human prehistory, even if the rules of racial assignment are subject to change in each generation, as Anthony Appiah has argued.[39] The English *ethnic*, like the convenient French noun *ethnie*, derives from the Greek *ethnik-os*, which referred to a foreign people, normally in a somewhat disparaging way, like *heathen*. This holds true for the roots of *nation*, by which Romans referred to their non-Italianate subjugated peoples. The connotations were in each case different: *ethnikos* was linked both to the character and the customs of a people; *nation*, from the *Latin nasci, to* be born, indicated descent. *Ethnie* and *nation* are simply terms for any human group which counts, for itself or others, as a distinctive "people," by whatever criteria, such as race, language, culture, descent, manners, and so on. We must just remember not to confuse nationality with sovereign polity, a conflation to which the modern "nation-state" constantly tempts us. Peoples need not be self-ruling; that is the innovation of modern nationalism.

What then is the difference between group identity in a modern, pluralistic society and identity in an aboriginal tribe, or a minority ethnic enclave? If we try to imagine the most isolated and traditional human groups, we find two distinctive features. The first is social-cultural homogeneity, which means that society and culture are not differentiated, that is, rules of intelligibility and propriety, symbolic practices, and socio-economic institutions are integrated. Sharing one means sharing all three, which means that the criteria of membership are maximally thick. Second, membership is given and irrevocable. There is no routine of naturalization nor, except under extreme conditions, emigration. There were, of course, pluralistic polities in the premodern world, both cosmopolitan centers where the criteria of membership were differentiated—for example, language or race was not a condition—and empires and consociations, where, as Michael Walzer argues, sovereignty did not represent an *ethnie* to which distinctive homogeneous locales had to belong.[40]

But the pluralism of modern liberal republican societies is different. First, implicit in theories of modern social differentiation, from Weber to Berger, Habermas, and Luhmann, is the claim that modernity is marked by differentiation, both differentiation of socio-cultural spheres from each other, and differentiation of society from culture. In particular, economic organization, knowledge, and political power are released from cultural tradition, enabling progress.[41] Modern societies less are unified by symbolic practices and more by the state, socio-economic system, and mass communications culture. Such modern "cultures" tend, as MacIntyre has argued, to be thin and hence commensurable with each other.[42] A further effect is that since this system is progressive, all must assimilate again and again to the accelerating present which belongs to no one. That is, middle-aged Americans who trace their ancestry to the Mayflower and middle-aged Vietnamese-American immigrants are equally stupefied by the Internet and their children's taste in music. Second, the liberal polity makes membership largely elective. Individuals can routinely enter and exit. Primordialism is not thereby eliminated, but descent is no longer the sole means of membership. Hence a modern "nation-state," like France, is now non-exclusive, meaning that the conditions of civic membership must be highly differentiated or narrowed. In an immigrant society, like the United States, joint membership in more than one cultural group, or "hyphenated" identity, becomes the norm. Lastly, as Kedourie, Gellner, Anderson, and Greenfeld have argued, nationalism, the integration of ethnic groups under a large egalitarian polity subtended by a relatively homogeneous literate culture, is a modern, not a premodern, condition.[43] Modern nationalism diffused an official culture, hence a thinned ethnicity or peoplehood, across an expanded population, rigidly distinguished from that of other "nation-states." In the so-called modern polity ethnicity, nationality, primordiality, blood, and descent have not simply evaporated; rather, the character of the society and culture to which they are attached, and their relation to sovereignty, has changed.

III. CIVILITY AND CULTURE

We now turn to the relation of civil society and culture. The term *civic culture*, a natural focus of attention, turns out to be little help. As can be seen in probably the most famous exposition of recent decades, Gabriel Almond and Sidney Verba's 1963 book *The Civic Culture*, the dominant habit has been to identify the civic with the po-

litical, hence making "civic culture" into "attitudes toward the political system and its various parts, and attitudes toward the role of the
self in the system."[44] This is too narrow.

If civility is the minimal rules of citizen relations and behavior,
which condition membership, liberty, and dignity, then these certainly
are inherited across generations. Civility must be culturally interpreted, stored, transmitted, and legitimated, that is, culturally contextualized. Here again Shils precedes us. As he argued, "the system of
freedom . . . can flourish only if it is permeated with a largely unreflective acceptance of [the] rules of the game of the free society . . .
[and] must, at least to some extent, be based on" tradition.[45]

But civility must also restrain cultural tradition. If civility requires the collective self-consciousness and the interpretive inheritance provided by culture, it also requires that society tolerate, to
some extent, deviation from cultural tradition. Civility is about limitation; civil society is the society of "nothing too much." As Shils wrote,
"it . . . permits neither the single individual nor the total community
the complete realization of their essential potentialities. . . ."[46] It inhibits, for example, any cultural tendencies toward "ideology," or the
politicization of the sacred. The good, or civil, society inhibits the attempt to actualize the culturally perfect society, to realize heaven on
earth. But even here, Shils rightly denies there can be a "pure" civility,
a civility completely unconnected with ideology. That would mean
a purely procedural society, without substantive values or a sense of
supercivil legitimacy.

Philip Selznick makes the similar point that civility and piety
are jointly required for a "moral commonwealth," despite the fact that
they conflict. He recognizes that "their reconciliation is a prime object
of theory and policy."[47] Quoting Santayana, he understands piety as
an individual's "attachment to the sources of his being," the "spirit's
acknowledgment of its incarnation." Piety is essential to what Selznick
calls the "implicated self," the self that emerges "out of the meshing
of lives and activities . . . whose obligations are neither wholly voluntary nor wholly imposed."[48] This piety, in Selznick's hands is, like
Dewey's notion of "'natural piety,'" a reverence for the social and natural sources of the self, including loyalty to family, love of country, and
duties to institutions.[49] The objects of piety are "relatively uncon-
ditional bond[s]," including a "customary" or "conventional" morality,
which, while not exclusively traditional, is significantly composed by

traditional culture. All critical or reflective morality, with which civility is more closely tied, rests in part on traditional culture.

Both Shils and Alasdair MacIntyre have noted that liberalism is that paradox, an antitraditional tradition—in effect, an anticultural culture.[50] Given liberalism's common self-understanding this is correct, but, rightly conceived, the paradox is merely apparent. For once liberalism is understood as a valued set of institutions and practices within a larger cultural inheritance, the conflict of liberal civility and culture as a fruitful, if troublesome, feature of our tradition can be recognized. Toward that end I would argue for a "holist liberalism."

Holism is the conservative view, in the Burkean sense, that the political is not independent of the social, the economic, and most importantly the cultural. Holism rejects the neutralist attempt to insulate politics from culture. Minimally, holism endorses what is called perfectionism, that awful term for the recognition that liberalism, despite itself, does imply a substantive account of the good. As perfectionists like Salkever and Galston recognize, this account of the good must be plural.[51] But holism adds that this account must be suprapolitical and supraliberal: the goods for which a liberal polity legitimately strives are *not* restricted to "political" and "economic" goods, that is, individual self-determination, self-government or participation, and progress or prosperity. Holism accepts that these must be contextualized by other culturally transmitted ends, and that the polity can and must endorse these. Contrary to many liberal writers on culture, who try to fit culture into a pre-given liberal anthropology, holism starts with a cultural conception of selfhood and tries to locate liberal republican values within it. Holism accepts the legitimacy of a culture's attempt to reproduce itself over time, including the use of law, government, and politics.

I would argue that holism is justified on internal and external grounds, externally because it is anthropologically, epistemologically, and politically superior to neutralism, internally because even principles and institutions liberals hold dear themselves presuppose holism. To take one example, the liberal harm principle, which says that an individual's liberty may only be limited if it threatens harm to others, cannot even be applied without distinguishing harms that offend rights or duties and those that do not, and those rights and duties, being not solely political, themselves depend on a suprapolitical moral theory bequeathed by cultural tradition.

Oddly enough, a concept from Rawls can be appropriated here. In his book *Political Liberalism* Rawls introduced the idea of an "overlapping consensus" of "reasonable," that is, tolerant or liberal, comprehensive doctrines that citizens might hold which would each endorse liberal political values but on the basis of a distinctive religious, metaphysical, or moral conception. Thus the reasonable Muslim, Baptist, and agnostic could agree on the importance of liberal tolerance. Rawls's overlapping consensus was purely political. Instead, for holism, civil society must be subtended by an overlapping cultural consensus, an overlapping consensus supporting a common set of institutions, practices, and values not restricted to the political. Within the "overlap" we can distinguish three complexes of interpretation and valorization: first, of the institutions, practices, and ends of liberal republican *civitas*, including market and democratic institutions, along with liberty, membership, civility, and dignity; second, of progress, prosperity, technological innovation, pragmatism, etc.; and, third, supraliberal commitments that explain, interpret, and contextualize the foregoing as contributing to the achievement of the good life.[52]

Holism does not imply that the goods supported by the polity can be simultaneously maximized. It is perfectly compatible with the "incommensurability" of ultimate goods claimed by Isaiah Berlin.[53] The ultimate irreconcilability of human goods does not imply the necessity of neutrality; it implies that goods must be *balanced.* The supraliberal goods of the overlapping consensus must be balanced among themselves, and must be balanced against the political and economic goods, hence limited by the liberal republican procedures and institutions they valorize. There being no hierarchy among these goods, the balancing act cannot be dictated by formulae. It can only be accomplished by practical reason, *phronesis.* And practical reason cannot be conceived but as operating against a background of inherited culture.[54]

As communitarians seem wary to admit, holism *does* threaten restrictions on individual liberty. Any step away from neutralism increases the ability of the polity to curtail the negative liberty of members. Here William Galston's distinction between promotion and coercion is basic.[55] He rightly says it is the nature of a liberal polity to limit coercion to a minimum, but this does not require the polity to avoid promoting or discouraging forms of life. Some violations of the overlapping cultural consensus must be tolerated on grounds of the civil liberty of members, but not all. Which are to be tolerated is a matter of culturally informed negotiation. To the response that this puts us on the famous "slippery slope" toward tyranny I would say only that *life* is a slippery slope; the point is not to slip, and that is a matter of judgment.

The relation of civil society and culture is thus a *dialectical* one. Civil life cannot mean without culture, and a culture of citizens must be civil. We *meet* as citizens; we *mean* as bearers of a culture. Each layer of civil life—the neighborhood, local institutions and practices, voluntary associations, and the mega- or meta-*civitas* of state—must be culturally interpreted and valorized. Culture is the meaning-inheritance of the *civitas*. Culture and civility must each support, and be limited by, the other, and that balance must itself be culturally interpreted and valorized.

This raises the question of cultural diversity within the liberal polity. Conservatism, hence holism, has been associated with the view that immigrants must assimilate to the dominant culture, which is "established" by the state.[56] Until recently, the liberal view oscillated between "neutrality" and what Bhikhu Parekh has called a "civic assimilationist" or "bifurcationist" model, demanding assimilation to a "civic culture" while maintaining official neutrality toward noncivic cultural differences.[57] Both have been criticized by a new pluralism or multiculturalism, which regards neutrality, hence bifurcationism, as a cover for the "assimilationist ideal," which is claimed to include not only nativism but even, in the American case, the famous "melting pot" metaphor, no doubt to the posthumous chagrin of its author, Israel Zangwill.[58] Rather than regarding citizens as equal *despite* their cultural differences, pluralists insist on equal public recognition *of* cultural particularity. In this spirit some have tried to reconceive liberalism as diversity-friendly. Iris Marion Young's characterization of "city life," Will Kymlicka's "differentiated citizenship," Charles Taylor's "deep diversity," and Galston's "diversity state" are but a few examples.[59] I conclude with some remarks on this discussion, particularly employing the work of Bhikhu Parekh, who has gone further than anyone in imagining the working relations among cultural groups in a liberal polity.

Citizenship can indeed be "differentiated," that is, different citizens can feel tied to the polity in different ways. Participation in the components of the overlapping cultural consensus can be complex, a Wittgensteinian family resemblance. In America, the old Anglo-Saxon-Protestant assimilationist ideal has proved largely unnecessary. That our culture valorizes cultural diversity is both legitimate and compatible with civility. And the overlapping cultural consensus is open, as Parekh has argued, to ongoing negotiation among cultural groups, including new immigrants.[60]

But diversity has its limits. It is always relative to sameness. Permitting or encouraging diversity in one respect is bought at the price of ensuring sameness in other respects, for example, uniform tolerance taught in public schools. In fact, most versions of multiculturalism rely on some version of neutralist bifurcationism, the insistence that government treat all equally as citizens irrespective of somatic-cultural identity, even if at another level they promote official accommodation of particularity.

Further, the condition of cultural dominance is unavoidable. Some cultural elements, inevitably more central to the identities of some citizens rather than others, will at any one time be dominant over others. Negotiations are often won by majorities. Taking culture into account means taking majority culture into account, too, as Parekh has rightly noted. This means that what Galston calls "cultural disestablishment" is not possible.[61] Liberalism cannot erase this establishment; it can only limit it.

We cannot forget that human socio-cultural identity is finite and never all-inclusive. Professor Parekh writes, "A white Briton who does not understand the cultural accents of his Muslim or AfroCaribbean fellow-citizen is just as incompletely British as the Indian ignorant of the way his white fellow-citizens speak. . . . Only he is fully British who can honestly say that no British citizen, black or white, Christian or Hindu, is a cultural stranger."[62] Oddly enough, like the conservative assimilationist, Parekh here demands too much from Britishness. No one in a diverse modern society can say that no fellow citizen is a cultural stranger; if he or she can, diversity is minimal. If I move to Beijing, naturalize, and my neighbors cannot relate to my American habits, do they suddenly become insufficiently Chinese?

Lastly, we cannot require with Professor Parekh that negotiation over the acceptability of minority cultural practices be ultimately "rational," that is, a debate in which arguments from loyalty and authority, failing to justify themselves in a noncircular fashion, are illegitimate.[63] This liberal rationalism is suspect. An approach to politics that accepts that humans are fundamentally cultural beings must accept that the "grammar of life" cannot be rationally justified except in terms it can recognize. Citing Shils once more, "Rationalization has thus far been successful because it has not been completely successful."[64] The cultural perspective requires that, with MacIntyre and Gadamer, we see rationality itself as an intracultural practice.

NOTES

1. See Alan Wolfe, *Whose Keeper? Social Science and Moral Obligation* (Berkeley: University of California Press, 1989).

2. See, for example, Nancy Rosenblum, *Membership and Morals: The Personal Uses of Pluralism in America* (Princeton, N.J.: Princeton University Press, 1998); Andrew Arato and Jean Cohen, *Civil Society and Political Theory* (Cambridge: Massachusetts Institute of Technology Press, 1992); Stephen Carter, *Civility: Manners, Morals, and the Etiquette of Democracy* (New York: Basic Books, 1998); and Krishan Kumar, "Civil Society: An Inquiry into the Usefulness of an Historical Term," *British Journal of Sociology* 4 (September 1993): 375–95.

3. Samuel Huntington, *The Clash of Civilizations and the Remaking of the World Order* (New York: Simon and Schuster, 1995), p. 95.

4. See John Stuart Mill, *On Liberty*, esp. chap. 3, "Of Individuality"; and John Rawls, *Political Liberalism* (New York: Columbia University Press, 1996).

5. Aristotle, *Politics*, trans. Carnes Lord (Chicago: University of Chicago Press, 1984), 1252a6. The Latin translation as *societas civilis*, while standard, is controversial. Its story is told by James Schmidt in "A Raven with a Halo: The Translation of Aristotle's *Politics*," *History of Political Thought* 7 (Summer 1986): 295–319.

6. Niklas Luhmann, *The Differentiation of Society*, trans. Charles Larmore and Stephen Holmes (New York: Columbia University Press, 1982), pp. 332–44.

7. Norbert Elias, *The Civilizing Process: The History of Manners and State Formation and Civilization*, trans. Edmund Jephcott (Oxford: Blackwell Pubs., 1994).

8. Desiderius Erasmus, *De civilitate morum puerilium* (Loudinie: Rogerie Danielis, 1661).

9. Immanuel Kant, "Idea for a Universal History with a Cosmopolitan Intent," in *Perpetual Peace and Other Essays*, trans. Ted Humphrey (Indianapolis: Hackett, 1983), p. 36.

10. Jürgen Habermas, *The Structural Transformation of the Public Sphere*, trans. Thomas Burger and Frederick Lawrence (Cambridge: Massachusetts Institute of Technology Press, 1989), pp. 19ff.

11. Elias, p. 36.

12. Karl Polanyi, *The Great Transformation: The Political and Economic Origins of our Time* (Boston: Beacon Press, 1944).

13. J. G. A. Pocock, *The Machiavellian Moment: Florentine Political Thought and the Atlantic Republican Tradition* (Princeton, N.J.: Princeton University Press, 1975).

14. G. W. F. Hegel, *Philosophy of Right*, trans. T. M. Knox (Oxford: Oxford University Press, 1952).

15. Ibid., pp. 314–20.

16. See Habermas, *The Structural Transformation of the Public Sphere*, esp. chap. 12.

17. Alexis de Tocqueville, *Democracy in America*, trans. George Lawrence (New York: Harper & Row, 1969), p. 513. See the rest of his discussion in vol. 2., pt. 2, chaps. 4–7.

18. Nancy Rosenblum has recently challenged that view; some forms of civil association are "congruent" with democracy and some are not. She argues that even illiberal associations are legitimate and can be beneficial. See her *Membership and Morals*.

19. See Kumar, "Civil Society."

20. Habermas, *The Structural Transformation of the Public Sphere*, p. 28.

21. Lon L. Fuller, *The Morality of Law* (New Haven: Yale University Press, 1969).

22. Andrew Arato and Jean Cohen, *Civil Society and Political Theory*, p. 451. Unfortunately Arato and Cohen regard civil society, in my view oxymoronically, as a "self-limiting utopia."

23. See Oakeshott's masterful formulation of civil association in Michael Oakeshott, *On Human Conduct* (Oxford: Clarendon Press, 1975).

24. See Michael Walzer, *Spheres of Justice: A Defense of Pluralism and Equality* (New York: Basic Books, 1983).

25. See Christopher Lasch, *The True and Only Heaven: Progress and Its Critics* (New York: W. W. Norton & Co., 1991); and *The Revolt of the Elites and the Betrayal of Democracy* (New York: W. W. Norton & Co., 1995).

26. Rosenblum, *Membership and Morals*, p. 46.

27. As James Schmidt has been quick—*very* quick—to point out.

28. The republican tradition is currently represented by Michael Sandel, especially in his *Democracy's Discontents: America in Search of a Public Philosophy* (Harvard: Belknap Press, 1996). Benjamin Barber is perhaps the

most prominent participatory democrat; see his *Strong Democracy: Participatory Politics for a New Age* (Berkeley: University of California Press, 1984); and Jürgen Habermas, "Discourse Ethics," in *Moral Consciousness and Communicative Action*, trans. Christian Lenhardt and Shierry Weber Nicholsen (Cambridge: Massachusetts Institute of Technology Press, 1993).

29. Samuel Fleischacker, *The Ethics of Culture* (Ithaca, N.Y.: Cornell University Press, 1994), pp. 115–22; and Ernst Cassirer, *The Philosophy of the Enlightenment*, trans. Fritz Koelln and James Pettegrove (Boston: Beacon Press, 1955), pp. 228–33.

30. A. L. Kroeber and C. Kluckhohn, *Culture: A Critical Review of Concepts and Definitions* (New York: Vintage Press, 1952).

31. See Fleischacker, *The Ethics of Culture*, pp. 115–22.

32. By *public* I mean actually or potentially accessible to multiple social members.

33. The term is partly inspired by the work of Pierre Bourdieu, although I do not claim it reflects his view.

34. See Immanuel Kant, *Fundamental Principles of the Metaphysics of Morals*, trans. James Ellington (Indianapolis: Hackett Pub. Co., 1981).

35. Bhikhu Parekh, "British Citizenship and Cultural Difference," in *Citizenship*, ed. Geoff Andrews (London: Lawrence and Wishart, 1991).

36. Yael Tamir, *Liberal Nationalism* (Princeton: Princeton University Press, 1993).

37. Will Kymlicka, *Liberalism, Community, and Culture* (Oxford: Oxford University Press, 1989) and *Multicultural Citizenship* (Oxford: Oxford University Press, 1995). See also Stephen Macedo, *Liberal Virtues: Citizenship, Virtue, and Community in Liberal Constitutionalism* (Oxford: Oxford University Press, 1990).

38. Edward Shils, "Primordial, Personal, Sacred, and Civil Ties," *British Journal of Sociology* 8, no. 2 (June 1957): 130–45.

39. "Race, Culture, Identity: Misunderstood Connections," in *Color Conscious: The Political Totality of Race*, ed. K. Anthony Appiah and Amy Gutmann (Princeton: Princeton University Press, 1996).

40. Michael Walzer, *On Toleration* (New Haven, Conn.: Yale University Press, 1997).

41. See Peter Berger et al., *The Homeless Mind: Modernization and Consciousness* (New York: Random House Press, 1973); Jürgen Habermas, *Theory of Communicative Action* (Boston: Beacon Press, 1984, 1987); and Max Weber, "Science as a Vocation," in *From Max Weber: Essays in Sociology*, trans. H. H. Gerth and C. Wright Mills (Oxford: Oxford University Press, 1946); Luhmann, *The Differentiation of Society*; and Jean-François Lyotard, *The Postmodern Condition: A Report on Knowledge*, trans. Geoff Bennington and Brian Massumi (Minneapolis: University of Minnesota Press, 1984).

42. See Alasdair MacIntyre, *After Virtue: A Study in Moral Theory* (Notre Dame, Ind.: University of Notre Dame Press, 1981) and *Whose Justice? Which Rationality?* (Notre Dame, Ind.: University of Notre Dame Press, 1988).

43. Elie Kedourie, *Nationalism* (Oxford: Blackwell Pubs., 1960); Ernest Gellner, *Nations and Nationalism* (Ithaca, N.Y.: Cornell University Press, 1983); Benedict Anderson, *Imagined Communities* (London: Verso, 1983); and Liah Greenfeld, *Nationalism: Five Roads to Modernity* (Cambridge, Mass.: Harvard University Press, 1992).

44. Gabriel A. Almond and Sidney Verba, *The Civic Culture* (Princeton, N.J.: Princeton University Press, 1963), p. 13.

45. Edward Shils, *Civility: Selected Essays on Liberalism, Tradition, and Civil Society*, ed. Steven Grosby (Indianapolis: Liberty Press, 1997), p. 110.

46. Ibid., p. 49.

47. Philip Selznick, *The Moral Commonwealth: Social Theory and the Promise of Community* (Berkeley: University of California Press, 1992), chap. 14, "Civility and Piety," p. 387.

48. Ibid., p. 205.

49. John Dewey, *A Common Faith* (New Haven, Conn.: Yale University Press, 1934), p. 25.

50. It was Shils, not MacIntyre, who actually used the phrase "antitraditional tradition," but in recognizing that liberalism is antitraditional, yet a kind of tradition, MacIntyre recognized the same phenomenon. See Edward Shils, *Tradition* (Chicago: University of Chicago Press, 1981).

51. Stephen Salkever, "'Lopp'd and Bound: How Liberal Theory Obscures the Goods of Liberal Practices," in R. Bruce Douglass et al., *Liberalism and the Good* (New York: Routledge Press, 1990); and William Galston, *Liberal Purposes: Goods, Virtues, and Diversity in the Liberal State* (New York: Cambridge University Press, 1991).

52. The idea here is related to Martha Nussbaum's notion of a "thick but vague" conception of the human good, although the particulars of my conception would be different from hers. See Martha Nussbaum, "Aristotelian Social Democracy," in R. Bruce Douglass et al., *Liberalism and the Good*, pp. 203–52.

53. See for example Isaiah Berlin, "The Pursuit of the Ideal," and "Alleged Relativism in Eighteenth-Century European Thought," in *The Crooked Timber of Humanity* (Princeton, N.J.: Princeton University Press, 1990).

54. Here I follow Samuel Fleischacker.

55. Galston, *Liberal Purposes*, p. 180.

56. David Miller attributes this view to Roger Scruton (in Miller's *On Nationality* [Oxford: Oxford University Press, 1995], pp. 124–27), drawing on

Scruton's *The Meaning of Conservatism* (Totowa: Barnes and Noble, 1980) and on "In Defense of the Nation"—Scruton's critique of some of Bhikhu Parekh's work—in Scruton, *The Philosopher on Dover Beach: Essays* (New York: St. Martin's Press, 1990), pp. 299–328. I should say that I do not think this is an entirely accurate way of describing Scruton's position.

57. Bhikhu Parekh, "Integrating Minorities," in *Race Relations in Britain*, ed. Tesse Blackstone et al. (London: Routledge Press, 1998), pp. 1–21.

58. Israel Zangwill's play "The Melting Pot" ran in New York in 1909. See Israel Zangwill, *The Melting Pot: A Drama in Four Acts* (New York: Macmillan, 1921), and especially the author's Afterword.

59. See Iris Marion Young, *Justice and the Politics of Difference* (Princeton, N.J.: Princeton University Press, 1990), chap. 8; Will Kymlicka, *Multicultural Citizenship*, pp. 173–92; Charles Taylor, "Shared and Divergent Values," in *Options for a New Canada*, ed. Ronald Watts and D. Brown (Toronto: University of Toronto Press, 1991), pp. 75–76; Bhikhu Parekh, "The Rushdie Affair: Research Agenda for Political Philosophy," in *The Rights of Minority Cultures*, ed. Will Kymlicka (Oxford: Oxford University Press, 1995), pp. 303–20 (see also Parekh's other essays referenced below); and William Galston, "Two Concepts of Liberalism," *Ethics* 105 (April 1995): 524.

60. Bhikhu Parekh, "Cultural Pluralism and the Limits of Diversity," *Alternatives* 20 (1995): 431–57, and "Minority Practices and Principles of Toleration," *International Migration Review* 30, no. 1: 251–84.

61. Galston, "Two Concepts of Liberalism," p. 528.

62. See Parekh, "British Citizenship and Cultural Difference."

63. See Parekh, "Cultural Pluralism" and "Minority Practices."

64. Shils, *Tradition*, p. 316.

Trust, Confidence,
and the Problem of Civility[1]
ADAM B. SELIGMAN

VLADIMIR ILYCH LENIN is famously said to have remarked: "Vertraun ist gut, Kontrol noch besserer"—that is, trust is good; control, however, is much better. In this saying we find a distinction critical to any preliminary understanding of trust—the distinction between trust and confidence, or control in Lenin's terms. Control or confidence is what you have when you know what to expect in a situation; trust is what you need to maintain interaction if you do not.

Now confidence, and the knowledge necessary to confidence, can be based on many different things. It can be predicated on the ability to impose sanctions and the knowledge that one's partner to an interaction also knows that sanctions will be imposed if he or she fails to live up to the terms of an agreement. Note, too, that sanctions may be formal or informal; they may be based on an intricate web of kinship obligations or on the veritudes of contract law. They may be immediate or intergenerational, symbolic or material. In all cases my confidence is based on knowledge that our interaction and/or exchange is set within a system that will impose sanctions in the case of an abrogation of agreements. This is true whether agreements are based on principles of the market contract between free agents or on status responsibilities among kin group members. Hence, when I say that I "trust" the doctor, that is not quite correct. Rather, I have confidence in her abilities, in the system that awarded her the degree on the wall—especially if the degree is from Cornell University rather than from a West Coast mail-order address—as well as in the epistemological assumptions of American medicine. Of course I may also lack such confidence and take my daughter to Lourdes instead, or trust in the Lord if, for instance, I am a Christian Scientist. Similarly, when Virginia Held says that she "trusts the plumber to do a nonsubversive job of plumbing," that is also not quite true.[2] For she knows that if he does a "subversive" job she will not only not hire him again, and tell her neighbors not to hire him, but she will also complain to the local Better Business Bureau. She may even refuse to pay him. In short, she can impose sanctions formal and informal. She knows this, he knows this, she knows that he knows, he knows that she knows that he knows, and so on. Their interaction and exchange is entered into by mutual interest and maintained by mutual confidence in the system within which the exchange takes place. Now if she were to rush off to meet a colleague and had to leave her baby with the plumber until her husband came home, that would be a very different story, one involving both parties in a relationship of trust. But I will return to this a bit later.

Confidence, to reiterate, is predicated on knowledge of what will be. And this knowledge may in turn be based on the ability to impose sanctions. It may also be based on what we may term familiarity. Because John over there played stickball on East 13th Street as a boy, and I also played stickball, he shares with me certain codes of conduct, certain moral evaluations, certain ways of being and acting that bring me to have confidence in him. We are alike, and hence I can predict his actions. Knowledge of what will be, confidence, and prediction are here based not on sanctions but on sameness, on familiarity. The relevant other may not be "the same" at all; but we will often draw certain conclusions from modes of dress, speech, where he went to school, neighborhood, religion, and so on that constructs a narrative of sameness that inspires confidence. Often, indeed, we combine as many possible bases of confidence before entering an interaction. Formal sanctions may be costly and involve too great transaction costs, so we like to know we can impose informal sanctions as well. How often, indeed, does conversation turn to place of origin, school background, family, or sports—all icons of familiarity, ways to demonstrate some underlying sameness, to the other as well as to ourselves. We do this all the time, in choices ranging from whom to sit next to on the bus, to what architect to employ in redesigning our house. It is the warp and woof of our public life.

Trust, however, is something very different. Trust is what you need when you do not and cannot have confidence or predict behavior and outcomes. Trust is what you need when you interact with strangers. Trust is what is necessary if the other is unknowable. And the other is unknowable when you cannot impute or predict behavior because either a) there is no system within which sanctions can be imposed or b) there is no underlying familiarity or sameness which would allow such prediction.

Interesting light can be shed on this proposition through a brief review of the work carried out by the anthropologist Keith Hart on the Frafas in Ghana.[3] The different tribes comprising this group of migrants were caught, as Hart so brilliantly explains, between two different types of system: the traditional form of social organization predicated on ties of kinship and a more modern one based on the workings of markets and contracts. Faced as they were with the task of "build[ing] economic relations from scratch in a world lacking both orderly state regulations and the segmentary political structure of their customary society," the Frafas were literally coerced into finding a third mode of establishing social relations—one determined by what Hart terms trust.[4] "Trust," he tells us, "is located in the no-man's land between status and contract."[5] It was a "last resort" when recourse to confidence in either long-standing (but now eroded) ties of kinship or nascent (but not yet institutionalized) bonds of contract could not be had. Trust then emerged at system limit, as the only way to maintain economic exchange relations.

This notion of system limits is critical to what I would like to argue about trust and about the very modern nature of trust as a mode of relationship. For system limits are really the limits of our ability to predict the behavior of the other, and as such they are a particularly modern phenomenon. Traditional societies organized around kinship bonds were societies with very high levels of prediction, hence high levels of confidence based on a combination of familiarity and sanctions. Thus to say that traditional societies are societies with high levels of trust is, I would argue, a misnomer. They are rather societies with high levels of confidence based on well-known and mutually reinforced kinship obligations. Predictability is high, variability low. Systems of obligations, responsibilities, and mutuality are clear and visible, and hence confidence in behavior is remarkably high. The corollary to this is that whatever is outside the system is totally unknown and hence dangerous. Boundaries are clear and relatively well marked. When situations arise that do not fit into system categories—such as friendship between individuals in a system that can only "think" in term of ascriptive, primordial categories—these are immediately translated into terms the system can accommodate. Hence the phenomenon of blood-brotherhood where friendship is symbolically transmuted into a primordial tie.[6]

Modernity is, of course, precisely the opposite of this. It is life among strangers, those we do not know and who do not know us. Strangers are not necessarily dangerous. Interaction is risky; and trust, as Niklas Luhmann noted, mediates risk, but not danger.[7] Unable to assume familiarity (though we constantly attempt to do so), and rooted in a "system" of much greater cognitive instability than one based on kinship, we nevertheless enter into myriad interactions with others on the basis of something akin to trust.

True, we do not forfeit the power of sanctions, but we would do well to recall Tallyrand's dictum that "you can do anything with bayonets except sit on them." Force and coercion are aspects of social order (Lenin's control), but you cannot maintain a social order based solely on these considerations. Social order rests on those precontractual elements of solidarity that Durkheim posited as the source of the sacred. This sense of solidarity has often been confused with trust, but the basis of solidarity may be different in different systems. While some minimum degree of solidarity is necessary for a system to work, the terms of its workings will be very different in a system organized by kin exchange, one organized on the basis of a Christian *ekklesia*, or one of the market exchanges of autonomous self-regarding agents. The self-regarding aspect of individuals in modern capitalism is precisely what makes them strangers and hence, in some ineluctable sense, unknowable.

Contract, as the basis of social order, registers this lack of knowledge and so may well register a lack of trust as well, but its emergence registers the triumph of that unknowable and autonomous individual for whom terms of trust may exist.[8] For the first time relationships built on trust become possible on a large scale.

Trust becomes necessary in the face of the free, autonomous, and hence unknowable individual. This self-regarding individual stands at the source of the new terms of civility and friendship that define the modern age. These terms of friendship and of civility now mediate between individuals no longer tied by traditional and ascribed sets of obligations and responsibilities. It was the breakup of local territorial and primordial ties that accompanied Europe's entry into the modern era and it was the destruction of the bonds of local and often primordial attachment to kith and kin, to territorial and local habitus, that forced the establishment of new terms of generalized trust in western Europe. This made the idea of the "promise" central to early modern political theory and to the revival of modern natural law theory with Puffendorf, Grotius, and later in the thought of John Locke, David Hume, and Immanuel Kant.[9] For what else is a promise but an act of will that invites trust among strangers who share no ties of affinity, kinship, or even shared belief. It is "a speech act whereby one alters the moral situation" by incurring new obligations.[10] The social ties predicated on these obligations and the moral force of one's commitment to them thus forge a new model of political community based on a shared belief in the act of promise keeping.

It is only when agency, in the freedom of promise keeping, can come to play a major role, that trust must also come to play a part in defining interpersonal relations. This is of course the connection between trust and risk. Trust is not only a means of negotiating risk; it implies risk. The risk implied is precisely that which is inherent in the other person's realization of agency, since action is no longer circumscribed by role expectations and normative definitions. Trust, by contrast, implies the risk that is incurred when we cannot expect a return or reciprocal action on the part of the other. In Luhmann's terms, "trust cannot be demanded, only offered and accepted." What it is that cannot be demanded but only offered must then be something existing beyond role expectations. This something is connected to that aspect of personal identity not so circumscribed by roles, which is tied to a recognition of the other's agency.

Here is the place to return to Ms. Held and her plumber. Where their interaction is defined by publicly recognized reciprocity—that is, plumber and customer—there is little room to speak of trust. It is really confidence in that system of meanings which define the mutual roles of plumber and client. However, when they step outside those bounds, when she entrusts her baby to him, they leave the restrictions, obligations, and sanctions of system and step into that arena of risk that can only be regulated by trust.

For example, before the prohibition on smoking in public places I always asked people in line at the bank or market if my smoking bothered them; if it did I did not light up. However, when smoking began to be banned from public spaces I stopped asking the people around me if it bothered them. From my perspective the matter had been taken out of my hands; it was no longer something to be negotiated by the partners to the interaction but was now solely a legal matter. Where I was legally prevented from smoking I did not, of course, smoke; but where it was legally permissible I stopped thinking to ask people if it bothered them. If I could smoke, I did. I was no longer negotiating the boundaries of acceptable behavior. Freed from the burden of concern, indeed of civility, the field of smoking was henceforth ruled by law—that is, by system—rather than by negotiation and trust. Why trust? By voluntarily refraining from smoking and so circumscribing my will in favor of the interests of a stranger I was establishing, in however passing, fleeting, and inconsequential a manner, a social bond. Both of us were granting one another a measure of symbolic credit to be redeemed at an unspecified time by a third unspecified party. Precisely this type of symbolic credit is what maintains that social capital that Fukuyama identified with trust.[11] However, the increasing inability of people to engage in such negotiation and trust leaves more and more interaction defined solely by system constraints which are, in their very nature, inimical to the development of trust. I have, in any case, quit smoking.

Note, however, the significance of the story, which is twofold: a) its very everyday nature, just the type of action and interaction that makes up the warp and woof of our daily life like queuing for a bus; and b) recognition of the actors as individual agents, responsible for their own behavior and capable of negotiating its effects. This negotiation is mediated solely by civil recognition of one another as individuals, curbing our desires (or not) in recognition of one another's preferences.

Yet another realm where we may see a similar dynamic at work, seemingly inconsequential, is in the rules of etiquette and civility. What, after all, is the difference between asking someone to "Please pass the salt" as opposed to the demand of "Give me the salt"? When asking and prefacing our request with "please" we are, however formally, acknowledging the possibility of the other to refuse. We are, in a sense, recognizing the other's agency and in so doing recognizing the other's selfhood. Any parent who has struggled to teach her or his child manners can attest to just how important that recognition of selfhood is to their relationship. Anyone who has been through that stage of child rearing knows just how important a request prefaced by a "please" (even an unmeaningful one) is. How easy to acquiesce to demands so phrased and how one's back goes up when demands are put in the perennial "gimme" form.

We have internalized this type of speech over such a long period of time that we have become blind to its essential meaning, which is, however, clear as soon as we take time to think about it. Bracketing a request with the terms "please" and "thank you" is a recognition of the contingent nature of that request's fulfillment, making of even the smallest of matters a sort of symbolic gift. In so doing it recognizes the fact that the other could have refused to carry out our request and carried it out "of his own free will," as it were. Recognizing choice we thus recognize agency and in so doing, in essence, recognize the selfhood of our interlocutor. In some sense it may be claimed that the codes of etiquette are a democratization of deference. Deference, once restricted to those above us in the social hierarchy, is transformed into an aspect of all interaction as mutual recognition becomes an aspect of modern social formations. Those are the same social formations which place the individual at the center of their conception of moral agency and orient the terms of trust toward individuals.

The point here, as with the smoking story, is one of recognizing and valuing the individuality of each. It is of course a formalization of the smoking story and, needless to add, the breakdown of such civility leads to the type of legal intervention noted above.

The whole of civil society, of what the eighteenth-century Scottish thinker Adam Ferguson termed *polished* society, turns on just this sort of mutual recognition. Individuals, no longer embedded in collective groups, no longer viewing the stranger as necessarily dangerous, no longer hostage to traditionally defined terms of membership, group, and participation, meet, in the confidence of the nation-state—and, paradigmatically, of the city. This is the urban universe of life among strangers, among those whom we do not know and those who do not know us, among those who if unknown are nevertheless not dangerous. This meeting of self-regarding and autonomous individuals and their mutual recognition formed the basis of that approbation and moral sentiment which for the thinkers of the Scottish Enlightenment made social life possible at all.

To indulge only briefly in a quote from Ferguson:

> The mighty advantages of property and fortune, when stripped of the recommendation they derive from vanity, (or the more serious regards to independence and power), only mean a provision that is made for animal enjoyment; and if our solicitude on this subject were removed, not only the toils of the mechanic,

but the studies of the learned, would cease; every department of public business would become unnecessary; every senate house would be shut up and every palace deserted.[12]

Vanity is crucial here. For even our self-conceit, our *amor de soi*, rests on the social nature of our existence and on our individual validation in the eyes of others. The realm of civil society is thus not simply a "neutral" space for market exchange, where already fully constituted individuals meet to exchange property or develop commerce, manufacture, or the arts. It is also an ethical arena, in which the individual is constructed in his or her individuality through exchange with others. Vanity is that which links us to the social whole as we become who we are through the other's perception of us. These individuals of Ferguson and Smith's civil society were thus both emergent from group identities on the one hand and, on the other, not yet eviscerated of all mutual approbation and recognition by the proliferation of legal norms and dicta—those constraints of abstract systems of communication and exchange which are defining our own lives.

The early modern shift from confidence (in overwhelmingly shared primordial and territorial attachments) to trust (in autonomous individuals), from system regulations to system limits, is reflected in the move from public to private realms, from lesser to greater degrees of role negotiation. For it is at system limits that roles, behaviors, obligations, and definitions of reciprocity and mutuality all become negotiable. And it is there, consequently, that trust is most liable to be found, as it is there that the risk is greatest.

Existing in that arena of risk that arises at the limits of system, trust is a phenomenon of both private and public interactions. The complexity of system makes it impossible to predict the other's role performance.

We moderns have an almost infinite number of different social relations whose obligations are continually clashing and conflicting. This makes it impossible for us to maintain confidence in any system. Compare this to premodern societies where, as Ernest Gellner has pointed out, "a man buying something from a village neighbor in a tribal community is dealing not only with a seller, but also with a kinsman, collaborator, ally or rival, potential supplier of a bride for his son, fellow juryman, ritual participant, fellow defender of the village, fellow council member."[13] This is very different from the "single-stranded" relations we enter into when purchasing a particular commodity.

For example, as a member of contemporary American society I fulfill more roles than a contemporary Bedouin or a twelfth-century peasant in Languedoc. Moreover, my role as a university professor probably contains a greater number of role sets than occupation positions in nonmodern societies. Together these factors would account for giving me a broader set of potentially conflicting reference groups. Yet within any particular role my relations with role set members will be defined solely by expectations defined by that role and not by others. Thus my filial obligations to my sick mother will be only marginally relevant to the different members of my professional role set—though, to be sure, within any one role, my different obligations to different role set members will maintain a certain relevance. I could, for example, discuss my obligations to my students with colleagues—let us say to explain my research unproductivity—in a way that will perhaps carry a certain legitimacy that reasons based on family obligations will not carry.

Thus, the greater the number of roles in a system, the greater the potential for conflict, contradictions between roles, and the differential privilege of different roles.[14] The greater the proliferation of roles, the more it becomes possible to assign a degree of instability to any particular role. Consequently a certain degree of negotiability of role expectations becomes possible—perhaps even necessary. This leads to the greater possibility of trust (and mistrust) as a form of social relations. If confidence in a system of role expectations cannot be taken for granted, it becomes very difficult to establish role reciprocity which can only be met by the establishment of trust.

Indeed, we in the United States are more and more in need of "system experts"—such as lawyers and social workers—to help mediate the most minimal sets of obligations and definitions of role performance. Too many criteria of role definitions clash too often. As social systems become more and more complex within families, in schools, between genders, and so on, the need to trust increases at a dizzying pace—as familiarity and stories about stickball become less and less binding.

A multitude of private realms emerge which can no longer be negotiated without the imposition of public, standardized role definitions. For without a shared universe of expectations, histories, memories, and affective commitments, no basis of trust can exist. In a situation of private and therefore radically incommensurate life-worlds, the trust necessary to negotiate role expectations is lacking. What are beginning to emerge in its place are the increasingly public definitions of roles and role expectations. In the absence of trust, we have "speech codes," housing association regulations, smoking laws, and other forms of formal regulation of interpersonal behavior. The fact that much of this is framed in term of collective identities (of ethnicity, gender, or even sexual preference) is indicative of the fragility of collective representation based solely on the private. It is a return of collective identities rather than individual selves as modes of representing public culture.

Whether in the emergence of new forms of family life (single parents, same-sex parents, couples married for the third or fourth time), or in the new norms of "distributive manufacturing," small-batch production, personalized payment systems, and labor diversification spread out over a global market, or yet in the cultural forms of a postmodernist consciousness that abjures all "narrative structure" and celebrates the "porousness of experience" of "hyperrealities," "local determinisms," and the polymorphousness of "particular interpretive communities," what we are witnessing is the loss of that familiarity and confidence in social role that had characterized high modern bourgeois culture.[15] We are observing, in short, an end to those shared "strong evaluations" which had been the touchstone of the relation between individual selves and a culture of democratic civility and civil society.

The period of classical modernity was, by contrast, characterized by a "strong" fit between role and person. The social actor was seen as fundamentally constituted by the different role complexes which made up the components of personal identity. This premise stood at the heart of all legal, social, and economic relations and is expressed in the literature of Fielding and Richardson through Balzac, Zola, and Thomas Mann. In this period, the era of the individual par excellence, the idea of the individual and the uniqueness of each rests, not only on the progress of role differentiation, negotiability, and reflexivity, but on the fact that roles were viewed as constitutive of each unique individual identity. Behind whatever front stage was presented (at theater, stock exchange, CGT meetings, or Republican clubs) there stood a back stage which was perceived of as a self, an identity, deeply rooted in one's social role complex. In the broadest of terms this model of self corresponds to Riesman's idea of the inner-directed self, while the more contemporary situation is characterized by what Riesman referred to as the other-directed type.[16]

The proliferation of "role making" and the infinite possibility of self-reflexive regression through an endless array of curtains behind an endless series of stages calls into question the very idea of the stable individual. Note here Robert Wuthnow's respondent in his research on contemporary spirituality, ". . . a 26-year-old disabilities counselor, the daughter of a Methodist minister, who describes her religious preference as 'Methodist, Taoist, Native American, Quaker, Russian Orthodox, Buddhist, Jew.'" As Wuthnow notes: "She appears to have so many religious identities that all or none are likely to matter little when the chips are down. Interesting as she might be, she raises doubts about how seriously religion can be taken when it becomes a mixture of everything, and she contrasts sharply with the unitary moral self on which most conceptions of democracy have been based."[17] This, what Wuthnow terms the "multispherical self," is, however, a phenomenon with implications on more than the religious plane. It is an aspect of our increasing role incumbencies. It calls into question those more traditional ideas of the individual that we identify with the civil component of bourgeois culture.

At some point self-reflexivity must come home; at some point actors must remove their paint and find a face that cannot be twisted to any script; at some point one must settle on a name, hair color, gender, body dimension, percentage of fat and muscle tension, that are not a function of a given job description but are in essence a self. If the idea of the individual can no longer provide this, something else will, and that something may well be renewed allegiance to group identities.

In fact, I wonder if ethnicity, race, gender, sexual preference, "New Age," and so on, are not simply separate interests akin to corporate groups acting in the public arena. Are they not rather "lifestyles" which represent a mode of identity contrary to those classic ideas of the individual that we associate with bourgeois political forms and were indeed essential to that mode of social organization? If so, we may well be left with bourgeois political forms as modes of organizing social life, but forms devoid of that principled conception of the individual upon which the rights and duties, liberties and obligations of a civil polity and society were seen to rest. What this may mean for the concrete organization of society may well remain an open question. It will, however, herald an end to trust as a form of sociability and inter-action, making life that much more nasty, short, and brutish.

NOTES

1. Parts of this argument first appeared in *The American Journal of Economics and Sociology* 57, no. 4 (October 1998): 391–404. For the full context of the argument presented here see my *The Problem of Trust* (Princeton, N.J.: Princeton University Press, 1997).

2. Virgina Held, "On the Meaning of Trust," *Ethics* 78 (January 1968): 157.

3. Keith Hart, "Kinship, Contract and Trust: The Economic Organi-zation of Migrants in an African City Slum," in *Trust: Making and Breaking of Cooperative Relations*, ed. Diego Gambetta (Oxford: Basil Blackwell, 1988).

4. Ibid., p. 178.

5. Ibid., p. 188.

6. S. N. Eisenstadt, "Ritualized Personal Relations," *Man* 56 (1956): 90–95.

7. Niklas Luhmann, *Trust and Power* (New York: John Wiley and Sons, 1979).

8. On these aspects of contract law see P. S. Attiya, *The Rise and Fall of the Freedom of Contract* (Oxford: Clarendon Press, 1979).

9. On the role of promise keeping in the modern natural law tradi-tion, especially as it formed the basis for the development of contract law, see Attiya, *Rise and Fall*, pp. 140–43. This theme is also dealt with in P. S. Attiya, *Promises, Morals and the Law* (Oxford: Clarendon Press, 1981), chap. 2, and in his *Essays on Contract* (Oxford: Clarendon Press, 1986), p. 32. See also A. I. Meldon, *Rights and Persons* (Berkeley: University of California Press, 1980).

10. Annette Baier, *Postures of the Mind: Essays on Mind and Morals* (Minneapolis: University of Minnesota Press, 1985), p. 174.

11. Francis Fukuyama, *Trust: Social Virtues and the Creation of Pros-perity* (New York: Free Press, 1995).

12. Adam Ferguson, *An Essay on the History of Civil Society* (London: T. Cadwell in the Strand, 1782), p. 52.

13. Ernest Gellner, *Plough, Sword and Book: The Structure of Human History* (Chicago: University of Chicago Press, 1988), p. 44.

14. In this discussion of roles I follow the nomenclature of Robert K. Merton in his *Social Theory and Social Structure* (New York: Free Press,

1968), which has become standard within sociological writing. These usages are also followed by Rose Laub Coser who, in her *In Defense of Modernity: Role Complexity and Individual Autonomy* (Stanford, Calif.: Stanford University Press, 1991), develops arguments similar to those worked out below.

15. On these aspects of postmodern culture see David Harvey, *The Condition of Post-Modernity* (Cambridge: Basil Blackwell, 1989); and Scott Lasch and John Urry, *The End of Organized Capitalism* (Cambridge: Polity Press, 1987).

16. David Riesman, *The Lonely Crowd* (New Haven, Conn.: Yale University Press, 1961).

17. Robert Wuthnow, "A Reasonable Role for Religion? Moral Practices, Civic Participation and Market Behavior," in *Civil Society and Democratic Civility*, ed. R. Hefner (New Brunswick, N.J.: Transaction Press, 1998).

Beyond Courtesy: Redefining Civility

ADAM McCLELLAN

THERE IS A fairly widespread sentiment that in recent years the United States has witnessed a decline in civility. This decline is said to be manifest in a variety of ways: sociopathically rude drivers, dour customer service, an increasingly fractious political culture, and a society-wide focus on the assertion of individual rights, accompanied by a general disinterest in the carrying out of social responsibilities. However, while there is a broad consensus that our contemporary society is less civil than its predecessors, there is considerable confusion as to what precisely makes it uncivil. We have a nebulous conception of civility as including the treatment of others with a certain deference and courtesy, but cannot pin down what it is that makes a set of behaviors civil rather than simply courteous. The etymology of the word implies a certain grounding in the *civitas* and civil society; however, to limit civility this way makes it equivalent to a sort of social grease that arises from a semi-enlightened self-interest, rather than characterizing it as a type of virtue. For that matter, the very concept of civility as a virtue is problematic—can one person be civil, or is civility like friendship a disposition that must exist between two or more people? And is civility even good in and of itself, or can it in fact be opposed to the pursuit of justice, and thus best cast aside at times?

I will argue that civility is best understood as a community-building impulse or mood which requires the fulfillment of three criteria: the recognition of the full humanity of both one's self and the other; the awareness of one's interdependence with the other; and the desire to make common cause with the other.

I. TRADITIONAL UNDERSTANDINGS OF CIVILITY

Both *Webster's* and the *American Heritage Dictionary* give a two-word definition of civility, equating it with courtesy and politeness. This sense of the word has earned it a bad reputation among those who insist that civility can serve as a tool of oppression, and thus must at times be trumped by justice. Courtesy and deference, when practiced by a Salvadoran *campesino* towards the landowner who exploits his labor, act to preserve the status quo and the structures of a society that dehumanizes a great number of its members; thus, considerations of justice dictate that civility be discarded in favor of self-realization and a revolutionary consciousness. Similarly, this sentiment is behind Sartre's statement that in order for the colonized to become fully human, he must kill his colonizer.[1] In this reading, civility can become something of a false consciousness—a pernicious hiding behind the skirts of decorum in an attempt to avoid the truth of one's oppression at the hands of the other.

It is also civility-as-courtesy that people seem to be talking about in large part when they lament the currently uncivil state of our society. Complaints about cashiers who refuse to acknowledge your presence other than sticking out a hand to accept your payment, drivers who honk and swear at you because you stop for a yellow light rather than running it, or students who speak to teachers disrespectfully suggest that people are concerned about a society of individuals that seem increasingly unwilling or unable to follow simple rules of courtesy and proper conduct in their interactions with one another. On its most basic level, this understanding of civility implies acting towards the other with a certain good-heartedness and consideration; however, this approach may also become increasingly formalized, until finally civility is understood as being the observance of the rules of etiquette in a given society in all their arcana. To negotiate the more subtle points of civility in such a situation, one must fall back on authorities—whether that be the nineteenth-century guidebooks for train travelers that Stephen Carter mentions fondly,[2] or Judith Martin's Miss Manners newspaper columns. Civility can thus begin to take on connotations of urbanity and *savoir faire*, so that, "in the presence of others, [to] sing . . . to yourself with a humming voice"[3] becomes not merely an eccentricity or display of mild rudeness, but positively uncivil.

To define civility as courtesy, however, is to treat it superficially, and presents problems on a number of levels. For one thing, there is something quite unsatisfying about opposing civility to justice. There will always be a degree of injustice in the world, so such an opposition leaves us perpetually open to the discarding of civility in the name of a greater social good, and forces us to ask the question of how justice is supposed to flourish in an uncivil society. Further, to reduce civility to courtesy is to trivialize it, and to give short shrift to the etymologies of both words. As Lawrence Cahoone points out in his essay in this volume, Norbert Elias has noted that courtesy (from the Old French *cortesie*, and later *courtoisie*) arose in the context of medieval royal and noble courts, and refers to "increasing restraint, self-consciousness, 'affective neutrality,' the heightening of shame and repugnance, and the concealment of a range of bodily functions."[4] The focus is on the process of domesticating and polishing a warrior nobility, and transforming warriors into courtiers. Civility, on the other hand, has its root in the Latin *civis* (meaning "citizen"), and shares this common origin with the words *city, citizen, civic*, and, more obviously, *civil*. There is here a latent implication of not merely bringing one's behaviors into line with what is expected at court or any other particular social setting, but of facilitating the common enterprise of living together. Such a goal cannot be met by the mere following of social niceties. Something deeper is involved.

In pursuit of this something deeper, it seems worthwhile to explore the relationship of civility to the *civitas*. Robert Pippin characterizes civility in its idealized form as "the distinctive virtue or excellence of the civil association." He asserts that it must be characteristic of participants in an ethical community, and thus distinct from a broader respect for all other human beings.[5] Here, civility becomes closely linked with civil society. On this reading, the question becomes one of how to define the civic realm and the society that characterizes it. Lawrence Cahoone traces the origins of civil society to the emergence of the burgher class during the late Middle Ages and the notion of a "public realm of equal members" that arose with it—a realm that was not dependent on church or king, but emanated from the various social interactions of individuals. This culminated in Hegel's influential formulation of civil society as standing between the "private, biological realm of the family and the public, political realm of the state."[6] Any civil society will correspond to certain geopolitical boundaries; thus, insofar as civility is tied to civil society, it too will be exclusive and bound by human geography. Thus, I may treat a Tuareg tribesman with respect and deference; I may greet him and ask after his family in the proper manner; I may love him like a brother; but, failing a decision on my part to emigrate to Mali, I cannot be civil to him no matter how hard I try, simply because we have no recognizable socio-political construction to bind us.

Such a reading of civility was certainly appropriate during the period when, in the West in particular, there came into being a number of states and principalities with fixed geographical boundaries and, as time passed, an increasing sense of nationhood. Moreover, it retains a certain relevance for the present day, in that nationality and citizenship remain potent influences on human behavior and our sense of community. However, the importance of borders in any contemporary definition of civility should lessen just as their significance has decreased in the affairs of the modern world. The extent to which our world has become truly "global" has been overstated by some, but the fact remains that we live in a world where problems observe our geopolitical boundaries less and less. This is true not only of the environmental issues that have arisen due to our mismanagement of the earth, but of economic and political issues as well. Two hundred years ago, you would have been hard pressed to find more than a few hundred people in the entire United States, all of them merchants and traders, who could have cared about the economy of Siam; in the current world, the precipitous decline of the Thai economy set off a chain of events that traveled throughout southeast Asia, hit Japan, moved on to Russia, and took a good-sized chunk out of the investments and pension funds of many in the United States. Franklin Pierce would have never considered rallying a coalition to make war on a state five thousand miles distant in the name of humanitarianism and democracy, as we observed in the NATO strikes on Serbia. None of this is to say that we are witnessing anything as dramatic as the beginnings of a world state, or even a global society. However, it does suggest that at the very least we are expanding our conception of community to include human beings who share little if anything with us geopolitically, and that our conception of civility should be revised accordingly.

II. CIVILITY REDEFINED

Put most succinctly, civility is a disposition that one individual may have towards another or, increasing the scope, a mood that obtains in a given group of individuals or a society, when the following three criteria are met by both or all sides in a human relationship: the individual acknowledges the full humanity of both him- or herself and the other, recognizes his or her interdependence with the other, and desires to make common cause with the other.

A. *The full humanity of the self and others.* For an individual to act civilly, he or she must recognize the full humanity of both him- or herself and the person toward whom he or she is acting. This vague notion of viewing someone as fully human has traditionally implied something positive—an awareness of their fundamental worth and dignity, and a refusal to give in to the all-too-common temptation to view the other as embodying humanity in a lesser manner than we do. Such an awareness or the lack thereof can take place in a number of spheres of life. The classic example is perhaps the question of racial or ethnic differences. The twentieth century has witnessed in America the beginning of the dissipation of the once-cherished notion that white Americans are superior to people of color. Although the issue is by no means resolved, there is unquestionably a greater awareness of the fact that African-Americans, Hispanics, Asians, and American Indians are human beings in the full sense of the word; insofar as this truth has gained a foothold in our society, the society has become more civil. Obviously, this form of denying the humanity of the other is not limited to the United States; two of its more virulent manifestations have recently come to a head in Rwanda and the former Yugoslavia. However, such a denial need not be limited to the confines of a particular nation or society to qualify as uncivil. In a redefined civility, it makes no absolute difference that Serbia lies five thousand miles away, or that I share no real cultural heritage with the Serbs; I still must consider the Serbs as fully human despite the atrocities that some of their number have carried out over the past decade.

The denial of the full humanity of the other in the positive sense of the term need not be limited to racial or ethnic identity, either. Sexuality is an area that is particularly prone to this possibility. Despite my belief that homosexuality is a perfectly normal and acceptable mode of sexual behavior, I do not mean to imply that those who hold homosexuality to be somehow wrong are acting uncivilly. The key is in the way they consider those who are practicing homosexuals. The Kansas fundamentalists who showed up at Matthew Shepard's funeral with signs saying "God hates fags" are behaving in a manner that could scarcely be less civil; however, there is a profound difference between such behavior and the assertion of a Catholic priest who insists that homosexuals are behaving sinfully but nevertheless considers them to be as human as any other sinner. The fact that the priest may be making some people profoundly uncomfortable by his assertion, and may even be causing gay Catholics considerable pain by maintaining it, does not make his behavior uncivil. Civility is not synonymous with social comfort.

In addition, it is not merely the members of distinctly different social groups whose humanity we run the risk of denying; it can happen in our disposition towards those of whom we disapprove or those we view as our opponents in one sphere or another. This is particularly true in the case of religious and socio-political beliefs, as those who differ strongly from us in their vision for society are all too easily explained away as some force of backwardness or evil, rather than fellow human beings who happen to view the world differently than we do. Thus, when I pick up a newspaper, read an article about how a group of fundamentalists in Alabama has succeeded in getting *Macbeth* banned from the local high school library because it includes witches in its cast and thus endorses the occult, and in turn refer to them publicly as a bunch of inbred Bible-thumping cretins, I am acting uncivilly by letting my outrage at their actions cloud my perception of their humanity.

Finally, the humanity of the other can be denied through selfish neglect. This is the disposition behind much of the incivility that we lament in contemporary society. You need to know nothing about the person in the car in front of you in traffic in order to treat him or her uncivilly by tailgating and honking incessantly—it is enough to know that they're driving too slowly and keeping you from getting home as quickly as you would like, and the faceless nature of the encounter makes the incivility easier to perpetrate. Self-centeredness causes much incivility and can either be a conscious arrogance or an unconscious self-absorption.

The phrase "full humanity" is not restricted to the positive senses noted above, however; it also involves an acknowledgment of human sinfulness, or in more secular terms an awareness of our status as fundamentally flawed beings. This human imperfection plays out in a number of ways. For one, due to our status as finite creatures, even the most perceptively intelligent among us lack the ability to see things in their totality, and are as a result condemned to a limited understanding of any issue.

Our sinfulness is not simply lack of knowledge, however. It is also what the Christian tradition has called human depravity. We are beings simultaneously capable of envisioning the highest ethical ideals, yet we are utterly incapable of fulfilling them. Part of this is due to the imperfection inherent in our status as finite beings. At the same time, however, there is a certain self-serving baseness and duplicity embedded in the human character, which may be lessened but never extinguished entirely.

We as a species are capable of acts of generosity, good will, and limited self-denial, but we rarely approach the level of genuine self-sacrifice. Even self-denial and self-restraint are difficult for us. We are capable of a wide variety of rationalizations that allow us to neutralize our moral principles when doing so facilitates a desired end or pleasure. If I know that the best pair of basketball shoes available is a pair of Nikes made by a Vietnamese sweatshop worker, all too often I will be able to construct a rationale ("supporting the Vietnamese economy," envisioning similar abuses perpetrated by Reebok, Adidas, or New Balance) that allows me to justify the purchase of the shoes to my conscience. The aisles of Wal-Mart are filled with shoppers who both cause and lament the demise of small-town downtowns and family-owned stores.

Nor is it only our self-serving impulses that are prone to this moral duplicity—even our attempts to come to the service of others carry within them an attempt to propagate a social, political, economic, or moral principle that we hold to be of great importance, and whose exalted status in our thought has a tendency to blind us to the needs of those we seek to help. The free marketeers of the International Monetary Fund, contrary to the assertion of many leftists, are not all rapacious capitalists who wish to cause the misery of the peoples of other countries in order to line their own pockets. At least some of them have a genuine desire to set all of the world's economies on a footing that will provide them with a high level of prosperity. However, their focus on the free market as *the* answer prevents them from adequately taking into consideration the effects of the reforms they suggest, and also steers them away from seriously considering the possibility of alternative methods of ensuring the flourishing of the citizenry of the societies that they attempt to treat.

Thus, any acknowledgment of the full humanity of oneself and the other should take into consideration the depth of the negative sense of the phrase and its implication of human sinfulness. This is not a call to human self-loathing, but to a self-awareness that we are fundamentally flawed creatures and that even our best intentions may cloak agendas that seek to serve the ego rather than the greater good.

The awareness of the dual connotations of full humanity is only one part of this precondition for civility, however; this awareness must be combined with an acknowledgment of the full humanity of both the self and the other. This holds true on a number of levels, including the classic pop-psychology observation that a person who doesn't feel good about him- or herself is not likely to treat others well. For that matter, a person who considers others, but not him- or herself, to be fully human will not be capable of acting in a civil manner—obsequiousness is not civility. We tend to view our friends, loved ones, and allies as human in the positive sense, and our opponents and enemies as human in the negative. By viewing the other solely through the lens of negative humanity, we begin to consider them as less than fully human, while we overestimate our own goodness and worth. The result is a cognitive imbalance that further skews our assessment of any social situation and allows us to justify the ill-treatment of the other. This holds as true for businessmen who complain about the stupidity and laziness of the poor as for liberation theologians who advocate a preferential option for the poor and thus facilitate the demonizing of the moneyed classes who do not share such a viewpoint. In all such cases, the sense of common humanity necessary for civility is undermined, and the greater human community suffers.

B. *Recognition of interdependence with the other.* Definitions of civility seem to be incapable of escaping at least some connotation of enlightened selfishness—for example, the claim that civility is a social lubricant that facilitates the smooth living of one's life in a given society. Vestiges of this viewpoint can be seen in the assertion that a recognition of one's interdependence with the other is necessary for civility to prevail.

There is some truth to the claim that action in accordance with a recognition of interdependence is self-interested—it does, after all, improve the quality of our relations with others, and this undoubtedly makes our lives easier. However, a genuine recognition of interdependence not only views things in terms of how one's individual fate is interlocked with the fates of others, but attempts to regard relationships in terms of a greater community. An Irish Republican Army member's awareness of the extent to which his own well-being and the success of his cause lie in the hands of his comrades is likely to inspire him to treat them civilly; however, his blindness to the extent to which the lives and fates of Protestants and Catholics in Northern Ireland are intertwined means that he is incapable of acting civilly in the social sphere.

There is of course a hierarchy of interdependence; not all individuals are equally interdependent with one another. This is true even within small societies, and becomes more apparent as the net of interdependency is cast wider. I am more interdependent with my wife than I am with the man who runs the convenience store across the street. In turn, I share a stronger interdependence with him than I do with the woman who runs a similar store in Oakland, California. I am not equally interdependent with this Californian woman and an Uzbek shepherd. The Californian and I are citizens of the same nation and that ties us much more closely together. This hierarchy of interdependence is reflected in the fact that one may speak of civility in a variety of contexts ranging from a neighborhood to the globe. But true civility is not given greater intensity when it is directed towards those with whom we are more closely linked; rather, it is affectively neutral and makes note of the state of interdependence in a yes/no fashion and acts accordingly. If I treat the shopkeeper across the street more civilly than I treat the one in California (should I happen to meet her), I am undermining the mood of civility in the greater society. Similarly, if I treat my fellow citizen with a greater degree of civility than I accord a Mayan citizen of Guatemala, the mood of Pan-American or global civility suffers as a result. For civility to flourish as a community-building impulse rather than a mere self-interested social lubricant, there must be a simple acknowledgment of one's interdependence with the other, accompanied by an attempt to act in an appropriate and affectively neutral manner.

C. Desire to make common cause with the other. On one level, this can be seen as overlapping with a recognition of interdependence, and in a perfect world this desire would necessarily follow from such a recognition. In our imperfect world, however, it remains necessary to consider the desire for common cause as a separate condition for the establishment of civility.

In its simplest sense, the desire to make common cause refers to the human urge to band together with those of like mind or similar goals, and is reflected in groupings as disparate as communes, political parties, neighborhood watch organizations, and the Allied Forces during World War II. Similarly, certain nations may feel a sense of common purpose that serves to bind them together, particularly when other nations arise as threats to their security. The common cause need not be something tangible. It may be a national mythology or civil religion, or the unspoken desire to work in concert for the perpetuation and well-being of the community. These causes lend themselves to social cohesion. For civility to obtain in a given community, however, it is not necessary that all members of the community be sworn to the same cause. What is important is that they wish to join with their fellow human beings in some cause or other, rather than viewing them as impediments to be overcome, or independent agents with their own unique point of view to be left alone.

This desire to join with the other is insufficient for civil communal life, however. It must be accompanied by an awareness of one's interdependence with the other. The former gives a sense of direction and engagement with the other which is essential to civility; the latter facilitates the horizontal aspects of living together which a succession of common causes is incapable of providing.

Lawrence Cahoone argues that "civil morality is . . . horizontal, not vertical. More brazenly, it is metabolic or vegetative: its goal is living with."[7] But civility seeks to facilitate living together through the structures of community. Thus, it is not sufficient to acknowledge our interdependence with others and then do nothing in coordination with them if we hope to act civilly. Rather, we must seek to engage them in the process of community building. Such engagement will involve at the least an implicit vertical morality—a vision for the common life that is to be constructed over time. A failure to engage the other in this manner will result in a community that will be prone to falling into the lazy "tolerance" that Edwin Delattre decries,[8] and runs the risk of ultimately turning towards a violent sectarianism if the societal appreciation of interdependence ever diminishes. In any case, the community whose members fail to engage one another in this way cannot be said to be civil, no matter how courteous or pleasant the interactions of its citizens may be.

At the same time, a focus on common cause and action that takes no account of the interdependence of actors not only is oddly short-sighted but runs the risk of not adequately providing for the more static elements of living together that Cahoone mentions in his essay. Such an approach will tend to lack stability, and is likely to fall into a pattern of pragmatic and self-interested alliance-making-and-breaking that focuses on shorter-term goals at the expense of community building. The desire to make common cause will always be frustrated to some degree, as there are limits to the extent to which human differences may be overcome. At moments of high frustration, it is important that there be an awareness of our interdependence with others to provide a check on our tendency to dehumanize our most recalcitrant opponents. It is after all not only the desire to work for a common goal, but also a sense of interdependence that lies at the heart of community, and it is a sense of community in one form or another that is necessary to the practice of civility.

III. CIVILITY EMBODIED

What, in fact, are the forms of civility? I suggest examining it in three contexts: first by comparing civility to courtesy, second by exploring its relation to justice, and finally by discussing some of the limits of civility.

A. *Civility and courtesy*. As noted earlier, civility has often been treated as synonymous with courtesy. Clearly, there must remain a reasonably intimate bond between the two; otherwise the attempt to redefine civility moves too far afield, and becomes the addressing of a different question. Insofar as courtesy is the treatment of others with respect and deference, it overlaps with civility. However, when courtesy becomes mere attention to the etiquette of a given society, it can become profoundly uncivil. Civility can involve a degree of confrontation and discomfort that have not traditionally been considered forms of courtesy, but which may nevertheless be done civilly.

Civility should be understood as the recognition of the full humanity of the self and the other, an acknowledgment of interdependence with the other, and the desire to make common cause with the other. In the majority of social situations such a disposition will make individuals prone to the respectful and deferential treatment of one another that in large part comprises courtesy. If I fulfill the conditions of civility in my view of another human being, I am likely to hold the door open for them when I see them coming with an armful of packages, I will tend to address them in a way that conveys a basic sense of respect and with which they are comfortable, and I will avoid telling a dirty joke that I find particularly funny if I do not know the other well enough to share this level of intimacy. By extension, a society where civility obtains will tend to observe similar acts of courtesy. Despite the assertion of many a rebellious teenager, such courtesy is not an act of phoniness or dishonesty. Rather, as Adam Seligman points out, as simple a component of courtesy as the word "please" is in fact a recognition of the selfhood and agency of the other.[9]

But courtesy has generally not been limited to a fulfillment of universal and abstract conditions of positive human engagement. It has also included following the rules of etiquette specific to a given culture. Thus, if in Saudi Arabia it is socially unacceptable to ask a woman her opinion on political matters, one who wishes to remain courteous must accept and follow this rule. Similarly, if in the South Carolina of the 1930s it is considered appropriate for a seventy-five-year-old black man to call a twenty-three-year-old white man "Mister Gaffney," and for the young man to address his elder as "Jimmie," a person concerned primarily with courtesy will find some way of acting accordingly and respecting the custom. In acting courteously in these ways, however, one is acting uncivilly—in both cases by giving in to societal norms that insist on treating the other as less than fully human. Despite the fact that we may be acting courteously to the husband of the Saudi woman or to Mr. Gaffney of South Carolina, we are canceling out these limited "civilities" by our egregious incivility to those individuals who in the accepted social rules are relegated to a less-than-human status.

The civil response to such oppressive courtesies is not a passive acceptance of cultural peculiarities, nor is it an explosion of moral indignation and condemnation. Rather, an individual who hopes to act civilly must simultaneously refuse cooperation with uncivil social norms and attempt to engage those who hold such norms to be correct. A civil response acknowledges the deep wrong and even at times evil of the actions of these people, and confronts them with it, but attempts to keep such an acknowledgment separate from the assessment of their humanity. The confrontation of the perpetrators will rarely if ever be pleasant or comfortable, and cannot be said to fall within the range of normal human courtesies; however, it can be deeply and essentially civil.

B. Civility and justice. Civility is regarded by some as a luxury which we can afford when justice reigns, but which must be foresworn when opposing injustice. Such an argument presents two fundamental difficulties. First of all, the finite character of our existence means that any earthly justice is foredoomed to be an approximation of our ideal of justice. Second, an uncivil justice is, if not in fact absolutist, at the least a peculiar and unstable form of justice.

Our achievement of perfect justice is hampered by our finitude in at least two major ways. One is the partial character of the perspectives of all finite human beings combined with the incredible diversity of human experience. This means that any sort of genuine and detailed consensus as to what perfect justice is will be unattainable. Thus, we will inevitably find ourselves able to envision a better and more just world, but forced to live with those we perceive to act unjustly. So we must act with an awareness of the limited way in which ideal justice may be embodied as well as an acknowledgment of the inevitability of living in community with the perpetrators of injustices both real and perceived. Thus, civility may not simply be cast aside due to its supposed inefficacy in the pursuit of justice, but should continually inform all attempts to make our world a more just one.

A classic example of the civil pursuit of justice is the civil rights movement that took place in this country during the 1950s and '60s. The participants in this movement had no doubts as to the rightness of their goal of equal treatment under the law, and were not willing to cease in their struggle until this goal had been achieved. Their opposition was formidable, permeating the entire South. It was quite explicit about its hatred for the members of the movement, and murdered three voter registration volunteers, attacked an unarmed busload of Freedom Riders, bombed a church and killed four little girls, beat a pregnant woman to the point that she miscarried, turned dogs and fire hoses on young children, and more. The members of the civil rights movement had good cause to hate, but as a movement they refused to do so. Rather than denounce Bull Connor and his white Alabama supporters as a cancer on the American body politic, Martin Luther King and his colleagues in the movement asserted that these segregationists were the misguided perpetrators of a profound wrong, but they were to be confronted in a spirit of brotherhood and brought into the Beloved Community.[10] This sentiment was of course profoundly influenced by the philosophy of nonviolence, but what made the movement civil was not the renunciation of violence *per se* but the spirit of engagement and self-sacrifice for the greater good that King's philosophy of nonviolence implied. The pursuit of justice was not compromised. It was informed by an awareness of the humanity of the self and other, a sense of interdependence with the other, and the desire to make common cause with the other.

The alternative to having civility inform the pursuit of justice is the development of an absolutist form of justice. Such a justice ignores the communal components and finite character of human life and superimposes abstract principles of rightness and justice which it then attempts to force human beings to live by. It is no longer human life but conceptions of justice that are considered as sacred. This is problematic on two levels. Such a vision of justice will have a tendency to blind its devotees to the necessity of using just and civil means to achieve it. The result is often the legitimation of considerable abuses in the pursuit of "justice." A classic example of this is the Algerian war of independence, in which the French insistence on the justness of a French Algeria ultimately led to the use of torture by French police on the Arab and Berber population, and the FLN goal of a "free Algeria" legitimated in their eyes the terrorist bombing of streetcars and French night clubs. In addition, such a conception of justice may lead to a more subtle dehumanization, whereby opponents of such a vision are perceived to lie outside the promised community. Thus no attempt is made to engage the other or to treat them as fully human, and the society gradually becomes increasingly factional and fractious. Justice must be informed by civility if there is to be any sort of stable society.

C. The limits of civility. Civility will inevitably be limited in at least two major ways. First, it is an ideal which may be approximated but never perfectly realized. Second, there are circumstances where civility breaks down and the resort to war on either a literal or metaphorical level becomes necessary.

The attainment of a perfect civility is hampered by our finite condition in the same way that a perfect justice is. We lack sufficient powers of love and objectivity to view those who oppose us as fully human or to desire to make common cause with them. Even the most pure-hearted attempt to engage the other civilly may be misread as a repudiation or rebuke, with a resultant decline in civility. A white politician who publicly suggests that the black community needs to take steps to address the terrible problem of gang violence among black youths is, regardless of his intentions, likely to be perceived as the latest in a line of white demagogues who play on the fear of black crime for their own political success, and decried accordingly. In this manner, our status as finite and historical creatures will limit our achievement of civility.

Civility is also confronted with limited power in the face of co-ordinated and unrestrained evil. That is, there are certain situations in which civility ceases to be a legitimate option due to the presence of a threat that has no desire to abide by the principles of civility and which attempts to destroy all those who oppose it or fall outside its vision of the ideal society. The classic examples of this in the twentieth century are communism and Nazism, both of which made the pretense of participation in civil society a means of maneuvering their way to absolute political power. When movements such as these represent only a small portion of a given society and present no real threat, it remains a reasonable option to attempt to engage them according to all of the principles of civility; however, once they approach the level of power at which they are able to begin carrying out their program, it becomes futile, if not in fact self-destructive, to engage them in this manner—one thinks of the European Jews who hoped until the very end that negotiation and cooperation with the Nazis would ease their fates. In such cases, otherwise civil human beings will find themselves forced to resort to war on some scale if they are not themselves to be destroyed, and war represents a breakdown in civility.

CONCLUSION

Civility, therefore, is best understood as the mood that obtains when there is an acknowledgment of the full humanity of the self and the other, an awareness of interdependence with the other, and a desire to make common cause with the other. Courtesy is part of such a civility, but only insofar as it does not serve to relegate certain groups of individuals to second-class status. Justice is compatible with such a civility, but only insofar as it is not an absolute justice that insists on the priority of principles to human beings.

NOTES

1. "The rebel's weapon is the proof of his humanity. For in the first days of the revolt you must kill: to shoot down a European is to kill two birds with one stone, to destroy an oppressor and the man he oppresses at the same time: there remain a dead man, and a free man . . ." Jean-Paul Sartre, Preface to Frantz Fanon's *The Wretched of the Earth* (New York: Grove Press, 1963), p. 22.

2. Stephen L. Carter, *Civility: Manners, Morals, and the Etiquette of Democracy* (New York: Basic Books, 1998), p. 4.

3. "The Rules of Civility and Decent Behaviour in Company and Conversation" http://www.nationalcenter.inter.net/WashingtonCivility.html.

4. Lawrence Cahoone, "Civic Meetings, Cultural Meanings," in *Civility*, ed. Leroy S. Rouner (Notre Dame, Ind.: University of Notre Dame Press, 2000), p. 42.

5. Robert B. Pippin, "The Ethical Status of Civility," in *Civility*, ed. Leroy S. Rouner (Notre Dame, Ind.: University of Notre Dame Press, 2000), pp. 103, 105.

6. Cahoone, "Civic Meetings," p. 44.

7. Ibid., p. 45.

8. Edwin J. Delattre, "Civility and the Limits to the Tolerable," in *Civility*, ed. Leroy S. Rouner (Notre Dame, Ind.: University of Notre Dame Press, 2000).

9. Adam Seligman, "Trust, Confidence, and the Problem of Civility," in *Civility*, ed. Leroy S. Rouner (Notre Dame, Ind.: University of Notre Dame Press, 2000), p. 70.

10. John Lewis, *Walking with the Wind: A Memoir of the Movement* (New York: Simon and Schuster, 1998), esp. pp. 80–374.

The Belligerence of Dogma

STEPHEN TOULMIN

ONE THING IS SURE. Those who use phrases like "The Age of Enlightenment" and "The Age of Romanticism" to refer to the culture of western Europe in the eighteenth and nineteenth centuries will not look back to the twentieth century and call it "The Age of Civility." For the core meaning of this term—setting aside for the time being the historical senses "connected with citizenship, and civil polity" that the *Oxford English Dictionary* recognizes as obsolete—refers to "behaviour proper to the intercourse of civilized people; ordinary courtesy or politeness, as opposed to rudeness of behaviour; decent respect, consideration." If the record of two world wars, from 1914 to 1945, had left any doubt on the matter, the monstrous practices of "ethnic cleansing" to which we have been introduced in the 1990s would settle it finally.

True, Adolf Hitler gave us a foretaste of these practices in the 1940s; but we were inclined to respect the optimistic claims about the *uniqueness* of the Holocaust so often insisted on by the Jews themselves, and it is with sinking stomachs that we watch similar atrocities unleashed by Hutus on Tutsis, Serbs on Croats and Muslims, and vice versa. None of this conduct displays consideration, let alone decent respect. None of it is proper to the intercourse of civilized people. Such policies and practices make the Enlightenment—even Romanticism— look like saintliness.

In the present essay, it is no use anticipating the judgments of future historians, who will recollect our emotions from positions of greater tranquility. At most, it is worth focusing on one shared feature of the issues that politicians and ideologues rely on to distract attention from the atrocity of their atrocities, namely, their insistence on the unique truth of the religious or nationalistic claims that are the themes of their propaganda—in a phrase, the *dogmatism of their dogmas*. This is not an exclusively twentieth-century subject. On the contrary, it is worth pursuing it back as far as the seventeenth century, or even earlier. So I will here allow myself the liberty of taking soundings from earlier stages in human history, in hope of casting some cool light on a hot topic.

Scholars recognize that the concept of *dogmas* itself embodies an etymological puzzle. To pose this puzzle as a question: what was the difference in classical thought between "doctrines," "dogmas," and simple opinions? In classical Greek and Latin alike, all three nouns (*doctrina*, *dogma*, and *doxa*) were cognate with the same verb, *doceo* ("I teach"). That verb was written in Greek with a *kappa* (*dokeo*)—a trivial difference—and all three nouns shared the core meaning of "what appears to be so" and is therefore an "opinion" or "judgment" fit to be taught. While their core meanings overlapped, their overtones progressively diverged across the spectrum ranging from "a mere conjecture" (*doxa*) to "a public decree" (*dogma*). The noun *dogmatias* came to refer to "a sententious person"; the verb *dogmatizein* meant "to lay down an opinion"; and so eventually, by the time of Quintilian, the adjective *dogmatikos* had the force—surprise, surprise!—of "didactic."

So much for etymological background. At this point, we need to look closely at the history of Christian belief, and the ways in which contentious issues of doctrine began to be framed and distinguished. In particular, we do well to recognize how differently the terms *doctrina* and *dogma* were related during the High Middle Ages, and from the Protestant Reformation on, respectively.

We have been encouraged to think of the medieval Western Church as enforcing "right opinion" (*ortho-doxia*, "orthodoxy") in a *dogmatic* manner, using this word in its modern sense. Often, indeed, the very term *medieval* is (like *scholastic*) used with derogatory implications. Historically speaking, the opposite is nearer the mark. Before 1500, debates about theology and philosophy left room for a variety of views. Quite apart from the differences among the parallel scholarly and monastic traditions, teachers within the ambit of the Church's *magisterium* (teaching function) were free to interpret doctrines more or less narrowly or liberally: from a "rigorist" standpoint, which insisted on one single, generally supported interpretation, across a spectrum by way of a "tutiorist" or "probabiliorist" to a "probabilist" or even a "laxist" reading, for which the support of only one authoritative *doctor* ("teacher") is all that was needed. Further, the teachers to be cited as authorities need not be Christians. Aristotle and Cicero were the source for arguments and cases that were offered for debate without any embarrassment. Finally, the Schoolmen learned from Aristotle to attach weight, on suitable occasions, to "common opinion," even to what Ludwig Wittgenstein would, much later on, call "agreement in concepts."

To return to a familiar illustration, the five general lines of arguments Aquinas uses to elucidate our idea of God: his *quinque viae*, or "five ways"—were never meant as quasi-Euclidean apodictic demonstrations of the proposition "God exists," capable of converting an unbeliever. To this extent, it is misleading to refer to them—as is often done—as "proofs of the existence of God." Rather, Aquinas' claim is to articulate the ramifications of ideas that were embodied in medieval common sense: each argument therefore concluded, "This everyone calls God." If, in the thirteenth century, anyone baldly questioned the current belief in God, it could not be taken as a counter-assertion ("Is God an *existent* Being? No, God is a *non-existent* Being"). Given the shared understandings of people in general, such a challenge would have been unintelligible. The point of the Psalmist's lines, "The fool hath said in his heart, 'There is no God'; . . . like the crackling of thorns under the pot," is to register the fact that—even if it were as loud as speech—any such statement would, as late as Aquinas' time, be heard as "noise" rather than as a "signal."

It is as though a twentieth-century European were to say—without explanation—"There are no *forces*," or even "There are no *objects*." What would we make of this? We cannot simply "beg to differ," for we cannot "disagree" about something we do not even understand. Nixing an element in our currently assumed ontology is something that cannot be done without explanation, and we would indicate this breakdown of communication by replying, perhaps, "Huh?!" or at best, "I don't get it!"

Right up to 1500, that is to say, the action of God in the world was—to adopt Collingwood's phrase—an "absolute" presupposition. Just how God's action was manifested in particular situations was open to discussion, but the bare *fact* of His action was not open to question. As James Gustafson puts the point, our experience of living in the world is an experience both of agencies that bear down on us, limiting our powers, and of agencies that sustain us, making our action effective. Before the ecclesiastical schism of the Reformation and the Council of Trent, as a result, there were no clear criteria for telling

"doctrines" from "dogmas": it was up to the Church to teach the faithful as best it could, and all its doctrines and dogmas were, on mature
reflection, revisable or reformulable.

The years from 1517 on saw the debate enter a new period of
contentiousness, culminating in the bloody events of the Thirty Years
War from 1618 to 1648. Instead of a conceptual framework unthink-
ingly expressed in *theistic* terms, rival theologies, which were grist for
the new scientific intelligentsia of the late sixteenth and seventeenth
century, grew up to challenge thinkers from all congregations and denominations. This was a brand-new situation: "God exists" ceased to
be one of the *truisms* of the Age—one constitutive element helping to
define the conceptual framework of European thought—and became
an *assertion*. The Origins of Modern Atheism, as Michael Buckley has
explained, were thus all of a piece with the Origins of Modern Theism.

Meanwhile, issues of religious affiliation became politicized.
Doctrinal differences became grist for the sovereigns of the time. At
first, the effects were not too severe. The Polish Constitution of 1555
imposed toleration toward all denominations, though this toleration was abandoned under Jesuit pressure from the 1630s on. Meanwhile, the comparatively liberal terms of the Treaty of Augsburg (also
in 1555) granted each sovereign the right to choose an established
church for his or her territory. After 1618, matters were more oppressive. The Austrian Habsburgs made support for Catholicism a test
of loyalty to the regime. This led to a persecution of Protestants under
Austrian jurisdiction no less severe than that which would be experienced by French Huguenots later in the century, following the Revo-
cation of the Edict of Nantes. (Outside Vienna, few readers, or even
scholars, realize what a large fraction of the Viennese had become
Protestants by the year 1600; when I inquire from my Austrian colleagues, the figures I repeatedly hear run as high as 75 percent!)

From 1618 on, the Emperor and the Court were sincerely
committed to the Catholic cause; but the professionals, craftspeople,
and skilled artisans were largely Lutheran, and found themselves
faced with the alternatives of nominal conversion, emigration, or persecution. (There are those who see in this choice one source of the
Gemütlichkeit—the willingness to say whatever one's hearer is hop-
ing for—that is a familiar feature of Viennese social relations.) So
began a shift that finally led to a redefinition of *dogmas* as marking off
those *doctrines* about whose foundations good Catholics were not

even permitted to ask questions, so allowing the papacy and Curia to control the core content of the *magisterium*—at least in theory.

For some two hundred years, until the 1840s, this control was more complete in theory than in practice, and there was little to stop different Provinces of the Roman Church going their own ways. Under Richelieu and Mazarin, the French Church acknowledged the authority of the Pope in Rome in words more than deeds. The reasons why this was still possible for so long were technological, not organizational. Until the introduction of the electric telegraph, the fastest way to send or receive long-distance messages was what it had been ever since the height of the Roman Empire, some 1500 years before—namely, by courier—and its speed was the pace of the nimblest post-horse.

The thing that made centralized Church authority practicable, not just theoretical, was the worldwide spread of Samuel Morse's invention, Morse code and all. From then on messages could be exchanged among the authorities of Church or State some hundreds of miles apart in minutes, not days or weeks. Ambassadors or cardinals might remain "plenipotentiary" in title, but the reality of their independent power was largely stripped away. This change became powerfully influential only with the First Vatican Council. The seeds of centralization, sown at the time of the Counter-Reformation, turned into the effective authority over Church teaching exerted nowadays by Cardinal Ratzinger and his colleagues. No wonder Pope Pius IX, who watched over the First Vatican Council and became more conservative the more he reflected on the political implications of the French Revolution—especially after the events of 1848—is known to liberal-minded American Catholics even today as "Pio NoNo." It was he who elevated the *doctrine* of papal infallibility into a *dogma*, and so supposedly set it beyond challenge.

A certain irony surrounds the changes initiated by Samuel Morse's electric telegraph. Quite aside from this invention, and his Code for telegraphic messages, Morse was well known in his time for two other things. He was a very competent painter, and he was a committed anti-Papist. No twentieth-century Southern Baptist was more suspicious of the power or policy of the Roman Catholic Church than Morse himself. He would have gone on the warpath against, say, John Fitzgerald Kennedy's candidacy for President. Yet, if his personal conviction that the papacy was the hub of a worldwide conspiracy to undermine the

Constitution of the United States had been realistic, his own telegraph would have given the conspirators an indispensable instrument. Instead of sending all messages by trans-Atlantic steamboat, taking a couple of weeks in each direction, he had provided a technical means for keeping even the most distant fellow conspirators under supervision and control.

Unfortunately, the same instruments that might have supported the relatively benign power network based in the Vatican, of which Samuel Morse was so distrustful in his own time, played a part throughout the twentieth century in sustaining the malignities of fascism, Nazism, the mid-century Holocaust, and our contemporary ethnic cleansing. So, the rival dogmas of political dictators like Lenin or Mussolini, Hitler or Milosevic, have been free to do much more harm, and used to justify killing many more millions of "non-Aryans" (or other nonpersons) by excluding them from the protection given to other human beings as a matter of mere civility: namely, "ordinary courtesy or politeness; decent respect or consideration."

As the twentieth century passes into history, many people are worried about the new powers conferred on potential malefactors by their access to the Internet or cyberspace. If I have spent a little time here on the political and cultural consequences of Samuel P. Morse's electric telegraph, it is because (as I see it) the political goods and ills we owe Morse are more obvious than anything for which the Internet is responsible, up to now.

The bitterest lesson of our century is that it is possible to make an ideological issue of just about any difference between our own community and another, suspect group, between us and them. The same hostility and scorn concentrated in the Middle Ages on the Jews—whose skill in occupations that Christians were unwilling to undertake, like banking, was turned back on all Jews, as tainted by those occupations—has been turned onto Kulaks and Tutsis, Bosnian Muslims, Kosovars, and other non-Serbs, with no less belligerence and brutality.

In the notable essays making up his book on ethnic conflict, *The Warrior's Honor*, Michael Ignatieff borrows a phrase from Freud, when he writes about "the narcissism of minor differences." From a distance, few outsiders can see the differences between Serbs and Croats as warranting the mutual mayhem that characterized their relations on the ground during the disintegration of Yugoslavia in the early 1990s; nor could those who were actually caught up in the fighting, as Ignatieff himself found when he visited both sides of the front line at Vukovar in Eastern Slavonia.

Jonathan Swift (you recall) makes the same point well enough, in locating an issue of seemingly ultimate triviality: when he pits those people who open their boiled eggs at the wide end against those who open them at the pointed end. It would be good if we could be confident that Swift's Fable of the Big-Enders versus the Little-Enders is exaggerated, but, to our cost, we know better now. Triviality itself can be odious.

In the long run, the secret of survival lies with the skeptics, who refuse to allow any doctrine to be set beyond challenge, or elevated into a dogma, and who recognize that the very act of turning a legitimate belief into an unquestionable axiom is too often the prelude to belligerence. In this respect, patriotism is easily corrupted into dogmatism, and dogmatism into sloganeering. We had better watch our steps.

PART II

The Civility Debate

The Ethical Status of Civility [1]

ROBERT B. PIPPIN

I

Civility, as its name implies, denotes a quality or social form characteristic of a particular kind of human association—a civil society. In its idealized form, civility can be said to be the distinctive virtue or excellence of the civil association, in the way that courage is for military associations, or industriousness for enterprise associations.

This means that civility can be discussed in any number of ways, depending on what one understands by the notion of civil society. Minimally, a civil society can simply designate the rule of law, and civility would then mean law-abidingness, or an enduring, stable disposition toward law-abidingness, together with various manifestations of such a disposition. Any fuller understanding of the meaning and various dimensions of civil virtues such as patriotism and their relation to civility will then depend on one's theory of the *civitas*, in order to define the nature of a *civis* and the various virtues of such a human type. Here the original question would be: what makes a human association a civil or political one? Such a question leads quickly to the land of philosophical giants, to the likes of Aristotle, Hobbes, and Hegel and to very daunting, intimidating issues.

There is also a historical dimension to the question. Virtues *like* civility, such as hospitality, decorum, dignity, and politeness, have often been desiderata of various societies at various times. Civil society is, however, a modern notion, meant to refer to a public sphere, a certain ethical bond among free individuals, distinctly characteristic of modern societies, committed in common to the value of a free life as the highest good.

However, the question of civility can also be detached from the issue of the rules of civil association, and the virtue in question can mean much more than accepting and abiding by those rules as one

103

goes about the pursuit of one's private ends. It can mean much more than law-abidingness. There need be nothing illegal about such things as sarcasm and hostility in academic exchanges, rudeness in cab drivers or waiters, insensitivity in the telling of ethnically offensive jokes, screaming fits and "road rage" on the highways, suggestions, just this side of the libel law, that a political opponent is a criminal or a cheat, and so forth, but something is clearly going wrong in such exchanges and that wrong seems natural to characterize as a lack of civility. This seems more important and far-reaching than issues of politeness but also not a sanctionable violation of rights, not the sort of injury we think subject to the state's great coercive power. This is the sort of notion of civility, or the virtue of "appropriateness" in public conduct affecting other free subjects, that is my topic. It is the sort of category that often comes to mind in questions of what is "offensive," and why it is wrong to be offensive, as in the issue of "appropriate" language or content in television shows or advertisements, obscene messages on t-shirts, and so forth. The issue arises as well as more subtle forms of indifference to others that do not qualify as moral harm, but as an absence of solidarity or acknowledgement of others that we nevertheless consider morally important in some way. As already intimated, this "virtue" sense of the issue of civility is today inseparable from the "legal" sense of civil regulation. But that will introduce a special problem in what follows.

And, as already apparent, civility in this sense can be very hard to identify. The moral phenomenology and category problems introduce phenomena intertwined with issues of decorum, politeness, beneficence, and respect and so make a simple categorization difficult. In a rough and ready sense, we can all recognize incivility as a kind of disrespect, disregard of or indifference to others, a disrespect that is serious but does not rise to the level of immoral treatment of others. Of course, such things as assault or cheating are also "not civil," but what we are trying to understand are forms of incivility that are not illegal or immoral but, in some sense yet to be identified, still wrongs. Imagine, for example, that you are teaching a seminar, and imagine three scenarios: (i) a student attempts to steal a fellow student's purse; (ii) he or she attempts to lean over and copy from another's paper; or (iii) he or she expresses contempt at the contributions of others, rolls eyes, sighs loudly, mutters obviously sarcastic, giggling side comments to a neighbor when another speaks. I think it is reasonable to note that (i) is illegal, (ii) is immoral, and (iii) is uncivil, and although a form of impoliteness, not quite like arriving late or leaving early, or forgetting classmates' names, or other common forms of impoliteness.

Conversely, we can initially note a few positive characteristics. As the name implies, we are looking for the distinctive form of association among participants in some sort of ethical community, and, therefore, civility should not be confused with a universal respect for and decorum towards all others. *Civil* acknowledgement always rests on an appreciation of some commonality and mutual dependence. Indeed civility itself could just be said to be the lived enactment of a dependence on one another, and a way of regarding and being regarded that takes this dependence into active account. Aristotle's claim is worth calling to mind: that civility's closest kin is friendship, albeit a "watered-down" form. Such an acknowledgement of this "watery friendship" avoids the great pretense or fantasy of incivility: the possibility of self-sufficiency. The thesis here is that incivility can look like the necessary cost of a society of free, competitive agents in honest, aggressive exchanges and relations. Rather, it evinces a false and fantastic sense of independence and self-sufficiency. By examining the nature and importance of civility, we can learn something about the collective nature of a free life, and the more mediated, complex relation between social dependence and individual autonomy.

The further assumption in this way of stating the problem is that public life in modern societies cannot be understood as extensions of familial or tribal groups, nor as directed or wholly "steered" by coercive state power, or law. As developing societies dominated by familial oligarchies, and post-Communist societies emerging from the legacy of state totalitarianism have discovered, modern societies require a distinct social bond, something other than kin-loyalty or submission to legal authority, or even "self-interest rightly understood," a kind of trust and fellow acknowledgement among, essentially, strangers, even if members of the same community. These fellow *cives* aspire in their trade and professional associations, universities, civic clubs, corporations, and charities to a kind of distinctive ethical relation with one another, a civility, a relation we hope will also hold society-wide, not just in such private associations. There are three points that I would like to make about this ethical relation.

II

First, it has a *distinct* ethical status. Modern societies are able to function because of some reliable expectation of civil treatment among their participants, and this expectation is a normative one. It is what ought to happen; a society is better, more like what it ought to be, if there is a high degree of civility, and such civility is a form of trust and mutual respect or recognition. As already noted, it is of course hard to isolate exactly what is expected in the expectation of civility. The notion is loose and imprecise enough to look like many similar valuable aspects of human sociality. But being civil is more than being polite, and different from being morally righteous in general.

Even so, such expectations are clearly normative or moral expectations. They would be misunderstood if reduced to social strategies of interest satisfaction. If I offer you the signs of respect and trust only because I want you to offer them to me, and that only because that will simply help me get what I want, then we are not being civil, but pretending to be civil in order to gain a certain end.

However, this expectation also cannot be understood as a moral claim or entitlement. Persons *are* entitled to respect as moral "ends in themselves," to use Kant's well-known language. No one is morally permitted to make use of another as a mere means in the pursuit of one's ends, or as an "object," not a fellow "subject." And one is thereby morally obligated to respect another's freedom, the other's entitlement to pursue his or her own ends, all in like acknowledgement of the claims of all others. But this requirement basically expresses a moral duty to do no moral harm, and a society in which persons were morally righteous in this sense, simply refrained from injuring or interfering, in which we all minded our own business, would not necessarily be a society with a high degree of civility. Being civil to one another is much more active and positive a good than mere politeness or courtesy, but like many other important goods, such as generosity, gratitude, or solidarity, it is not the sort of thing that can be "demanded" as a matter of duty, like a moral entitlement. Being generous only because you have a moral duty to be generous, for example, is not *being* generous. It is simply giving more than strictly required in some context, something that can be done reluctantly or fretfully and *not* "generously." The same is true of gratitude, and of civility.

That a morally righteous society need not be a particularly civil one is a point made with great regularity in American literature; the point is almost part of our national mythology. In one familiar representation, persons who are products of New England Puritan societies—ever on the watch for the radical evil or original sin in human nature, harshly judgmental about egoism and the failure of moral intentions, obsessed with guilt and the prevalence of sin, as well as driven by genuine passion for moral rectitude (as in the abolitionist movement)—are often portrayed in our literature as cold, unloving, isolated, alienated, spiritually deformed in some way, however righteous and public-spirited. Their social lives are proper, and while not uncivil or hostile, are full of enough suspicion, wariness, and separation to make the point about the possibility of a general lack of civility, even in the presence of politeness and moral rectitude. On the other hand, Southerners are often portrayed as the very embodiment not only of chivalry and courtliness and a warm charm and regard for others, but of civility, some form of life that actively embodies the sort of recognition and trust associated with that virtue. This has something to do with the role of British and French aristocratic culture in the South in America, and the contrast with the culture formed by denominational groups fleeing religious persecution in the North, but that is another story. So are similar manifestations of this mythic image, as in the contrast between urban incivility and small-town or rural hospitality and civility, and so on. The point now is the simple if still controversial one: that this mythic contrast helps one see that civility can be an ethical or normative matter without being a matter of moral entitlement, and that morally righteous societies need not be, and in many interesting ways just are not, civil societies. Perhaps the best book that one might use to make this point would be one that focuses on this North-South contrast and the problem of civility and moralism in Boston, Henry James's *The Bostonians*, with the contrast there between Olive Chancellor and Basil Ransom. The idea shows up, however, in the treatment of moralism in America in everyone from Hawthorne and Melville to Faulkner.

Second, there is another point that separates civility from such similar social virtues as generosity or gratitude: the degree of its importance. Civility is of fundamental importance in a modern civil society, because the end of modern civil societies, our highest good, is a free life and civility is of vital importance in the collective pursuit of a free life. As a social form, it is not a marginally good thing but indispensable in the possibility of a worthwhile common life in a modern world so committed to freedom as its supreme value. To understand this, one needs to try to imagine what in fact would go missing, would be so wrong, if a society were either only rationally cooperative and only apparently, not really, civil; or if persons were individually morally righteous, but not, in the loose and imprecise sense so far discussed, particularly civil. What would be amiss, in the context of this issue—a modern commitment to a free life—without civility?

Third, there is the question of contemporary American society, and the question of the compatibility of a social virtue like civility within an extremely competitive, relatively anomic, ethnically diverse, rapidly self-transforming, consumer culture. The proper form of an ethical relation of trust and acknowledgement among strangers is one thing; when the strangers are intense competitors or also very different culturally, even more difficult questions are raised. (Or to invoke the occasionally more optimistic suggestions of Mr. Smith, when the strangers are all potentially customers, does the situation look better?) The question also looks different if we assume an important emphasis on romantic notions of originality, individualism, and above all authenticity, by contrast with which a code of civility can look conformist or repressive or stultifying.

I am particularly interested in this last question about America and civility since I have just again spent a year living in Germany and, like many Americans who have had this experience, come away mightily impressed with the daily rituals of civility one encounters in German, as well as in Italian and French, communities. People, even strangers whose eyes simply meet randomly, greet each other more frequently and warmly than they do here; forms of greeting and departure are elaborate and regular (lots of handshaking and *Auf Wiedersehen's*); conversations on buses and trains are quieter, more respectful of others; bikes are left unlocked outside stores; people are willing not only to give directions to a lost stranger; they will often walk out of their way for a while to point someone in the right direction. The honor system on buses and trams functions quite well. (In the two and a half years that I have lived in Europe, on almost all the occasions that I have ever been on a bus or Strassenbahn that was controlled, all the passengers had their tickets.) Billing for services is much more relaxed; people trust each other, without much paperwork, to pay with a bank transfer in the next few days, and easily and without anxiety give out their bank account and bank transfer numbers. (We once were a few hundred dollars short at a department store in paying for some bedding. The sales woman, without checking with anyone or asking for identification, took our name and address and asked us to please transfer the rest of the money in the next few days.) Customers still don't have to pay first at gas stations. Sale and consumption of beer and wine are much more prevalent in public, on the well-founded assumption that everyone will indulge responsibly. There is no need, at movie houses, that some announcement be shown reminding people that they shouldn't chat loudly with each other. And so forth.

Let us designate these problems as: the question of the distinct *normative status* of civility; its degree of *importance;* and the *conditions* under which it flourishes or is threatened.

III

I have suggested that the distinct feature of such a norm is that it cannot be demanded as a right or entitlement. Even though one "ought to be civil," one need not be immoral in not being civil, and civil treatment is certainly not something one can claim as a legal right with the coercive force of law as a sanction. Indeed one way to state the uneasiness many people feel about so-called political correctness legislation is that it makes precisely this mistake. It tries to inspire with sanctions and punishment what simply cannot be secured by sanctions and punishment. A society so regulated and so coerced is not civil; it merely looks that way.

To understand why this should be so, we need to explore the elusive question of the nature of civility itself. As already suggested, the social form in question amounts to a very general way of regarding and acting toward others; and that way has something to do with an active acknowledgement of each other as fellow members of some sort of common, important enterprise—in the broadest, most relevant sense, in "civilization" itself. If this is so, it already means that such an expectation must be conditional on the actual prior existence of this common ground. There must be some basis on which we can recognize each other as part of some fellowship in general. This is part of the reason why it is so easy to imagine natural, seamless relations of openness and trust so similar to civility among members of the same tight neighborhood, or among members of an ethnic group with a common history and common experiences, or even among alumni of the same military unit or university. "They" are part of what "we" are, almost as if I cannot have become "me" without an equally intimate acknowledgement of "them." Such a commonality is not the sort of thing one can demand as a moral or legal entitlement, as if it could be constituted or created by will or out of duty. It either exists already or it doesn't; and if it does, then not acknowledging it in one's actions might be dishonest in some existential sense, but not in any immoral sense. This in turn means that civility in general involves a kind of en-actment of mutuality. It is a way of acknowledging that we are *not* wholly independent; a way of avoiding a dishonest pretense of solitary independence. A society of suspicious or sarcastic or cynical or judg-mental or self-involved persons—let us say a world full of Seinfeld characters—need not at all be immoral or even unvirtuous, as long as they develop their talents somewhat and are marginally beneficent; and they are certainly not criminal. In this sense, part of what is wrong in such incivility is not only the dishonesty just mentioned, but that such indifference or disregard corrodes and undermines the depen-dencies and reliances central to the modern *civitas*.

Civility then involves some sort of appreciation of the depen-dence of my life on others within some community of dependence, and the enactment of social forms appropriate to that dependence. It is not what we owe others as their right; it manifests an already ex-isting social bond. If there is such dependence, we can expect it to be manifest in the rituals of daily life. We ought to be able to expect that such daily life not involve the pretense of self-sufficiency, indiffer-ence, suspicion, and hostility typical of that classic model of American incivility, the average New Yorker.

But what form of dependence, at what level, are we talking about and, to anticipate the second question, why should it be very important, as opposed to it simply being a "nice" feature of daily life in small towns? Why especially should it be important in our ability to lead free lives? In the context of modern civil society as sketched above, it is easy enough to begin to understand how a collective com-mitment to a free life entails certain legal and moral constraints. We depend on each other in collective support for a system of law that protects individual rights. We are morally entitled to demand from each other equal treatment as moral subjects, always one among many equally entitled, self-determining subjects. What more in the collective, mutually dependent pursuit of freedom is required?

This can turn out to be a very broad question, for what we are asking is something like the following: if, within a democratically elected regime, individual liberties were legally secured and constrained as little as possible, enough to ensure a reasonable level of common welfare and equal opportunity, what else might be lacking, in order to secure the full realization of a just civil order, or even for the empirical stability and reproducibility of that society itself? The Hegelian name for that lack would be a lack of "recognition," some experience of solidarity, civility, and mutual respect without which individual free lives in that society *could not* be effectively or meaningfully led. At least that is the kind of claim that would justify taking civility, understood as such mutual recognition, so seriously.

Then the question is: what argument might show that civility, properly understood in this way, is not merely a matter of politeness and decorum, or important for psychological health, but an essential element of the possibility of any individual's own "free life"? Why should we believe that there is a distinct form of harm—disrespect, say—that must play its own role in the evaluation of social processes at some foundational level, especially in modern civil societies committed to freedom as an ideal?

IV

Civility has now become, it would appear, a fairly abstract topic. We are still talking about active forms of respect and affirmation and solidarity, and all of that is still linked with our intuitive understanding of civil conduct, but the direction of these last remarks suggests an importance to the issue that might now appear unmotivated, far out of proportion with a simpler claim defending civility as one of many sorts of social goods it would be better to have than not to have. The link in question is between civility and the supreme good in modern societies, that capacity upon which all respect is based, individual freedom, and the conditions under which individuals could lead free lives and sustain such freedom.

For incivility, disrespect, the presumption of unequal status and privilege, have come to be understood in modern societies as an implicit or often explicit disregard of the other's status as an equally free subject. Here, again, I am not talking about actual abuse or immoral treatment but about a more general incivility. This need not imply any problem with the assertion of authority or hierarchical relations of real or socially constituted inequality where they are appropriate, like that between parent and child, teacher and student, officer and soldier, and so forth. The issue is still that these hierarchical relations must also be exercised "civilly," with proper regard for the status of the other as an equally free, end-setting agent. And, as a final qualification, there are obviously moral and social limits to any such claim for the importance of civility. The general good of social respect need not imply moral neutrality, or the weak, uncertain, timid toleration of anything that, say, Nietzsche worried about as a consequence of liberal societies. A student's indifference to the cultural sensitivities of others, their own moral code, their ability to converse on the beach next to his loud boom box or to hear the class discussion because of her conversation with a friend; a teacher's willingness to humiliate a student for a laugh, or even to stress a pedagogical point, and so forth, are now understood as ways of disregarding that other as a subject with his or her own ends, freely set and freely pursued, just like mine. And, fnally, of the many dimensions of freedom current in the modern self-understanding, what seems particularly relevant here is that the other's status as a free subject is being disregarded because the other's status as a reason-giving and reason-responsive being is disregarded. Rather than simply offer objections to a point made, the uncivil student we began with attempts to manipulate conduct and reaction by expressions of contempt and impatience that cannot be rationally responded to because they have no rational content.

But this interpretive point still just pushes the issue back a step or two. If civility is understood this way—as the enactment in daily rituals of our equal status as free agents, within a cooperative enterprise that seeks to realize and protect such individual freedom—then what would be so *wrong* with a city of uncivil individualists? If I *could* moderate my conduct in a civil way but do not, because I want to express myself more vigorously, or because of my passion for some issue I care about, what is the "wrong" done if this sort of indifference to the other is not legally wrong or morally injurious?

There are, of course, various psychological and other empirical ways of stating the "damage" done by widespread, frequent expressions of the disrespect we are discussing. At the social level, one might try to establish that such phenomena "manifest" a disintegration of precisely the individual free agency the uncivil agent insists on so stridently, and, as an empirical fact, undermine and gradually make less likely the social will necessary to sustain such a social good. One might also try to show, on the psychological level, that the successful formation of a stable individual identity is a complex and fragile process. It may be that a necessary condition for any successful social identification is the existence of some social community willing to recognize and affirm such a role. A civil state of tolerance, mutuality, and active recognition may be necessary for "internal" confirmation of individuality; it may be that, as a matter of psychological fact, one just *isn't* who one takes oneself to be unless "recognized" as such. There is certainly evidence of something like this in studies of childhood development and in other accounts of socialization, and it isn't too far a stretch to make use of the claim in discussing our deep dependence on others, and the importance of manifestations and acknowledgements of it in civil conduct.

More philosophically, one might also appeal to arguments like those used by Kant about the virtues, or appeal to our broad, imperfect duties towards others. I know, as an empirical, psychological fact, that it is quite possible that the morally significant respect I owe all others might well be undermined were I to live in an uncivil, socially hostile, overly competitive community. I cannot count on myself to do the right thing, always, automatically; dispositions must be trained, emotions guided, habits cultivated, sensibilities educated, and so forth, if I am to be better able to appreciate what I must do and to be better able to do what I must do. (This is the Kantian version of the "Mayor Giuliani philosophy" about how large problems can grow out of small ones, and it is not an insignificant argument in favor of civility as an imperfect duty with broad discretionary latitude in judgment, but basically a duty nonetheless.)

Finally, though, the importance of such civil recognition can also be stated in quite a philosophically ambitious way. This has to do with the status of freedom itself, the nature of the link between freedom and rationality, and the social character of rationality. Is freedom a categorial, metaphysical, substantive issue, on the one hand, or a social norm on the other hand; not a property we possess, but a norm we train ourselves to abide by? In the former case, the question of freedom, especially in the Christian tradition and its philosophical descendants, was treated as a question about substance, usually the immaterial substance of the soul. It was also about the possibility of a kind of causation exempt from the necessary determinations of nature. Such a voluntarist position usually tries to show that our normal intuitions about agency, and especially blame and responsibility, require this "uncaused cause" or "always could have done otherwise" notion of agent causality, and the problem is then how to defend such a requirement, with either traditional or "practical" metaphysics.

On the other hand, being a free agent might be understood to be a *norm* subjects hold each other to, a constraint in our actions that is best understood as a result of subjects binding themselves to such constraints, to responding to others and initiating actions on appeal to reasons. Being such an agent would not be a natural metaphysical kind, like being a featherless biped or being female, but would be better understood as a social category and norm, like "being a professor," or a practice "being the collection of rent"; not a part of the furniture of the universe, but what some parts of that universe have determined to hold themselves to.

The most radical implication of this way of thinking about the issue, and its relevance for our topic, are both immediately clear. The implication is that *being a free individual somehow just consists in being regarded as one,* and the relevance is simply that, without the modes of civility that make up such forms of recognition, the decisive aspects of such a self-description can get no purchase. Were we not to treat each other as rational and so self-determining and free beings, we could not be such beings. That is the nature of the dependence mentioned above and already indicates the role civility must play in such a realization.

All the objections to such a historicist claim easily come to mind. There may be nothing more to being a college professor, say, than the social system and rules establishing the practice, and the actual practice itself of certification and daily recognition. Without the satisfaction of such rules and your regarding me as one, I just couldn't be one, no matter who I thought I really was. But it seems a great and dangerous stretch to make similar claims about an issue which is more like a matter of scientific or metaphysical fact: whether my deeds happened because of my decision, and whether I could have decided otherwise, or what I am entitled to because of who I am.

It is worth keeping in mind why the "demand for recognition" has become so crucial a theme in so-called identity politics. The strategy crudely sketched above was always central in post-Hegelian accounts of class consciousness and of true human liberation—being a free or nonalienated subject by being in a *condition* where one could be *taken* to be such a subject. Many of the underlying premises of that tradition are still at work in such contemporary claims about the centrality of recognition to identity itself, where such recognition is not now only the "watery friendship" of civility, but the constitutive condition of freedom itself. What has changed, though, has been the odd coupling of such claims about identity with the language of rights and entitlement and the whole agenda of liberal democratic politics, as if something could be done to "manufacture" such mutuality and civility. Understanding the centrality of civility in the way suggested above may be leading somewhere interesting, but, as we have seen, it cannot be leading towards a moral or legal demand to be recognized or treated civilly.

V

A few last words about the American context and the problem of civility. I have already tried to suggest why a more intuitive American understanding of sociality—a "mind your own business" individualist attitude and a morally proper set of social forms—could not really count as the virtue of civility. The term is of course loose enough to define in various ways, and I have no real counterargument to anyone who wants to insist that such a negative state—the avoidance of the improper and the absence of unwelcome intrusions—-is "civility" enough. But I have tried to suggest that the virtue in question has traditionally been more affirmative and positive; it involves somehow being able to count on each other, all on the assumption that we depend on each other in both interest-based and even more fundamental ways. But the modern issue of this dependence and trust is obscured by the admittedly artificial invocation of the Latin roots of the notion: the nature of the *civitas*, the status of the modern *civis*, and so forth. We are really talking about the virtue of the good modern "burgher," the bourgeoisie and its so complicated modern representative, the bourgeois gentleman and lady.

The connotations of that term already suggest an important American resonance: the ambiguous standing of bourgeois virtues, and so the ambiguous standing of civility itself as a virtue in modernity. If you tell a contemporary American college student that a practice or some aspect of conduct is bourgeois, he or she will think you mean conformist, hypocritically righteous, timid, or perhaps even soulless, materialistic. That same worry about conformism, the same concern with a more desirable individualism, also underlies our experience of the claims of civility, even as so much of our popular culture attacks the incivility of the city. The ideal of a civil society, both law-abiding and actively cooperative, has an uneasy hold on the American imagination. It is sometimes held up as an ideal, often as a small town or rural (perhaps premodern) ideal against an urban (perhaps modern) individualism perceived to be a rootless form of egoism (the Frank Capra version). Just as often, though, especially in modernist and high culture novels and films, such cooperation is portrayed as regulatory in the extreme, thoughtless, repressive, and secretly obsessed with what it regulates and bans (the Woody Allen version).

Of course as Tolstoy long ago pointed out, successful bourgeois life is not a very interesting aesthetic subject, so it might not be a good idea to take one's bearings from the way modern bourgeois societies aesthetically represent themselves to themselves. It would, though, be quite hard to establish empirically whether, in particular, American society, given this ambiguity, was in fact more or less civil than other modern societies in the West, or than any other modern societies, like Japan, under similar economic and historical conditions. I have already suggested that my own intuition is that it is less civil, and, if we can simply consider that a hypothesis for the moment, some of the considerations introduced above might be relevant in understanding why.

If civility can be understood as an enactment in daily life of an active attempt to recognize and help promote each other as free beings, then such a commonality must already exist in daily life. If we return to European examples and more mediated, traditional forms of civility, we should not neglect the important role played by long common traditions and even ethnicity in the experience of the social bond of civility. Germans are quite civil to each other, and to most other Europeans who have become part of their societies.[2] But even third-generation Turks or Arabs in Germany report different experiences. The strains on French civility are obvious after the last provincial elections. It seems quite an open question whether in America, still quite a young country, the idea and experience of being "fellow Americans" can overcome the misunderstandings and often suspicions characteristic of a community with so many different national traditions, experiences, and religions. Civility, I have tried to suggest, cannot be understood as a duty, a responsibility, or an entitlement. It is already a manifestation of something else not subject to moral will or legal coercion. It is an indispensable human good, but no amount of moral lecturing or moral education, and certainly no amount of legislative constraint, can create it.

Secondly, as already noted, there is also the question of how much civility we really want. This has to do with the way we understand the great orienting ideal of our polity, leading a free life, and the various, complex dimensions that can have. At least one way to interpret incivility is that it reflects or betrays a false, self-deceived sense of self-sufficiency and independence. This already presupposes a contrary view, a view of a free life as an unavoidably collective achievement, or, said in its most paradoxical forms, that one cannot be free alone, that being free must involve being recognized as free. A civil order would then be, and be experienced as being, not a restriction on individual entitlements but a way of leading a free life in the only way it can be led: civilly, or in common.

NOTES

1. I am grateful to Charles Lanmore, Ralph Lerner, and Nathan Tarcov for their comments on and criticisms of an earlier draft.

2. There are also of course still serious class tensions, and the enormous problem of "identity," the complex problem of belonging, affirmatively, to Germany, given what "Germany" has come to mean on the world and local stage. See the discussion in Norbert Elias, *The Germans: Power Struggles and the Development of Habitus in the Nineteenth and Twentieth Centuries*, ed. Michael Schroeder, trans. Eric Dunning and Stephen Mennell (New York: Columbia University Press, 1996), pp. 405–33.

Response to Robert B. Pippin

DANIEL O. DAHLSTROM

AFTER THE MEETING of the House of Representatives committee deliberating whether to release Clinton's videotaped testimony in the Monica Lewinsky affair, Henry Hyde and Barney Frank both spoke to the press. Hyde said: "The session was civil and nonpartisan," to which Frank immediately quipped in reply: "It was civil but partisan." Thus, Hyde seemed to understand *civil* in a way compatible with, even akin to, *nonpartisanship* while Frank punctuated the difference between them. This discrepancy immediately raises the question of the nature and place of civility in a context that is of vital concern to us as a nation, namely, in the context of policy conflicts and public debate. It would be instructive to consider these uses of the term in light of what Rawls calls "a natural duty of civility" not to invoke the faults of social arrangements, even including unjust laws in some cases, as an excuse to avoid complying with them.[1] The issue is a pressing one. Throughout the contemporary body politic the level of incivility, by almost any definition, appears so distressingly high.

Of course, the uses of *civil* do not only part ways along partisan lines, as in the cases of Hyde and Frank. In a recent work, Stephen Carter argues that civility is "the sum of the many sacrifices we are called to make for the sake of living together. . . . Rules of civility are thus also rules of morality."[2] In stark contrast to this allegedly moral sense of *civility*, there is the use made of the term by Morris Dickstein in the book review section of the *Sunday New York Times*. Speaking of Lionel Trilling, his former colleague, Dickstein refers to "the barrier of civility that shielded" Trilling and that Dickstein never got past. Here the term *civil* means no more than "politeness" or "good manners," and decidedly not in the moral sense in which Hume characterizes the latter, but more in the sense of that etiquette once defined by Emily Post. This use of the term comes closer to what the French call *civilité* or *politesse* (and what many Germans understood as the very

118

antithesis of manly *Kultur*).[3] Such, too, is the sense of *civilitas* in Erasmus' *De civilitate morum puerilium* (literally, "On the civility of manners of boys"); licking one's dirty fingers or wiping them off on one's shirt is "uncivil," Erasmus proclaims (though he also recognizes limits to civility as when he observes: "Only fools who value civility more than their health would repress a sound conveyed by nature.") In contemporary American usage, there is yet another use of *civil* that has little to do with the foregoing sense of civility. Thus, the term *civil* in talk of "civil rights" clearly extends to more than manners; it extends to issues of public access and openness. Moreover, the term, so used, is understood in a way that affects individuals as citizens, the actions and well-being of whom fall under the law. Hence, the violation of civil rights does not simply or perhaps even primarily indicate incivility so much as criminality. The difference between these uses of *civil* and *civility* should also make us wary of being too ready to link civility with civil society. Hobbes's "status civilis" becomes what Kant critically reinterprets as "bürgerlicher Zustand," and Ferguson's "civil society" becomes what Hegel reconstrues as the "bürgerliche Gesellschaft," but "Bürgerlichkeit" is rarely, if ever, a synonym for "civility."

This brief survey of the varied uses of the term *civil* brings me to Professor Pippin's rich, provocative, and probative paper. I am grateful to Professor Pippin for his comments, especially since they are the reflections of someone who has speculated masterfully, that is to say, both critically and sympathetically, on the ongoing significance of German idealism for contemporary thought. At the same time I shall suggest that this very line of speculations distorts his interpretation of civility.

Professor Pippin begins his remarks with a distinction. There is, he advises us, a way of understanding civility in terms of civil society whereby civility has something in common with the orientation of the rule of law in that society, even though civility would not always be coercible like legally sanctioned actions and omissions. He contrasts this interpretation of civility with the kind of civility that is the proper theme of his paper, namely, civility as a kind of "appropriateness" that neither is coercible nor necessarily shares any orientation with a particular rule of law. He does not seem to sustain this valuable distinction throughout his paper but his intention is nonetheless clear: he wants to argue for a normative or ethical notion of civility that is distinct from questions of legality as well as questions of decorum and politeness.

Surprisingly, however, he also wants to distinguish civility from morality, or at least what he variously calls "moral righteousness in general." Or, as he puts it more negatively, he is concerned with forms of civility that are "not illegal or immoral," that "do not qualify as moral harm." Being civil is not, he maintains, a "moral duty"; similarly, he contrasts "civility and moralism," "civil societies and morally righteous societies" (note the alignment of "civility" and "civil society"). In his example, cheating is immoral, while laughing at others or speaking derisively of them is supposedly uncivil but not immoral. He accordingly insists that "one need not be immoral in not being civil."

Few of us would probably quarrel with Professor Pippin's conception of a sort of civility that goes beyond politeness and decorum, on the one hand, and yet lies outside the realm of what can legitimately be coerced, on the other. At the same time, however, there seems to be something highly counterintuitive about the claim that civility is not a matter of morals. The lack of civility among some Boston drivers and European soccer fans is a moral outrage! We have moral duties to try to be cheerful, to try to be silent during a public performance or address, to try to refrain from obscenities, to try to be sensitive to others. If there is a reason to say that these are not matters of morality, then a set of intuitions about the nature of morality quite different from mine is at work.

In Professor Pippin's defense, he does not make the claim about the moral neutrality of civility unqualifiably. He muddies the waters by suggesting that expectations of civility are "broadly speaking, still moral" and that an absence of civility is "morally important in some way." So there apparently is, after all, some broad sense in which civility is a moral matter ("morality lite"?) and Pippin's project can be construed as an attempt to say just what it is, broadly speaking, that is morally right about civility and morally wrong about incivility. Nevertheless, this strategy leaves us with the problem of distinguishing two senses of *morality*. I have a hunch as to how Professor Pippin understands this distinction but, rather than put words in his mouth, I would raise as my first criticism that he has not sorted out for us the two senses of *morality* that he has in mind.

Pippin pursues his project in terms of three questions or problems, "the question of the distinct normative status of civility; its degree of importance; and the conditions under which it flourishes or is threatened." It may appear that these problems are listed in order of importance, but in fact the reverse seems to be the case. Interpreting civility in what he takes to be a more positive sense, Pippin characterizes it as "an acknowledgement or lived enactment" of mutual dependence. "Civility," as he puts it, "involves some sort of appreciation of the dependence of my life on others within some community of dependence, and the enactment of social forms appropriate to that dependence." But this sounds remarkably similar to the kind of civility that Pippin says, at the outset of his paper, he is not considering, namely, civility understood in terms of not only law-abidingness, but "a stable disposition towards law-abidingness" and "the rules of civil association." A further indication that the notion of civil society continues to provide him with the clues to civility is the fact that he casts the notion of civility in terms of dependency. Civility appears to draw its normative status from its importance in manifesting, sustaining, and promoting that mutual dependence. Civility in the sense of mutual recognition is precisely what is necessary, in addition to "legal and moral constraints," in order to secure the supreme good in modern societies. That supreme good, he maintains, is "individual freedom," the status of equally free subjects.

To his credit, Pippin raises the crucial question for the ethical tradition out of which he works, a variation on what Kant calls "the problem of establishing a state even for a people of devils."[4] What is wrong with incivility if it is "not legally wrong or morally injurious"? Here we get to the heart of Pippin's argument. One might, he acknowledges, advance utilitarian arguments about the deleterious consequences of incivility (lack of trust, solidarity, and so forth) for the social good and for the formation of a stable individual identity as well as moral-psychological arguments about the way incivility undermines moral sensibilities and dispositions. Rawls gives a good example of the former sort of argument when he observes: "Without some recognition of this duty [of civility] mutual trust and confidence are liable to break down." However, Pippin seems more inclined to defend "the importance of civil recognition and so the nature of the wrong in its absence" by invoking the equivalence between being free agents and holding one another to a norm of rational self-determination. As he puts it: "The implication is that being a free individual somehow just consists in being regarded as one, being taken by others to be one, and the relevance is simply that, absent the modes of civility that make up such forms of recognition, the decisive aspects of such a self-description can get no purchase." Thus, the normative force and importance of civility lies in the fact that it constitutes precisely the forms of mutual recognition, without which freedom (always a jointly individual and collective notion) becomes an empty ideal. This norm of mutual recognition has obvious political implications that take us back to the notion of the conditions of civility. In order for this norm to be countenanced and embraced, it is necessary for individual subjects to be in a condition where they could be taken as free, autonomous subjects; in other words, they must be taken as members of a civil society.

Let us suppose that this reconstruction of Pippin's argument stands up. So what? Let us suppose that he succumbs to the all too natural inclination to take his bearings for his account of civility from civil society. What is wrong with that? In a sense, he is merely following the best philosophical instincts of Kant and Hegel. There are passages in the third part of the *Grundlegung*, for example, where Kant argues for the necessity of supposing the freedom of every entity endowed with reason and will, passages that are strongly suggestive of the equivalence of practical reason with the mutual recognition that becomes the centerpiece of Fichte's and Hegel's ethical and political theory.[5] The notion of mutual recognition in a prelegal sense (albeit in anticipation of a civil [*bürgerlich*] constitution) is present in Kant's remarks against Hobbes in his essay on "Theory and Practice."[6] The "struggle for recognition" also informs the dialectic of master and slave in the *Phenomenology of Spirit* as well as the "continuous historical narrative" of individual and collective self-determination that characterizes the Hegelian position, at least according to the nontranscendental, nonmetaphysical reading given it by Professor Pippin in *Modernism as a Philosophical Problem*. On the assumption that being a person consists in being self-determining, and that self-determination and a fully moral self-consciousness are in an important sense equivalent, not only to each other, but also to the recognition of that self-determination in others, there would seem to be every reason to interpret civility, in concert with Professor Pippin, as the actual, historical enactment of the mutual recognition required by two or more people insofar as they have come of age as persons. In other words, because civil society provides the ultimate condition and staging grounds for civility as the acknowledgement of mutual dependency, and civility in turn sustains that very society as the epitomization of individual and collective freedom, civility enjoys a distinct normative status.

What, then, could possibly be objectionable in Pippin's account of civility? My second major difficulty with the account is that it is fatally inadequate; it fails to consider paradigmatically moral instances of civility that need have little or nothing to do with mutual recognition. To make this claim is, of course, to invoke a conception of morality quite different from the senses of *morality* used by Professor Pippin and, indeed, probably both the broad and restricted senses announced but left unexplained by him. It would be "uncivil" of me at this point to marshal forth arguments for a different moral theory, not only because it is inappropriate to a commentary but also because I remain hazy about the differentiation of moral levels he presupposes. But allow me to outline a different conception of civility and suggest how it might be defended. I agree with Pippin that there is a paradigmatically moral or ethical sense of civility, not to be confused with senses of law-abidingness or manners. But civility, in that paradigmatically moral sense, is not the enactment of mutual recognition; there need be no mutuality at all in being civil in a genuinely moral sense. That is not to say that civility cannot lead to mutual recognition; indeed, it is precisely what facilitates friendship in a society, in the Aristotelian sense of the term.

At two points in his paper, Professor Pippin invokes Aristotle's description of civility as a "watered-down" sort of friendship (at the outset of the *Politics*). There are at least three places in the *Nicomachean Ethics* alone where Aristotle also speaks of something akin to civility,[7] but what perhaps corresponds most closely to that "watered-down" friendship is what Aristotle in Chapter Five of Book Ten calls εὔνοια, a kind of "inactive friendship." It is worth noting that the term translated as "inactive" here is ἀργός, also meaning "living without labor, idle, lazy." So εὔνοια might also be construed as a friendship that is not so much inactive as unworked, untilled, friendship that is not the result of work. According to Aristotle, εὔνοια (which is sometimes translated "good will" or *benevolentia;* in French *bienveillance;* in German *Wohlwollen*) is not identical to friendship, but it is the ἀρχή, the principle or beginning of friendship. εὔνοια, Aristotle tells us further, can be felt for strangers with whom we are unfamiliar and it can be unknown to the person who is the object of good will.

It is not my intention here to maintain that εὔνοια, as Aristotle describes it, is the paradigmatically moral sense of civility. But civility includes something like εὔνοια. As is neatly captured by the Latin translation, *benevolentia*, this good will is a wishing well or wanting what is best for another—where the other need not be aware of the fact. To be sure, Aristotle restricts εὔνοια to well-wishing that falls short of action and then moves on to another sort of friendship that is, indeed, closer to what Pippin has in mind as civility, namely, ὁμόνοια ("concord"; in German, *Eintracht*). In fact, I was puzzled why he does not mention ὁμόνοια. For the latter, namely, concord, is precisely that friendship between citizens that comes from wanting the same thing; it refers to "practical ends, and practical ends of importance, and able to be realized by both or all parties." Moreover, Aristotle depicts concord, again much like Pippin describes civility, in the context of social relations in a *polis* that are not clearly or necessarily governed by already constituted and shared laws or rules. Concord is, in short, friendship between citizens and, like friendship generally for Aristotle, it is reciprocal, a matter of mutual recognition.

But there seems clearly to be a category missing in Aristotle's account, namely, not merely good will or benevolence but action based upon good will that does not, however, involve any sort of mutual recognition. It is precisely this sort of action that constitutes, I suggest, a paradigmatically moral sort of civility. On this account, paradigmatically moral civility is not an enactment of mutual recognition, but a courtesy, a regard paid to others as a means of facilitating the good of others and friendly relations. In short, civility is benevolent action.

The devil is, of course, in the details. For one thing, it would be necessary to examine particular cases of civility at greater length. For another, it would be useful to unpack various senses of mutual recognition, tacit and explicit, and the degree to which benevolent action might be distinguished from them. I agree that civility can be mutual and that when it is, it accomplishes a good many of the things that he ascribes to it. But since I fail to see in mutual recognition the paradigm of moral civility, I am not ready to ground the ethical status of civility on mutual recognition. I suspect that the operative sense of morality for Pippin remains precisely the restricted sense that contrasts with civility, a legalistic conception of morality where moral norms and obligations are construed as matters of right or entitlement.

NOTES

1. John Rawls, *A Theory of Justice* (Cambridge, Mass.: Belknap Press of Harvard University Press, 1971), p. 355.

2. Stephen L. Carter, *Civility: Manners, Morals, and the Etiquette of Democracy* (New York: Basic Books, 1998), p. 11.

3. Norbert Elias; thanks to Nicolas de Warren for this insight.

4. Immanuel Kant *Werke* 8.366.

5. Ibid., 4.448ff.

6. Ibid., 8.289.

7. Aristotle *Nicomachean Ethics* 1126b11–1127a7 and 1166b30–1167b16.

Are We Losing Our Virtue?
The Case of Civility

ALAN WOLFE

CIVILITY IS A private virtue deemed to serve an important public purpose. The term *civility*, to be sure, is sometimes invoked as a social or collective property, as in the expression *civil society*. But even leaving aside the issue of whether *society* involves anything more than the sum of the collective properties of individuals, the *civil* in civil society rarely means the same thing as the *civility* whose lack is bemoaned in accounts of lost modern virtues. In its Hegelian form, "civil" is simply a more commodious translation into English of a word that could just as well have been translated "bourgeois." And even in its various forms deriving from the Scottish Enlightenment, the *civil* of civil society is not so much meant as a characterization of individual behavior as it is a metaphor for the benefits to be obtained from not living in a state of nature. "It is here," Adam Ferguson wrote of civil society, "that a man is made to forget his weakness, his cares of safety, and his subsistence, and to act from those passions which make him discover his force."[1]

When, by contrast, we turn to the question of lost virtue in the United States, we find many commentators bemoaning the absence of something called civility, by which they clearly mean a property associated with individuals. Stephen Carter's recent book on the subject, for example, begins with the account of a selfish passenger whose hurried rush through airport security in order to reach a flight resulted in an evacuation of the terminal to the detriment of everyone trying to travel that day—presumably including the selfish passenger himself. "Civility," as Carter defines it, refers to "the sum of the many sacrifices we are called to make for the sake of living together."[2] Here the plural "we," unlike the term *civil* in civil society, is meant to refer to a collection of specific individual behaviors, not to the properties of a group. Carter remains a social critic; his objective is to make claims about the

126

direction taken by American society away from a golden age—his term—in which there was a shared conception of the American experience, into one in which rules of rudeness and selfishness prevail. But to do this, he locates the problem, not in the institutions which shape social rules, but in the behavior of individuals who once presumably obeyed those rules but now no longer do.

However important it may be to understand the behavior of individuals, Carter's generalizations about their behavior are problematic. In part this is due to problems of measurement: What constitutes an act of incivility? How do we know that such acts are increasing? Where do we find the point of comparison with earlier periods? How much weight ought to be given to anecdotes? The difficulty of answering questions like these is revealed in the controversies swirling around a hypothesis very close to Carter's charge that America has become increasingly uncivil: the by-now-famous assertion by Robert Putnam that Americans are increasingly "bowling alone."[3] Unlike Carter, Putnam is a trained social scientist extremely competent in the use of quantitative methods. He has also assembled a gigantic data base covering a wide variety of American associations from the middle of the nineteenth century to the present. Yet despite careful empirical investigation, other scholars disagree, often vehemently, with Putnam, leaving us no closer to an answer to the question of whether Americans are becoming less social than we were when Putnam published the first version of his thesis.[4]

It is not, however, problems of measurement upon which I want to focus in bringing up Stephen Carter's account of America's presumed loss of civility. Carter's treatment of the problem illustrates an additional cause for concern in trying to grapple with a problem of the complexity of this one. For he assumes that civility is a good thing and that incivility is a bad thing, such that any manifestation of the former is to be welcomed as a virtue while any manifestation of the latter is to be condemned as a vice.[5] Thus it is not only behavior in airports which Carter cites as evidence for America's incivility, but also such divergent phenomena as the use of fighting words involved in issues of race and gender, the ideological controversies often held to be part of America's culture war, and the demonization of enemies by American presidents in times of war. Yet as much as we do not want people to be rude, we might very well want people to say what they really think about others, express their political disagreements sharply, and do whatever it takes to save American lives in international conflicts. Critics of political correctness on the American campus believe that we are too polite to each other as it is and that a little more incivility might advance the cause of both democracy and learning.[6] There can, in short, be goods more valuable than civility. Put even more strongly, we may sometimes have to act with incivility in our treatment of others to promote civility in our body politic, for we sometimes show our respect for fellow citizens by disagreeing with them, even when such disagreement is unpleasant. If so, then it is at least possible that vehement debate over an issue like affirmative action is an indication of more civility in our public life rather than less.

What is true of civility may also be true of other virtues which, according to a series of social critics, have been disappearing from American life. This story is by now a familiar one, popularized by the bestselling status of William Bennett's *The Book of Virtues*.[7] In that and other works, Mr. Bennett argues that such time-honored virtues as courage, honesty, fidelity, responsibility, and friendship are more honored in the breach than in reality. The result, in his view, has been a significant deterioration in the moral quality of American life, reflected in such depressing real-world events as rising rates of divorce, crime, abortion, and other indicators of moral relativism and secular humanism.[8] Mr. Bennett is not as shrill in his language as other critics, such as Robert Bork.[9] Still, it is self-evident to him that a society which no longer takes ideas of virtue seriously is a society on the brink of self-destruction. From his point of view, the failure of the American people to rise up and rid from office a President given to such serious vices as marital infidelity and persistent lying is even more depressing evidence of what happens when the virtues are no longer taken seriously.[10]

Bennett's account of lost virtue suffers from many of the same problems as Carter's. For one thing, there are also measurement problems, since many of the indicators of social decline he cites have actually reversed themselves in the past few years, a reversal that has not led Mr. Bennett to proclaim that the virtue crisis is over. Furthermore, one does not obtain from his treatment of this issue a sense that virtues can be in conflict, such that a decline in one could conceivably mean an advance for another. Courage, for example, is often demonstrated by the willingness of a troop commander to be less than honest with both his superiors and those under him, while perseverance, another of Bennett's virtues, can, if followed to an extreme, turn into the vice of stubbornness. If it is true that a gain for one virtue might result in a loss for another—or that too much of any one virtue can become a vice—then a statement to the effect that there is less virtue at one point of time compared to another begins to become meaningless. We need instead to ask under what concrete historical conditions which specific virtues are honored and which are not.

Both Carter and Bennett are too monistic in their approach to virtue to be fully credible. Both could benefit from more exposure to a thinker like Isaiah Berlin who stresses the inevitable conflicts between different conceptions of the good. Indeed, Berlin's essay on Machiavelli, in which he argues that Machiavelli's genius lay in recognizing the tragic incompatibility between Christian virtues and those required to serve the Florentine Republic, ought to be required reading for anyone writing about these topics.[11] An appreciation for pluralism in the study of virtue—the awareness, in Berlin's sense, that there is always more than one virtue to be admired and that one cannot pursue all virtues simultaneously—has implications for the hypothesis that in recent years we have witnessed a significant decline in civility, or, indeed, in any other virtue whose properties we admire. Even if one believes, with Kant, that morality represents a universal imperative unaffected by circumstances of time and place, virtue, which (at least in William Bennett's account) depends on literary and religious texts, is by definition a cultural product. Because virtue is a human quality, its presence will vary depending on, in Alasdair MacIntyre's phrase, the vibrancy of the practices which sustain it.[12] No wonder, then, that those who approach the subject of virtue do so with comparative instincts, determined to evaluate one period (usually the past) against another (usually the present) or to contrast one society's commitments to virtue (usually ours) with another's (usually our rivals). How should the comparative study of virtue proceed?

All of the problems I have been discussing—the translation of private behavior into generalizations about the state of society, difficulties of measurement, conflicts among virtues, and the need to avoid monistic accounts—lead to a caveat against any assumption that the most interesting thing to know about any good we value is that today (or here) we have more or less of it than we did yesterday (or they do there). Indeed, reading the literature of social criticism in the United States, one is tempted to want the word *decline* banished from the literature. At least among social scientists, notions of decline cause a reversal of the proper way to examine a hypothesis. Instead of being guided by data to find out whether a particular thesis is true, truth is assumed and data hunted down for purpose of substantiation. This is not to suggest that nothing of value has in fact declined. It may well be the case that specific aspects of American life have significantly worsened since some previous golden age. (I have no doubts whatsoever, for example, that grade inflation has increased as the overall quality of the students I teach has worsened.) But we—I mean here social scientists—cannot allow our roles as social critics and our roles as trustworthy analyzers of trends to become too confused. We must be open to the many surprises that careful investigation can yield— including even the possibility, however remote, that some things in life have actually gotten better.

Because virtue is a social or cultural practice which can and should change from one time and place to another, we ought to approach its study qualitatively rather than quantitatively. Our guiding hypothesis ought to be that just because things never remain the same does not necessarily mean that they get better or worse. Admittedly this is difficult to do because virtues are things that we care about, even though the few of us who are also social scientists want us to be somewhat clinical about them. But it does not follow that things we care about require precommitments. It is precisely because the virtues have so much to do with what it means to be a good person that we ought to respect a certain amount of dispassionate objectivity in studying them. One question at the heart of any study of the virtues involves the virtues we bring to that study. I do not propose to know what all of them should be, but a little humility ought surely to be among them.

LOYALTY, CIVILITY, AND OTHER VIRTUES

So what, then, can be said about civility? In what ways do Americans treat others around them differently compared to some point in the past? If indeed civility means, as Carter rightly argues it should mean, some sense of sacrifice for the sake of others, are there qualitative changes in the nature of the practices associated with such sacrifices of which we ought to take special note?

Any answer I provide to this question will have to be necessarily indirect, for two reasons. First, I have not studied, and cannot
say much about, the way people act; most of my recent work, including
my book *One Nation After All*, as well as the book I am writing at present, deals with how people talk about morality and virtue, and there
will always be some significant gap between what they say and what
they do.[13] Yet while acts and words are not the same thing, there is
no necessary reason to believe that actions are more important than
words. In a democratic society, legitimacy involves the words we use to
defend our values and our practices, which makes the public stories
people tell about their beliefs, including those stories they tell social
scientists, significant enough. If we therefore had a firm understanding of the way Americans talk about civility, we would be able to learn
something important—if, alas, not definitive—about the ways in which
civility has changed.

The second way in which I must be indirect is that questions
of civility are not the central focus of the research in which I am
presently engaged. That research involves interviews with randomly
chosen individuals in eight locations in the United States: Fall River,
Massachusetts; northern sections of Hartford, Connecticut; Dayton,
Ohio; Tipton, Iowa; San Antonio, Texas; Greensboro, North Carolina;
Castro and Noe Valley in San Francisco; and Atherton, California, in
Silicon Valley. My respondents are people of all ages and from many
different social classes and religious backgrounds. I have asked them
questions involving their understanding of human nature, their sense
of how character is formed, whether or not they use words like *virtue*
and *vice* in their ordinary language, what resources they draw upon
to know what is the right thing to do, and how they seek to put into
practice the specific virtues of loyalty, honesty, forgiveness, and self-
discipline. Because I have tried in these interviews to ask my respondents to reflect on incidents and illustrations from everyday life,
questions of civility inevitably arise, and I do have material on which
I can report about how Americans think about the issues raised by
Stephen Carter and others who, like him, think that we have a civility
deficit in America. But to do so, I must first give more of a flavor of
how Americans think about virtues other than civility, for these are the
ones to which most attention has been paid in my interviews.

One way to illustrate the ways in which Americans think about
the virtues in general can be found in their thoughts on the question

of loyalty. Americans, after all, profess to love loyalty, even as they design institutions exceptionally adept at discouraging it. Corporations, professional sports teams, and universities reward those most willing to move elsewhere. Young people are encouraged to serve their country by realizing the benefits to be obtained when their tour of duty is over. Term limits give politicians no reason to be loyal to the electorate—and vice versa. Whatever the theory, the practice could not be clearer: the loyal are nearly always the losers.

If ever a virtue were designed to be honored in the breach, it would be loyalty in a society which worships the market in economics and freedom in politics. Loyalty is feudal, not capitalist, in origin, evoking images of knightly chivalry on the one hand and codes of *omertá* on the other. Not only was the United States created through a singular act of disloyalty, it has been continuously replenished by immigrants willing to break the bonds of family, faith, and community. The largest mutual fund company in the United States calls itself "Fidelity," but it became so large only by weaning its customers away from their old-fashioned adherence to Christmas Club accounts at local savings banks. You do not build a country on the values of mobility, entrepreneurship, and dissent by placing too high a premium on loyalty.

The wonder is that critics have been bemoaning the lack of loyalty—"the central duty amongst all duties," as the philosopher Josiah Royce called it—since America was founded.[14] Often there was good reason to do so. "My country right or wrong" cannot serve as a moral injunction if, as during the Civil War, the question is which country is mine. Open societies, as we discovered during the Cold War, are indeed likely to find enemies within. Religious pluralism encourages multiple loyalties. Hyphenated Americans have at least two. Global capitalists often have none. Precisely because it values loyalty so rarely in practice, America must pay homage to loyalty in theory.

Of all the virtues presumed to be lost forever by contemporary social critics, loyalty often takes pride of place. "Thanks to the decline of old money and the old money ethic of civic responsibility," Christopher Lasch wrote in 1995, "local and regional loyalties are sadly attenuated today." Lasch pointed the finger of blame at upwardly mobile professional elites, whom he portrayed as "turning their backs on the heartland and cultivating ties with the international market in fast-moving money, glamour, fashion, and popular culture." Not only have they contributed to a gap in local loyalties, but their lifestyle contributes to a decline in national loyalty as well. "It is a question," Lasch wrote, "whether they think of themselves as Americans at all. Patriotism, certainly, does not rank very high in their hierarchy of values."[15]

Lasch is not the only critic to accuse Americans of insufficient appreciation of loyalty. We are, writes Barbara Dafoe Whitehead, living in a "divorce culture," in which loyalty to spouse and children is severely tested by the siren calls of personal self-fulfillment and liberation.[16] The problem with our politics, according to the political scientist Alan Ehrenhalt, is that we no longer have political parties or even political machines capable of imposing discipline by rewarding loyalty.[17] By focusing too much on the bottom line, American companies, business consultant Frederick Reichheld claims, are not taking advantage of what he calls "the loyalty effect," the benefits to be obtained by being faithful to customers, employees, and investors.[18] Left or right, although leaning definitely toward the right, the lament is persistent: a society which pays insufficient homage to loyalty will either self-destruct or be unable to offer its members anything worth living— or dying—for.

Is it true, as these critics would have it, that Americans no longer know how to practice the virtue of loyalty? In some sense it clearly is, but, at least in the minds of many of those with whom I have spoken, it is not people who are disloyal so much as institutions. Typical of those who think this way is Julius Taylor of Hartford, Connecticut, a forty-three-year-old African-American working as a computer programmer. He looks back to the days when, as he puts it, "employment with an employer usually meant lifetime employment with that employer." Under such conditions, it was important, in his view, for workers to demonstrate their loyalty to those for whom they worked. But this social contract has been broken, he believes, and it is not the workers who broke it, but the fact that "the almighty bottom line has become king." "You can't count on your employer to provide you with retirement benefits or to look out for your health insurance and your needs as you grow older," he says, not so much out of a sense of anger as out of a sense that this is the way the world now is. Under these new conditions, "you have to look out for yourself."

Because he stresses looking out for oneself, Mr. Taylor could be classified as one of those Americans increasingly unconcerned with the larger community around them. But this is not at all the sense one gets in talking to him. He is, for one thing, insistent on the importance

of loyalty in personal friendships. "I don't think friendships can exist
without loyalty," he tells us. In his view, anyone who says that they
have lots of friends—he puts the figure at twenty or so—does not
really know what friendship means. "A friendship takes a lot of maintenance," as he puts it, so co-workers or casual acquaintances do not
count. His test for a friend is a person he feels he can call at 2:00 A.M.
if he is in trouble and have them respond when he does so.

What applies to friendship applies even more to marriage, a subject on which Mr. Taylor has very old-fashioned views. Although he
cannot remember what it is called, he is aware of the trend toward
"covenant marriages," in which marriage partners take extra steps to
reaffirm their commitment to each other. For him this is a good idea.
As he puts it, if it is possible for couples to sign prenuptial agreements
specifying what will happen should they divorce, they also ought to be
able to sign an agreement underscoring their bond to each other. Of
course such agreements should be voluntary, he adds, for just as one
cannot be forced into friendships, one cannot be forced into a good
marriage. So if the marriage is not a good one, we ask him, should the
partners get a divorce? Yes, he answers. "If you're not happy and
you're not willing to work at it, then you should get out." (Mr. Taylor is
himself divorced.) Even if children are involved, we continue? Yes, he
goes on, even if there are children involved, for in such a marriage the
partners are "probably making each other miserable and the children
pick it up, so it's harder for the children, too."

I have chosen to illustrate Mr. Taylor's views because they are
so typical of many with whom I have talked. What should we make
of those views? At one level, his willingness to acknowledge the necessity of divorce when people are unhappy in a marriage would seem to
confirm the existence of a "divorce culture" in which loyalty is under-
valued, for he is clearly saying that personal happiness can trump
commitment. Yet nothing about his views indicates that they are frivolous or narcissistic, for he takes loyalty seriously as an ideal, knows a
great deal about what is happening in his society, and would impress
most people—or at least so I assume—as a morally thoughtful person.
It seems clear from my discussion with him that, for Mr. Taylor, loyalty
is an important ideal for which we ought to strive, but he also recognizes that there are realities with which we sometimes have to deal.
A virtue like loyalty, as important as it is, cannot—this is clearly not
Mr. Taylor's term—become an algorithm instructing us what to do in
any particular situation in which we find ourselves. It must instead be

a recommendation, one we ought to try our best to follow even while recognizing that sometimes we cannot.

Listening to Mr. Taylor and many others like him speak makes one wonder whether even those who emphasize the importance of virtues such as loyalty would insist that such virtues be followed unblinkingly, even at the cost of personal freedom. It turns out that they do not. Don't get me wrong, Barbara Dafoe Whitehead writes in her account of our divorce culture, "divorce is necessary in a society that believes in the ideal of affectionate marriage, and particularly in a society that seeks to protect women from brutality and violence in marriage."[19] Even William Bennett writes that loyalty "is very different from being a rubber stamp. Loyalty operates on a higher plane than that."[20]

Such caveats—coming, as they do, not only from ordinary Americans but also from many of those who bemoan the lack of loyalty in the United States—ought to make us question the notion that we once had so much more of a good thing and now have so little. Would the same conclusion apply to the question at hand: civility? Based upon my conversations with people, I think it would.

It is true that many of those with whom I have spoken find it easier to bemoan the lack of civility in America than they do the lack of loyalty. Ask people about rudeness or incivility and they are quick to respond. "Have you ever driven in Boston?" as Frances Milton Howard, a thirty-eight-year-old lawyer from Hartford, put the matter with some finality. Ms. Howard thinks that she is a civil person; she takes care to thank people for their troubles or to be polite. But often, she reports, people are stunned when she is nice to them, indicating to her that Americans have lost the arts of being nice to each other. Most of those with whom I spoke agreed. "I guess some of it came from the concept of the me generation," said Randy Cole, a forty-four-year-old African-American, who, like Mr. Taylor, is a computer programmer. "The eighties were, I guess, at fault. Very often, people got extremely selfish about things. And again, I would say that general moral decline we're talking about. Very little consideration for others. Very much concern for self." Hearing thoughts such as these expressed over and over again, it becomes clear that the complaint about civility registered by Stephen Carter is widely shared in the country.

Yet the very ease with which people slip into this complaint suggests a word of warning about it. For when pressed even a bit, a number of my respondents indicated that there was more to the story of civility than simple decline. Roger Donald, yet another computer programmer, was one of those who believed that Americans pay less attention to manners than they used to. But, also something of an iconoclast, he wanted more of a definition of rudeness before he would give his assent to the proposition that Americans are necessarily more rude. There are manners and there are manners, Mr. Donald suggests. For him, as, by the way, for Judith Shklar, behavior which, in being rude, causes harm to other people is surely offensive, but not all behavior generally considered ill-mannered does cause harm. So, he cautions, you have to make distinctions.[21] As he reflected on the matter, Mr. Donald also expressed the thought that, as important as civility may be, there are other values which are also important. One of them, in his opinion, was his ability to speak his mind. When he does so, he tells us, it is clear that other people think him rude. But what is more important: being polite or being honest? In his view, there is no question that the latter is to be valued, even if at the expense of the former. Whether he is right or wrong is less important than his recognition that a choice between competing goods must be made, a recognition, as I argued above, not always present in the views of theorists of the virtue deficit.

If we compare the way those with whom I have spoken talk about loyalty with the way they talk about civility, the differences are more of degree than of kind. My respondents are more skeptical of the notion that loyalty has been lost than they are of the idea that civility has been lost. But in both cases what emerges from discussions with them is the same underlying conflict: virtue is important, but that does not end the story. For one thing, it is never completely clear what virtue is. For another, goods can be in conflict. And third and most important, there will always be some conflict between the ideal and the reality. When we get down to concrete cases, people understand why it is sometimes necessary not to practice what we preach. There may be extenuating circumstances. The fault may lie in our institutions rather than in ourselves. But whatever the reason, we cannot always rely on external authority to tell us how to act but must also take into account who we are and what situations we find ourselves in.

CONCLUSION

Critics of America's virtue deficit, including those who feel that we have lost the art of civility, are clearly onto something real. Ameri-

cans are not listening to messages which instruct them in the importance of old-fashioned ideas about chastity, self-control, honesty, or
loyalty. We have, in short, come a long way from stories about George
Washington and the cherry tree or from ideas stressing "My country
right or wrong." But what so many writers see as a sign of our decadence could be interpreted as good news—even, perhaps, cause for a
certain celebration. For if Americans no longer turn to the Bible, to
their parents, or to great works of literature to find out what is right
and proper, they have no choice but to turn to themselves. And when
they do that, they discover that being virtuous does not consist in finding the right rule and adapting it to one's circumstances but instead
involves figuring out what the right rule ought to be. The missing ingredient in accounts of virtue lost is that Americans have been forced
by the circumstances in which they live to be *creative* when it comes
to knowing how to live. A people given to innovation and invention,
especially in their economic activities, Americans cannot be expected
to sit back and adhere to timeless notions of what is proper.

One person's lost virtue, in short, is another person's moral freedom. Americans—indeed all modern people—have been arguing for
over two hundred years about economic freedom. We all know what
those debates have involved: whether property rights guarantee other
rights, whether democracy can exist without a free market, whether
capitalism leads to inevitable instability, whether socialism or communism constitutes the wave of the future. For better or worse, the questions which preoccupied writers from Adam Smith and Karl Marx to
Joseph Schumpeter and Milton Friedman have by and large been settled: communism is disgraced, social democracy has its limits, and one
form or another of capitalism will remain the rule—despite the fact
that nearly all the governments of western Europe today call themselves socialist. It may have taken two hundred years, but the idea of
economic freedom has defeated all its rivals.

That has not yet happened with moral freedom. Indeed, many of
those who celebrate economic freedom and who call themselves conservative are uncomfortable with moral freedom. Looking upon the
refusal of Americans to live according to traditional ideas of virtue,
they conclude that people have failed morally, no matter how well they
may succeed economically. Yet is it really possible to instruct people in
taking charge of their finances and expect them not to take charge of
their virtues? What critics of our virtue deficit seem to have stumbled
on is that recent generations of Americans are among the first ever to

find themselves living in situations of unprecedented moral freedom. Compared to those who came before them, contemporary Americans cannot turn to the usual places in which moral authority was assumed to pass from generation to generation. Their churches tend to be absolutist in their teachings about moral truths. Their schools and universities have lost the confidence that they can recognize, let alone explain, something called reality. Members of their families care too much for personal satisfaction to accept the repression associated with classic ideas of renunciation and self-sacrifice. Were Americans to turn to institutions for instructions in moral guidance, they either would be unable to find them or would hear from them that they have little in the way of instruction to offer.

But let us also be clear why this has happened. When one reads many of the accounts dealing with the decline of virtue in America, two competing—and often contradictory—explanations are advanced. Sometimes, we are told, Americans are a deeply moral and religious people who have been sold short by their hedonistic and morally relativistic elite. In this explanation, the elite—by which is often meant academics at prestigious universities, journalists, and therapists—constitutes a "new class" governed by versions of liberalism completely out of touch with the needs of real people.[22] Were we able to appeal over the heads of the elite to Americans themselves, this point of view holds, we would find a people still committed to faith, authority, and old-fashioned values.

More recently, no doubt due at least in part to the American public's support of Bill Clinton despite his clear character flaws, a different view has been emphasized by theorists of our value deficit. This theory holds that the problem lies, not only with the elite, but with ordinary Americans themselves. Conservative writers like William Bennett are clearly disappointed with Americans.[23] They should, in his view, be expressing outrage at the moral decline which their country has experienced but instead they shrug their shoulders, refuse to pass judgment, and just go about the business of ordinary life. If there is a loss of virtue, from this perspective, it cuts especially deep, for the rot, if that is what it is, extends all the way down. We cannot reform America until we reform Americans.

Of these two explanations, my research convinces me that the latter is the more correct one—indeed, William Bennett relies on my book *One Nation, After All* for evidence of how indifferent ordinary

Americans have become to moral judgement. We differ, however, in what we make of what we find. As important as it is for institutions to possess moral authority—and if I did not think it important I would neither teach nor write—there is a legitimation problem when it comes to telling others how to live. What gives any elite the moral basis for the exercise of their moral authority? This is never an easy question to answer, but the answer cannot be, in a modern society, tradition. Moral authority is too important to people who have experienced moral freedom to be accepted just because those who would exercise moral authority claim that they have a monopoly over it. Moral authority must be earned before it can be exercised. As they look out on the world around them, not all Americans are convinced that their institutions—as well as their practices and their leaders—have done enough to earn it, which is why they reserve some of it for themselves.

When writers talk about civility, they do so, not just to make a point about manners, but to draw large conclusions about the nature of their society. Even Miss Manners (Judith Martin) believes that politeness, or its lack, tells us something about the balance between freedom and authority, as well as the problem of civility itself.[24] When we bemoan the lack of civility in America we will soon learn that what we are really talking about is whether people themselves will play a role in creating the moral rules by which their behavior will be governed. This being a modern democracy, it is likely that they will. It is time for America's moralists to recognize that fact and to incorporate it into their accounts of our lost virtue, or else they will find themselves talking only to each other.

NOTES

1. Adam Ferguson, *An Essay on the History of Civil Society* (Philadelphia: W. Fry, 1819), p. 32.

2. Stephen L. Carter, *Civility: Manners, Morals and the Etiquette of Democracy* (New York: Basic Books, 1998), p. 11. See also Deborah Tannen, *The Argument Culture: Moving From Debate to Dialogue* (New York: Random House, 1998).

3. Robert Putnam, "Bowling Alone," *Journal of Democracy* 6 (January 1995): 65–78; "Tuning In, Turning Out: The Strange Disappearance of Social Capital in America," *P.S.: Political Science* 28 (Winter 1995): 1–20;

"The Strange Disappearance of Civic America," *American Prospect* 24 (Winter 1996): 34–38; and "Bowling Alone Revisited," *The Responsive Community* 5 (Spring 1995): 18–33.

4. Nicholas Lemann, "Kicking in Groups," *Atlantic Monthly* 277 (April 1996): 22–26; Michael Schudson, "What If Civic Life Didn't Die?," *American Prospect* 25 (March–April 1996): 17–20; Everett C. Ladd, "The Data Just Don't Show Erosion of America's Social Capital," *Public Perspective* 7 (June/July 1996): 1; and Sidney Verba, Kay Lehman Scholzman, and Henry E. Brady, *Voice and Equality: Civic Voluntarism in America* (Cambridge, Mass.: Harvard University Press, 1995).

5. There are some writers who strongly disagree that civility is necessarily a good thing: Benjamin DeMott, "Seduced by Civility: Political Manners and the Crisis of Democratic Values," *Nation*, 9 December 1996, p. 11; and Randall Kennedy, "State of the Debate: The Case Against Civility," *American Prospect* 41 (November–December 1998): 84–90.

6. Alan Charles Kors and Harvey A. Silvergate, *The Shadow University: The Betrayal of Liberty on America's Campuses* (New York: Free Press, 1988).

7. William J. Bennett, *The Book of Virtues: A Treasury of Great Moral Stories* (New York: Simon and Schuster, 1993).

8. William J. Bennett, John J. DiIulio, and John P. Waters, *Body Count: Moral Poverty and How to Win America's War Against Crime and Drugs* (New York: Simon and Schuster, 1996).

9. See Robert Bork, *Slouching Toward Gomorrah: Modern Liberalism and American Decline* (New York: ReganBooks, 1996). For additional examples, see Robert Bork, "The End of Democracy?: The Judicial Usurpation of Politics," *First Things* 67 (November 1996): 18; and Mark Helprin, "To Fight for Principle," *Wall Street Journal*, 15 January 1997, p. A16.

10. William J. Bennett, *The Death of Outrage* (New York: Simon and Schuster, 1998).

11. Isaiah Berlin, "The Originality of Machiavelli," in *The Proper Study of Mankind* (New York: Farrar, Strauss, and Giroux, 1998), pp. 269–325.

12. Alasdair MacIntyre, *After Virtue: A Study in Moral Theory* (Notre Dame, Ind.: University of Notre Dame Press, 1981).

13. Alan Wolfe, *One Nation, After All: What Middle Class Americans Really Think about God, Country, Family, Racism, Welfare, Immigration, Homosexuality, Work, The Right, The Left, and Each Other* (New York: Viking, 1998).

14. Josiah Royce, *The Philosophy of Loyalty* (Nashville: Vanderbilt University Press, 1995 [1908]), p. xxiv.

15. Christopher Lasch, *The Revolt of the Elites and the Betrayal of Democracy* (New York: Norton, 1995), pp. 5–6.

16. Barbara Dafoe Whitehead, *The Divorce Culture* (New York: Knopf, 1997).

17. Alan Ehrenhalt, *The United States of Ambition: Politics, Power, and the Pursuit of Office* (New York: Times Books, 1991).

18. Frederick F. Reichheld, *The Loyalty Effect: The Hidden Force Behind Growth, Profits, and Lasting Value* (Boston: Harvard Business School Press, 1996).

19. Whitehead, *Divorce Culture*, p. 188.

20. Bennett, *Book of Virtues*, p. 665.

21. Judith N. Shklar, *Ordinary Vices* (Cambridge, Mass.: Harvard University Press, 1984), pp. 7–44.

22. See Bork, *Slouching Toward Gomorrah*, for examples.

23. Especially in Bennett, *The Death of Outrage*.

24. Judith Martin, *Miss Manners Rescues Civilization: From Sexual Harassment, Frivolous Lawsuits, Dissing, and Other Lapses in Civility* (New York: Crown, 1996).

Response to Alan Wolfe

LAWRENCE CAHOONE

ALAN WOLFE ARGUES that the diagnosis of lost civility in recent American life is mainly quackery. He objects to Stephen Carter's civility cure and to the dire prognoses of moral conservatives like William Bennett and Robert Bork. Their cries of moral decline are alarmist; their imagination of a golden age, a failure to do a good patient history. His interesting paper engages questions that would require a book-length response. Since I have not finished that book yet, I must be content with offering my own folk diagnosis and patent medicines.

I share some of Professor Wolfe's reaction to the moral critics. Stephen Carter never gives an adequate definition of civility, nor does he contextualize its apparent demise in a broader institutional analysis. As has been pointed out elsewhere, he pays scant attention to the historical and, especially, the class construction of manners. I believe William Bennett's elegy for outrage ignores the nuances of the arguably conservative American moral tradition, by which we often limit the reach of moral judgment for moral ends; but then I take the apparently idiosyncratic position that there is nothing conservative about making oral sex the main public business of the most powerful nation on earth for more than a year. As Professor Wolfe argues, conservatives who have never met a market they didn't like are responsible to notice the free market's role in undermining loyalty, civility, and other virtues. Thus I agree that no serious social critic can accept the critique of lost virtue at face value. But I also think that no serious citizen can doubt that it is in some important sense *true*. My task will be to make these claims consistent.

Professor Wolfe writes that "we ought to question the notion that we once had so much more of a good thing [that is, civility] and now have so little." He wants to banish the word *decline* from the literature of social criticism. But some clarification is required here. For he also cautions that "this is not to suggest that nothing of value has in fact declined." He himself asks, "Is it true . . . that Americans no longer know how to practice the virtue of loyalty?" and answers, "In some sense it clearly is. . . ." On a different score, while apparently questioning the relative value of civility, he suggests that our "vehement" political debates may be an indicator of *greater* civility. I might agree, but this is to argue not about the importance of civility, but about *what constitutes* civility. Has civility declined, or has a particular historical form of civility declined? We will return to this question.

Professor Wolfe raises three objections to the moral critics. First, "it is never completely clear what virtue is." Second, "goods can be in conflict." Third, "there will always be some conflict between the ideal and the reality. . . . People understand why it is sometimes necessary not to practice what we preach. . . ." Regarding the first objection, while the call for clarity is always welcome, if "complete" clarity is to be our standard, we might as well go home now. I do not know an important theory of social criticism whose key terms are not subject to questions of clarity. Even if the clarity of the moral critics is below the woeful state of the art, this is to fault the messenger and not the message, if the message can be put more clearly. I think it can.

It is Professor Wolfe's second and third criticisms that are the crucial ones. I will take them in reverse order. First he argues that to the extent that there is a decline in virtues like civility or, as he adds, loyalty, this loss is the rational response of individuals to social or institutional changes. Citizens are not "to blame" for this loss, and it cannot be remedied by moral education or exhortation. Civility has thus been trumped by "realism." Second, given Berlin's moral pluralism, lost civility or loyalty is the flip side of a moral gain in honesty or freedom. Here civility has been trumped not by amoral reality but by other goods. Thus, the contemporary liberal *Gesellschaft* or contractual society buys freedom and rationality in exchange for more *Gemeinschaftliche* or community-oriented virtues.

Professor Wolfe is partly right on both counts. Moral dispositions being shaped by institutions, it makes little sense to promote virtues that cannot cohere with them. It is also arguable that recent social changes that could count as moral losses are concomitant with moral gains. It is in this vein that Peter Berger argues that modernity entails the "obsolescence of the concept of honor," but thereby gains a notion of universal human dignity. The direction of institutional change puts pressure on traditional virtues, tending to make some ineffective, anachronistic, or even counterproductive, as Wolfe rightly notes in the case of loyalty. Michael Sandel makes a similar claim about symbiotic dependency, namely, that economic pressures and the rate of divorce tend to make it *irrational* for anyone, male or female, to devote themselves exclusively to unpaid childrearing.

But to describe this as a conflict between the ideal and the real is troublesome. This description is actually continuous with the moral critics' claim that ours is an increasingly amoral society. Following the language of this objection, Wolfe's difference with the moral conservatives would then be a Stoic acceptance of an amoral present versus nostalgia. But such acceptance would seem to deny the Durkheimian project of a morally concerned and informed social criticism that Professor Wolfe defends elsewhere. Further, while it is true to say that goods are plural, and that often one must be exchanged for another, this is surely a matter of degree and context. Professor Wolfe would no doubt agree that the exchange of, say, civility for honesty does not mean an exchange of *all* civility for *total* honesty. Rather, we have traded a certain level and kind of civility in certain contexts for some increment of honesty in those contexts. These homely points can, I suggest, serve to recast, not undo, the moral of Professor Wolfe's story.

Before proceeding to my main worries, two amendments. Professor Wolfe sets up his conclusion by saying that, since that great issue of political economy, the Smith-Marx debate, we might say, has now been resolved in favor of economic freedom, we ought now admit a like freedom in moral matters. Presumably this is a closing shot at conservatives who like their markets open but their moralities closed. I agree that true socialism, as opposed to a mixed economy, is now defunct. I for one do not mourn it. But while Marx's answer is defunct, the Smith-Marx *question* is not, for it was but one variant of a broader question, *the* eighteenth-century question: can a commercial society be a good society? The current debate over moral decline is part of that discussion, whose answer, it seems, we will forever be negotiating.

Second, there is the role of the elite, as explored by moral conservatives and, from a liberal-populist perspective, by Christopher Lasch. I agree that to the extent there has been moral decline it is largely due to systemic forces and not the action of an academic-journalistic-technocratic elite, "tenured radicals" plus the "liberal media" plus "Hollywood Babylon," or, dating myself, Spiro Agnew's "effete corps of impudent snobs." But this is not the end of the story either. One need not be a conspiracy theorist to recognize that like individuals pursue like self-interest. With Lasch, who followed Alvin Gouldner's analysis of the "new class," it is arguable that the absence of certain virtues, like loyalty, is class-distributed, that the class of, in Robert Reich's phrase, professional symbolic analysts is for objective reasons less loyal to clan, neighborhood, church, and flag. Granting this, it would be hard not to imagine that this class's special role in the "postmodern" information society tends to promote a deidentification with locale, kin, and country into culture at large. I would not, as some conservatives seem wont to do, regard the new class as the *first cause* of this phenomenon. Rather, they are its avant-garde, amplifying it, spreading it, and, given their medium, legitimating it. I think much of postwar liberal political theory has been an expression of this class's interests, or more fairly, its way of viewing everyone's interests. Not that this is all bad; Gouldner argued that, as ruling classes go, the new class has much to be said for it. But like all others, it has the vices of its virtues.

Now to civility itself: I think it both logically unnecessary and a moral error to imply, as Professor Wolfe does, that incivility is or can be a good thing *per se*. Certainly there are places and times where civility ought to be trumped by other goods. But that is not to deny the goodness of civility. To say that sometimes personal or social issues are so crucial that a departure from civility is justified is not to deny civility's value, but to honor it in the breach. I would restate the moral critics' position by saying that a decline in civility means, not merely that civility is in our society increasingly trumped, but that in some areas of our public life a shared sense of civility seems to have been *delegitimated* as a binding norm we can reliably invoke; that is, not merely that people behave uncivilly, but that the charge "That was uncivil" carries little or no weight. So I think there *is* a decline in civility and that this decline *matters*.

Likewise, I think it is a mistake to imply that civility and honesty are antonyms. Civility is, to be sure, a complex term, historically related to *civil society*, *civilization*, the notion of a *public* realm, *culture*, *cultivation*, and so on. In contemporary usage it simultaneously refers to the rules by which citizens relate and to refinement of manners, the latter being notoriously relative to history, culture, and class. Carter's notion of civility as "sacrifice" emphasizes the latter, and is continuous with Norbert Elias' analysis of civilization as the progressive control of affectivity and bodily presentation. In effect, Carter's "sacrifice" is what Freud called the instinctual renunciation intrinsic to the progress of civilization. Carter then fears a contemporary lowering of the level of renunciation. (I might say, as a historical aside, that this claim is not the sole property of the right; Herbert Marcuse saw such a contemporary "desublimation," although he claimed it served socially "repressive" ends.)

While I think this desublimation or lightening of renunciation might hold true at some level of our social life, the relativity of manners to society, history, and class should lead us to be tentative and limited in our judgments. I have no doubt that by the standards of some human societies in history—1950s America, or the culture of the American founders, to take two apparent models of civility—were remarkably uncivil. Every society, and every social subgroup, evolves its own rules of propriety and renunciation. An *utterly* uncivil society is hard to imagine; perhaps the Ik that Colin Turnbull described in his book *The Mountain People* are an example. We must not mistake a foreign civility for no civility. But this means, not that civility is too vague and relative to matter, but that it is remarkably flexible. As James Schmidt argued recently in this series, the moral critics are indefensible where they take particular historical standards of civility as *the* form of civility. But a concern for civility that is sensitive to history and variety would not fall to that critique.

Professor Wolfe's recounting of some of his interviews probes exactly the right point. Messrs. Taylor and Donald are unhappy with incivility and disloyalty, but they would not want restrictions on divorce, honesty, and so forth. Their conflict reflects, I agree, a realistically complex moral sense. I believe that many Americans believe that the authority of moral rules has declined, across most classes and social situations, especially regarding the public realm, and I believe they don't like this. Of course, lots of Americans do live in pockets of loyalty, civility, community—or whatever "virtue" or condition you wish to identify as what is progressively eroded by the direction of contemporary life. What such people fear is both that those pockets are easily undermined, and that outside those pockets all bets are off, that there is little or no shared moral context—or rather, an uncomfortably thin moral context. It is also true, I believe, that most people some of the time and some most of the time find alternative satisfactions in the *Gesellschaft* of declining civility and loyalty. The form of life in which individual liberty has been given greater scope has substantial benefits. This, coupled with the inertial dominance of this form of life, understandably makes many people loath to change it. Rather, they largely renounce unfulfillable hopes and, where they can, cathect uncivil society's compensatory pleasures.

Here we can reactivate two earlier points. First, while I criticized Professor Wolfe for using the language of morality versus realism as his own, it does seem an accurate *description* of what many people feel. People, and critics, often interpret our predicament as inherited moral expectations slamming into an amoral but prosperous reality. This leads them to accept a diremption between the moral and the practical; they avow civility or loyalty, but believe that *praxis* requires them to bracket parts of their moral sense. I think this is an interpretive error, a mistaken self-description, to which the nature of contemporary social life tempts us. It is also an unfortunate one; it lobotomizes us, morally speaking. To believe in the practical necessity of bracketing the moral sense is to deny the very plausibility of the kind of morally sensitive social criticism that Professor Wolfe has worked to promote.

Likewise, to describe such experiences as an exchange of one good for another *simpliciter is* also a misdescription. Mr. Donald says he likes civility, or politeness, but prefers honesty. I object not to his choice, but to the failure of our cultural language and of his imagination that leaves him with no other self-description than to say he is "giving up civility for honesty." I am willing to bet he does not mean that an honest remark requires utter incivility. He is not unfamiliar with the difference between saying, "No, I disagree," and, to euphemize the epithet increasingly on the tip of our cultural tongue, "F—— you." I hazard that Mr. Donald makes his *own* distinction between civil and uncivil honesty. He draws that line, but he draws it in *a different place* than those who find him rude. Unfortunately, he then accepts that his interlocutors' version of civility defines civility *per se,* hence feels forced linguistically, if not behaviorally, to jettison civility as a norm. In fact, he is not trading civility wholesale for honesty, but a certain expression of civility for a greater scope for honesty coupled with a modified civility. He is reinterpreting civility, not abandoning it.

In my version of the moral critique that Professor Wolfe proposes, our task is not the *anachronistic* one of exchanging present gains for lost virtues, nor the *Stoic* one of accepting the cloud of amorality about the silver lining of liberty and honesty, but the *hermeneutic* one of placing the gain and the loss in a moral language that can do justice to both, hence to continue the never-ending task of balancing goods. I claim this project both fits the facts better and serves the task of a normative social analysis. It is not a question of virtue versus reality, nor of civility and loyalty versus honesty and liberty *per se*, but of *what kind* of civility and loyalty balanced with *how much* honesty and liberty. The job is not to be civil and loyal the way we used to be, but to be civil and loyal in the way we *can be*. This we do as everyday citizens. When we struggle to be honest *and* civil we in effect create a *new way* of being civil. This means we must, as the moral critics suggest, attend to a strengthening of civility and loyalty, and, as liberals fear, also restrain honesty and liberty in some contexts, in some respects. Of course, we already do restrain them, but an increased civility and loyalty presumably means more restraint. This bothers some liberals who fear *any* rollback of liberty, however measured. But if moral pluralism, the rejection of a fixed hierarchy of goods, denies that civility can trump all other values, it *also* denies that liberty can trump all other values. According liberty the highest value is a *denial* of moral pluralism.

Professor Wolfe concludes with an ambitious suggestion. He says that *virtue* must not be conceived as "adopting a rule," as a sense of "propriety," supported by "authority" or drawn from "tradition." Taking the moral critics to imply an appeal to authority, he cautions, "As important as it is for institutions to possess moral authority . . . there is a legitimation problem when it comes to telling others how to live." Instead, we should "celebrate" the triumph of freedom because it betokens people's attempt to "take charge of their virtues." Reminiscent of John Dewey, he notes the failure to apply the freedom granted in other domains of modern life, like the market—or, for Dewey, science—to moral matters. He thus advocates a "moral democracy," where "the people themselves will play a role in creating the moral rules by which their behavior will be governed."

Now, if this means that a liberal republican morality is one in which people have a great deal of freedom, including scope not only for reinterpreting the moral rules governing their personal lives but also for contributing those reinterpretations to an ongoing public reinterpretation of morality, he is right. Since I deny the political view that thinks the polity can be neutral about morality, can leave morality a purely private matter, I agree that morality in a liberal polity must not permit liberty and change, but positively value them as well. All this is fine. But the call for "moral democracy" implies something more troublesome.

Even if it is the case that until now people have not "played a role" in creating their morality—which is already problematic—this cannot mean that from this day forward coercion will be absent from moral life. If "the people" construct moral rules, then the majority will impose them and minorities and individuals will feel bound by them. If institutions have moral meaning, individuals socialized in them will come to accept those meanings. Moral democracy cannot mean moral individualism, since moral rules intrinsically hold for more than one person. Moral democracy still means moral coercion. *All* morality suffers the "legitimation" problem of telling people how to live, including a morality of tolerance and rights. It is morality's job to tell people how to live, a job accepted by liberal social critics as fully as by conservatives.

Further, while I like a morality that values freedom, I am skeptical of a "free morality" devoid of authority and tradition. First, with most of those labeled communitarians I would agree that freedom and some of its alleged associates—like inquiry, critical thought, individuality—presuppose civility, not to mention loyalty, solidarity, and so forth. Freedom, individuality, and critique depend on a moral background that is communally constituted. Even if it is true that a liberal society rightly concerns itself to increase liberty, it must limit this project where it threatens the substructure of civility that makes liberty possible. More controversially, with Alasdair MacIntyre—whom Wolfe quotes approvingly—as well as Hannah Arendt, Edward Shils, Samuel Fleischacker, and David Selznick, I would argue that morality presupposes tradition and authority, that is, the acceptance of institutions, practices, narratives, and their implicit or explicit ends, without independent rational or critical assent. Our ability to debate, criticize, and choose some moral rules presupposes a shared moral background that cannot be entirely chosen, nor can it be rationally justified. This background is not sacrosanct; it can be reconstructed, but only one piece at a time, the reconstructionist standing on other unquestioned parts of the structure. Liberalism itself is such an authoritative tradition—albeit, as Shils and MacIntyre claimed, a paradoxically antitraditional tradition of antiauthoritarian authorities.

Normatively, then, what is to be done? As noted, the task is to find forms of civility and loyalty that balance with our form of liberty. Liberty has been reinterpreted so as to expand; so must civility be reinterpreted, rather than forgotten, and liberty re-reinterpreted so as to strike some balance with that reinterpreted civility. This may sound wimpy, but it would represent an improvement over the current situation, in which what we often see is the simple abandonment of the moral authority to judge incivility in the face of the real benefits, and the inertia, of the system in which we live. This lack of moral imagination is reflected in political theories which take discussion of the substructure of rights and the conditions of material prosperity to exhaust legitimate public moral debate. Professor Wolfe has rightly attacked that neutralist tradition, admirably calling attention to a minor topic often ignored in the Manichaean debate between the advocates of the Market and the advocates of the State, a little thing called "society." Civility and loyalty have something to do with that social substructure, and, I believe, always will.

Civility and the Limits
to the Tolerable
EDWIN J. DELATTRE

I CHOSE THIS TITLE because of the prevalence now in many schools and classrooms of direct and indirect instruction of students that tolerance, often called "tolerance of differences," is the highest virtue. Students are routinely told by their teachers that it is wrong to be intolerant—of anything except intolerance itself—and that intolerance of anything else is a form of incivility and, like other forms of incivility, never appropriate. Posters, bulletin boards, slogans celebrate both diversity and the celebration of diversity.

For at least the past decade, the lesson has been delivered by many teachers, school administrators, curriculum designers, textbook publishers, and advocacy groups that diversity among us is to be everywhere celebrated, honored, respected—and that criticism is by its nature intolerant, uncivil, and therefore wrong. Celebration of diversity, in turn, has emerged as one variety of the dogma visited on students for at least thirty years, to the effect that we are obligated to be "nonjudgmental" in our thinking about and conduct toward others. The implication of this dogma is that judging others or their ways of thinking, feeling, and acting is itself uncivil.

Nonjudgmentalism has been incorporated into education law, regulation, policy, and practice. The Massachusetts General Laws require that standards of instruction "shall be designed to inculcate respect for the cultural, ethnic and racial diversity of the commonwealth and for the contributions made by diverse cultural, ethnic and racial groups to the life of the commonwealth" (Chapter 69, Section 1D). This law requires efforts to inculcate respect, not for persons or for the achievements of individuals, but for "diversity" itself and for group identity.

Likewise, by law, curriculum frameworks developed under the authority of the Massachusetts Board of Education "shall be designed to avoid perpetuating gender, cultural, ethnic or racial stereotypes" and "shall reflect sensitivity to different learning styles and impediments to learning" (Chapter 69, Section 1E). Thus, if a student is averse in "learning style" to reading, teachers are required sensitively to find alternatives amenable to that style, even though no such alternatives can possibly enable the student to learn to read.

Sometimes "sensitivity to impediments to learning" becomes preemptively destructive pity. Deaf children need to learn to read and write well. Their intelligence varies just as the intelligence of hearing children varies, but many deaf college students have never learned to read high-school-level material. Deaf children need thoroughly competent schoolteachers who know written English, the best practices in reading and writing instruction, and American Sign Language. Deaf children do not need administrators, lawmakers, policymakers, or "advocates" who pity them or have "sensitively" low expectations of them.

In implementing the law to avoid perpetuating stereotypes, the Massachusetts Department of Education has established "Bias Review Committees." These committees are charged to make recommendations on state curriculum frameworks, state assessments of student performance, and state guides on pedagogy; but committee members often attempt to exceed their authority by making demands instead of recommendations. In one recent battle in which I was involved behind the scenes, a bias committee reviewing prospective test questions in history insisted that the word "ruthless" not be used in reference to Joseph Stalin, because "that might offend the emotional sensibilities of socialist students." Anyone who refuses to bow to such demands from a bias review committee can expect to be accused of incivility, intolerance, and disrespect for laws requiring sensitivity to diversity. Advocates of nonjudgmentalism can, and do, become judgmental when not allowed to have their way.

Curriculum frameworks prepared by the Massachusetts Department of Education under education reform law exhibit the determination to identify civility and tolerance with celebration of diversity and avoidance of distinctions. The framework for the study of foreign languages adopted by the state in 1995 has, of necessity, been dramatically overhauled under the leadership of the Board of Education composed in 1996. The earlier framework was carefully entitled "Making

Connections Through World Languages" so as to buttress indefensible ideological claims: "The term foreign language is a misnomer" (p. 5). "For the bilingual student, second language acquisition is easier when the children come to school knowing that their language and culture are just as important as English" (p. 16). "The learner is the center of World Language instruction" (p. 2). And "Proficiency-based programs assess proficiency in addition to accuracy. . . . If every item on a test evaluates accuracy (spelling, grammar, structural connections), that test does not give the student the chance to demonstrate his skill at negotiating meaning. Proficiency testing is personalized; it asks the learner to use thinking skills . . ." (p. 19).

Notably, the term "world languages" was intended to put all languages and cultures on a par in every respect—equal in importance in every respect—so that no priority could be given to any language in any context, except the native language of the child which, by implication, is just as important as every other, irrespective of circumstance. Making the learner the "center" of instruction was intended to safeguard the student from any feelings of deficiency or failure that might arise if learning subject matter were central, and so was trivialization of accuracy in spelling, grammar, and language use. The framework also said, "Teaching for proficiency allows students to experience the language in real ways," thus meeting such learning standards as "express[ing] likes, dislikes, and feelings" (p. 4). "Real ways," not incidentally, were sharply distinguished from "simply reading and writing language" (p. 1), both of which were treated with derision—as happens wherever educationists lapse into the idiom of "student learning styles" and "thinking skills."

More than once, when I publicly criticized these claims of the framework as untrue and threatening to worthwhile educational opportunity, I was accused by some advocates of the framework— not because of my tone or manner, but because of the content of my criticisms—of being insensitive, uncivil, intolerant, and condescending. No rebuttal was ever offered to my arguments, but only the accusation that my denying the claims of the framework was itself uncivil.

That accusation was mild compared to some of the reactions to my questions about the Massachusetts health curriculum framework. That framework declares that "affirming one's background, beliefs, and cultures is a key component in comprehensive school health education" (p. 8). I asked whether this meant health education should teach students to "affirm" backgrounds that exposed them to domestic violence and adult substance abuse; "affirm" beliefs that are racist, misogynistic, or transparently false; "affirm" cultures in which genital mutilation of girls and women, denial of educational opportunity to girls, enslavement of children, or genocide are practiced. Adverse reactions ranged from speechless shock to bluster about not being critical of other cultures. But not all reaction was adverse—some of the framework writers and teachers clearly saw that the text was not defensible as written.

In Massachusetts education reform, contempt for fact and deepseated fear that telling any unpleasant truth is insensitive and uncivil, intolerant of differences, find expression in the false but blithe insistence, "All students are capable of learning at high levels." Some people who say this genuinely believe it to be true—evidence notwithstanding; and some have even told me they are quite "comfortable" with the idea that everyone is far above average in some capacity or other to learn. Others do not believe it, but believe that they must say it in order to gain parental and teacher support for education reform—to give assurance that no child will be left behind, no student will ever have to come face to face with a limitation in capacity for learning. Either way, education reform is diverted from the aspiration to world-class standards, high expectations, and challenging instruction for students that both education reform law and massive state funding are designed to produce.

Those familiar with the ethos of schooling will recognize, in the reduction of civility to a demeaning sensitivity, the lengthy trend glorifying the promotion of student self-esteem under any and all circumstances—as if students were invariably too frail to bear learning of any personal error, wrongdoing, blameworthiness, shortcoming, or limitation. Thus are students told, "You can be and do anything you want"—as despicable a lie as telling students prejudicially that they are incapable of aspiring with hard work to significant achievement.

As indefensible as these lessons and positions are, it is difficult not to sympathize with teachers who affirm them and deliver them to students. Many teachers are poorly educated themselves and, because they are both well-intentioned and not very knowledgeable, they can be remarkably gullible. Never having learned the differences between respect and tolerance, they are oblivious to the fact that indiscriminate respect is no more justifiable than any other form of intellectual promiscuity; and they are unaware that tolerance normally presupposes judgment—in the sense that we tolerate what we have judged to be in some way wrong, deficient, or objectionable but not to merit our interference.

I hasten to add that in over thirty years of working in schools and with teachers, I have met many splendid teachers whose thinking is much more refined and reliable than what I have described. I have never visited or worked in a school—no matter how grim its circumstances—without meeting some outstanding teachers. Still, whether working in schools or serving, as I do, on the Massachusetts Board of Education, my experience has been cassandrine—not in the sense that I possess Cassandra's gift of prophecy, but in the sense that even when explaining the relatively obvious, let alone some more subtle point, or showing the bad practices and results to which yet another new fad or gimmick in education will lead, I meet skepticism and disbelief.

Many teachers believe that teachers and teaching—whether for political or conceptual reasons—must be "value-neutral," or else face the putative conundrum of whose values are to be taught. From this false premise, which no one could ever live down to, even if it were true, they infer that being civil means being nonjudgmentally tolerant.

At the same time, huge numbers of teachers have acquired from their own school and college teachers contempt for memorization—always called "rote memorization," as if memorizing had to be mindless and bereft of understanding. Likewise, they have learned contempt for facts—invariably called "dead facts"—and they have been taught that the essential purpose of schooling is to bring students to "critical thinking." But relatively few of these same prospective and practicing teachers, administrators, and curriculum and pedagogy specialists have ever studied logic or formed any specific sense of what it means to think critically. Neither have they been brought face to face with the brute fact that thinking critically about most matters depends on considered application of relevant factual knowledge. Made contemptuous of fact by their own teachers, many teachers do not know how to take either relevant facts or applicable principles into account in deciding what is tolerable and what is not, or in distinguishing candid and forthright criticism and refutation, even when politely delivered, from incivility.

Educationist jargon terms such as "critical thinking," "thinking skills," and "problem-solving skills" usually shelter disregard for accuracy and precision in grammar, vocabulary, and logic; and the jargon extols "student creativity." Just as meaning is "negotiated" rather than understood or learned, knowledge is said to be "created" rather than discovered or studied. Throughout, vague skills are supposed to take the place of factual knowledge, knowledge of language, and understanding of rigorous reasoning.

Such jargon is part of an idolatry of process. In school of education annual reports and other typical education publications that crossed my desk in a single day last month, I came upon the following supposed processes: "the critical thinking process," "the problem-solving process," "the education process," "the writing process," "the learning process," "a student's learning process," "the grieving process," "the counseling process," "the advising process," "the change process," "the enrollment management process," "the strategic planning process," "the discovery process," "the decision-making process," "the evaluation process," "the validation process," "the closure process," "the creative process," and, not to be forgotten, "the reform process."

Not long ago, I heard an education bureaucrat say, while promoting state budgets for instructional technology, "Students should be learning the word processing process." For the most part, such language is sheer puffery and obscurantism, not rooted in any discernment about what distinguishes a process from any other activity or sequence. The word "process" has become part of the educationist and broadcast journalist argot because it has a vaguely scientific ring to it; because reducing nouns to adjectives, like using nouns as if they were verbs, obviates the need for precision and attention to detail; and because government bureaucrats prefer to provide research funding for putative processes conjured by jargonistic sleight of hand than for homely-sounding topics. Better to fund research on the "authentic assessment process" than on teaching grammar.

It will not do, apparently, to say, "Ruth is knitting." We might be inclined then to ask, "What is knitting? How does one knit? What is Ruth knitting?" We are to say instead, "Ruth is involved in the knitting process." But what is the process to which we are to pay heed other than knitting itself? Many things may be going on in Ruth's mind when she is knitting, but the phrase "the knitting process" is pleonastic. It confuses by giving the impression that when someone knits, there is another process going on in addition to knitting that, while distinct, cannot be separated from knitting itself. I foresee, instead of "The elected official is lying," "The elected official is participating in the lying process." "Process" sounds more benign where lying is concerned, and our description more "value-neutral." "The child is making up a story." What's the story? Do you see traces of other stories the child has read in our class, or of what we have tried to teach about describing animals and people and places? But no: "The child is engaged in the creative process." "Ah," said Humpty Dumpty, "there's glory for you!"

The worn-out phrase "problem solving" does sometimes mean something specific—in geometry or computer programming, for example, or engine mechanics—but in current usage it often means nothing specific at all. The phrase serves as a summary and as shorthand for affirming the desirability of inculcating the belief or attitude that making one's way in the world is simply a matter of becoming a "problem solver." Here, we see a latter-day version of earlier calls for education to be "relevant."

In practice, inculcating this attitude often serves as a diversion from coming to know subject matter. One lesson recommended by the Massachusetts curriculum framework in science, now in revision, is supposed to draw younger students into the study of the physics of lift, as in aeronautics and aviation. The students begin by making paper airplanes at random and tossing them to see how they fly. The very next step in the lesson is for the students to consider the feelings of people who live in the flight paths of airports and to address the problem of how to avoid noise and other pollution. The lesson never returns to any idea or theory having to do with lift, such as the Bernoulli principle, or to any other concept in the study of physics and motion. Such diversions pass as instruction in "problem solving."

Again, there is a grain of truth in the idea that it is important to learn to identify, rank in significance, and solve problems. But no one is likely to become skilled at any of those without acquiring considerable detailed and relevant factual and conceptual knowledge. We do not learn to repair engines by studying problem solving, but rather by studying engines in the company of accomplished mechanics who can show us when and how we misread clues or otherwise go wrong.

Far more distant from the truth is the idea that living a life is essentially a matter of solving problems—that a life consists of little more than one problem or problematic episode on top of another. Life itself is not a problem to be solved; the elements of human nature that make deadly sins deadly are not problems to be solved but difficulties to be contended with; human finitude and mortality in a contingent world are not problems but facts of life with which we must come to terms. Our individual limitations and the inequalities of talent among us are not problems to be solved—as by equating civility with refusal to acknowledge failure, or by tolerating social promotion from grade to grade, or by pronouncing all homogeneous groupings of students in classrooms to be unjust. Our limitations and the fact that we are less or more talented than someone else are rather realities of our individual lives that call for self-knowledge and the aspiration to do the best we can with what we have for as long as we have it.

Everyone needs to learn such distinctions. Michael Downing captures them powerfully in his 1997 novel, *Perfect Agreement*. Downing's protagonist, Mark Sternum, says of his older brother, Tommy:

> My brother was cursed with an amazing capacity to invent practical solutions to almost any problem . . . . I did not count him a failure as a brother; he was no worse at it than I was. What failed Tommy was his attention span. He could muster energy enough to rescue a whole neighborhood from a zoning board decision to allow strip clubs near a school, but he had no abiding interest in his own life. Maybe it was too amorphous a challenge, or maybe he had found it resistant to practical remedies. He could not solve it.[1]

Moved by advocacy of "critical thinking," "problem solving," contempt for "dead facts," and the intolerable, destructive belief that listening is a form of passivity, many educationists eschew lecturing well as a part of the repertoire of the qualified teacher. They invoke dialogue as appropriate classroom practice (along with "group projects" and "cooperative learning"—as if individual study were somehow *un*cooperative), but few have ever studied philosophical dialogues or the nature of dialogue. Most cannot describe or explain differences between a dialogue and any other discussion, conversation, or classroom activity where students talk. In my experience, many teachers and administrators are shocked to learn that Plato and Socrates identified knowledge and candor as necessary conditions of participation in dialogue—as well as the good will or humility of recognizing one's own fallibility—rather than a mere spirit of uncritical cooperativeness and nonjudgmentalism.

For teachers laboring in such ignorance, as long as students are talking with some measure of politeness—and whether or not any of them are listening—the students are learning by participation in dialogue. In practice, much classroom talk, uninformed by serious homework, amounts to no more than the mutual perpetuation of ignorance.

Furthermore, many teachers, along with resident advisors in college dormitories, have been exposed to the ideology of conflict resolution programs which claim that to begin the mediation or resolution of conflict, it is imperative to recognize and explicitly acknowledge the legitimacy of the positions of all the disputants. This morally bankrupt prescription for living together—a prescription for peace at any price that does not work in practice in human affairs—likewise sails under the flag of civility, respect, and tolerance.

This ideology gains further purchase on the thoughts and dispositions of teachers who naively accept the exhortation or command of manipulative and deceitful "facilitators" who lead discussions of school policy and practice by requiring that all opinions are to be treated with respect. By respecting opinions, facilitators do not mean listening to them, giving them such consideration as they deserve, criticizing them with a due sense of proportion. They mean not being critical—not "devaluing" anyone's opinion and thereby, as the jargon runs, "invalidating" the person. But an opinion may in fact be foolish, stupid, benighted, false, unworthy of serious consideration, plainly refutable, unintelligible, or bigoted and otherwise shameful. Depending on the content of an opinion, proper responses may range from profound admiration to contempt. This is not the case, however, where criticizing an opinion, or refusing to tolerate it in silence, is equated with incivility to a person.

No doubt, some teachers would not be much wiser, even if their own educational opportunities had been more intellectually sound and fertile. As in other walks of life, including walks of life involving public service and obligations of public trust, some teachers are not very bright; and the teaching corps in the United States is to some extent undermined by the fact that many teacher preparation institutions, like the universities in which they are housed, have open admissions, widespread grade inflation, and little regard for advanced study by prospective teachers of the academic and scientific disciplines.

But even those teachers who are bright and reasonably well educated often face conditions that make it tempting to elevate mutual toleration, conceived as basic civility, to the highest good in classrooms. Often, some or many of the students they are expected to teach come to school ill-prepared, ill-mannered, undisciplined, inconsiderate, self-indulgent, lazy, misogynistic, vulgar, obscene, dishonest, brutal, predatory, or violent either by initiative or by reaction to the contrived or imagined slight. Some students bring with them to school what Charles Murray calls "the ethics of male adolescents who haven't been taught any better."[2] I would add that some of these students are females, and that some boys and girls, children and youths, in school today live their lives outside of school in conditions vividly pictured by Hogarth. Even supposedly advantaged children are coarsened by neglectful parents who leave them to their own devices in endless exposure to the vulgarity of popular culture as purveyed in the crude humor of the typical sitcom.

Many teachers must greet such students day after day—and must do so without benefit of administrators who have the knowledge and the courage to establish and maintain basic standards of discipline, conduct, safety, and civility in the schools for which they are responsible. Parents and members of advocacy groups can also be unbelievably nasty to teachers—and with impunity, where administrators are craven.

To add insult to injury, schoolteachers are often evaluated by their students as part of teacher performance reviews—in terms of whether the teachers are interesting, student-centered, stimulating, impartial in grading. To some students, "impartial" means fair only in the sense of not expecting too much. Such categories of evaluation are more appropriate to entertainment than to education. Far better to ask whether the teachers assigned substantial homework, required preparation for class, gave demanding tests, and graded student work in accordance with high standards of achievement. Current practices give students both opportunity and license to abuse and harm teachers who are in any way critical of their performance or who expect them to make efforts that intrude on their desires, likes, and dislikes.

So inflated has the status accorded student opinion become—however uninformed and irrelevant to educational quality—that Massachusetts requires by law the election of a secondary student to the state Board of Education. In my judgment, it is impossible for even a smart, conscientious, and reasonably well-educated high school student to know and understand enough to serve competently as a member of the Board.

Not surprisingly, when the state Board interviewed candidates for the Massachusetts Commissioner of Education on February 6 of this year, the student member of the Board—at the behest of her "constituency"—asked each candidate whether he would treat student evaluations as an important part of overall teacher performance reviews. Two of the candidates assured her that they would do so. The third said no; he explained that as a college academic vice president and dean, he had seen too much student evaluation that revealed nothing about quality of teaching and learning and confirmed only teacher popularity gained at the expense of high standards. Few school administrators—indeed, relatively few higher education administrators—have it in them to utter that truth straightforwardly, and teachers know it. It is unlikely that the supposed constituency of this student member of our Board will look favorably on her supporting the candidate who dared to say no.

Students are abetted in self-inflicted harm by advocacy groups whose members wear masks of sensitivity and benevolence. In the Boston University/Chelsea Public Schools Partnership, we have fought against enormous adult resistance in order to overturn the policy that high school students may fail two subjects in a term and remain eligible for interscholastic athletics. The argument? "For many of these students, interscholastic athletics will forever be the high point of their lives. Depriving them of athletic eligibility just for failing two courses verges on outright cruelty."

In this controversy, our earlier reversal of a profound injustice in the schools paid off in a way we had not foreseen. When the Partnership began in 1989, Chelsea had no interscholastic athletic programs for girls—none. We moved as rapidly as possible to establish parity in athletic programs for girls and boys. Then, at the height of the eligibility controversy, we confirmed that not a single girl would be disqualified by the higher academic standard for athletic eligibility. Not even the advocates of the "Two F-still eligible" rule were willing to defend the position that girls are simply smarter than boys and can reasonably be held to higher academic expectations and standards. Fatefully, boys thus benefited educationally from our establishment of athletic programs for girls.

Adult opposition to the new standards of eligibility is by no means gone. It is only temporarily muted. When we raise the standards for eligibility even higher, as we are poised to do, we will again face enormous adult resistance. Some adults who are more concerned about bragging rights in interscholastic sports than about student educational achievement will put pressure on teachers to inflate grades—to be "sensitive and compassionate"—so failing students remain eligible for sports.

Teachers in such conditions are expected to treat students as if they were customers who are always right and must be gratified. That civility should thereby collapse into not being judgmental at all, into pandering, into toleration of what students like and want—and into the tacit plea for reciprocal toleration of the teacher (provided the teacher is largely governed by student wishes)—is exactly what we should expect, giving us all the more reason to admire teachers who will have none of it.

Even in good teacher preparation institutions such as our own Boston University School of Education, it has been commonplace for years for students to evaluate demanding and rigorous faculty members negatively, to indict them for expecting too much, for criticizing student writing, for grading in accordance with high standards, for causing stress, for making students uncomfortable by their expectations, and even for insisting on regular attendance. Many students come to us with a dramatic overestimate of their achievements and competence acquired from teachers who dared not give, or were not competent to give, responsible criticism, and from parents who believed that high grades confirmed talent and achievement—even when their daughters and sons spent conspicuously little time doing homework.

In the School of Education we are finding a new student appreciation of criticism and instruction now that both we and the state are administering literacy tests—in our case, for graduation; in the state's, for teacher certification. "A rebirth of high expectations among students," one Boston University trustee called this change, as he has witnessed it in students he knows. "Better late than never," I replied. Still, we face an uphill struggle. The application essays of prospective students, most of them high school seniors, are filled with the jargon of "teaching styles," "learning styles," "making students comfortable," "promoting self-esteem," "celebrating diversity," and other shibboleths of educationism. By the time students reach college they seem to be as much in need of unlearning as of learning.

Where civility declines into indiscriminate, nonjudgmental tolerance, indiscriminate tolerance becomes wholesale indulgence, and education becomes a seedbed of incompetence, deception, and flattery. The multiple motives for equating civility with tolerance as the highest virtue—the different conditions that lend themselves to such simplism—inescapably lead to both conceptual and practical incoherence. Trying to draw students to the mannerly treatment of others without which classrooms run out of control, while simultaneously fearing offending students who consider any criticism offensive, is bound to result in incoherence and chaos—if not always in the classroom itself, then in hallways, lavatories, doorways, stairwells, and parking lots. In practice, the incoherence is masked by the substitution of the autobiographical revelation for the normative assertion or judgment—the casting of classroom discourse in terms that make error impossible, knowledge unnecessary, and criticism inapplicable.

It is now quite rare to hear a student or teacher say, "X is false," "X is wrong," "No one should do X," "We should not be willing to tolerate X." Instead, in discussions of "social studies" or literature, current events, policies, practices, attitudes, or ideas, we are much more likely to hear, "I am not comfortable with X." The assertion that X is false or wrong demands justification, the giving of reasons, respect for evidence, knowledge of relevant facts and principles that may be adduced; and such statements lend themselves to critical consideration, objection, refutation, disconfirmation, refinement. That is, they require the exercise of judgment and demand the study of the criteria for and the means of reaching the true, the probably true, and responsible judgment about truth and falsity, right and wrong.

By contrast, the autobiographical report "I am not comfortable with X" cannot be logically criticized. It is the first and last word, its truth apparently established by its being said. Some educationists even define incivility as "nonacceptance of others as they are" and as inconsiderateness toward the feelings of others—so that offering the suggestion that someone ought not to be made uncomfortable by X is itself uncivil. This exclusion of reason from discourse, this equating of civility with acceptance of others as they are, this elevation of autobiographical revelation of feeling to the apex of civilized discourse (with the presumption that the revelation is always truthful), make learning

what is objectively true about anything unnecessary; make considering what ought to be the case both presumptuous and extraneous; and
make systematic study of either fact or logic pointless at best and dangerous at worst.

In education so conceived, civility serves as the instrument of
our being "comfortable" and consists as much in sensitivity to our
own comfort as to the comfort of others. Now, we even witness, in
schools and elsewhere, rhetorical support of the content of speech, in
the forms, "I want to share with you" and "I want you to be comfortable with what I am saying." "Share" is a euphemism for "tell"—meant
to sound benign, generous, not intrusive or judgmental—but the euphemism merely impoverishes the meaning of "sharing." Genuine
sharing normally involves some sacrifice, as children need to learn, but
the euphemism blurs that fact. In this view of our lives together, to
appeal to an old meaning of civility as "seemliness," it is unseemly to
make anyone uncomfortable, even by acknowledging that we are
telling rather than "sharing."

This pathetic diminution of what we can civilly be and do with
and for one another is not confined to education, of course. Witness
the recent castigation of David Howard, the District of Columbia's
public advocate, for saying that he would have to be niggardly in the
distribution to his staff of scarce available funds. Maligned by colleagues for committing a racial slur—either because they mistakenly
believed that "niggardly" is a racial epithet rather than a completely
different word of Scandinavian origin meaning stingy or miserly, or
because they had it in for Howard on other grounds— Howard apolo-
getically resigned. Instead of defending himself against a false accusation, or trying to teach anyone anything about language and vocabulary, Howard—since rehired in another position by Mayor Anthony
Williams—spoke of the valuable learning experience and elevated
sensitivity toward others the events inspired in him.

Reluctance—no, unwillingness—to tell even a simple truth
about the meaning of a word seems to me to exhibit a stunningly low
estimate of what we can reasonably expect and hope of ourselves and
one another. When civility becomes a sensitivity that, like indiscriminate tolerance, casts aside regard for the truth, it bears little resemblance to civility understood as liberal learning, manners and morals,
behavior appropriate to the discourse of civilized people, or even plain
courtesy. Indeed, where the idea of civility is equated or conjoined

with the idea of sensitively coddling sensitivities that make us too frail to bear the truth, civility cannot any further be associated with our having any sort of genuine and decent respect for one another. It is, after all, an expression of pity, not of respect, to say of persons that they are too sensitive, too fragile, ever to bear learning that they have made, or are making, a mistake.

I have witnessed episodes in school classrooms that resemble the events involving David Howard and his staff in the District of Columbia. I have seen teachers turn such confusion, error, and resentment or indignation into opportunities to study and expand vocabulary, to root out error, and to enable students to discover the inappropriateness of their resentment. I have likewise seen teachers who never bothered to find out or teach what the words in question meant, and who instead exhorted students to be sensitive and mutually tolerant, as if some act of genuinely wrongful insensitivity had been committed at the outset.

I once sat in a classroom where one student criticized another for being "neutral" on a current events controversy the students had been asked to decide. The second student took umbrage, believing, or pretending to believe, he had been called sexless and cowardly—neuter or neutered. The teacher treated this as a "teaching moment"—a chance to promote sensitivity to the sexual identity and feelings of others. A few students tried to set the matter straight, and I sensed that some of them thought the teacher had been hoodwinked, but by then both the original topic and the attention of the class had been lost.

Associating civility with inordinate sensitivity and ubiquitous tolerance tends to turn civility, if not into sycophancy, at least into either naive or disingenuous flattery. Few prospective or practicing teachers and administrators of my experience have ever studied or reflected upon the school exercises that George Washington compiled at Ferry Farm in 1744 at the age of twelve under the heading, "Rules of Civility and Decent Behavior In Company and Conversation." I think some educators would be given at least brief pause by several of the 110 rules in Washington's boyhood list:

Be no Flatterer (17th); Superfluous Complements and all Affectations of Ceremonie are to be avoided, yet where due they are not to be neglected (25th); [I]n all Causes of Passion admit

Reason to Govern (58th); In visiting the sick, do not Presently play the Physicion if you be not knowing therein (38th).

I think, though, that many curriculum specialists and others would emphasize Washington's 65th rule of civility, perhaps to the exclusion of the others: "Speak not injurious Words neither in Jest nor Earnest. Scoff at none although they give Occasion." Some school personnel, I think, believe that the rule for playing the physician applies to all professional life—including teaching; but fewer see its full implications for the obligations of teachers and administrators to acquire advanced knowledge of subject matter. Legislators are often even more in the dark. One current Massachusetts legislative proposal requires administrators to study the teacher evaluation "process"—but not the academic subjects or what is known about the best practices in teaching and learning, without which no administrator can competently evaluate a teacher's work.

Well, Washington was only twelve. But the rules he had learned, in abjuring both flattery and scoffing, did not imply the unseemliness of courteously telling the truth. Neither did they proscribe designing curriculum and instruction to bring students into the systematic pursuit, understanding, and competent oral and written expression of the truth or the best reachable approximation of it.

But where facts are thought dead, memorization stultifying, values arbitrary, and reason either impotent or tyrannical, education guided by concern for the true, the appropriately precise, the eloquent and elegant, the overcoming of ignorance and the exposure of error, cannot flourish. Instead, the terrain of the classroom and the school can be, and sometimes is, clouded by a servile sensitivity, a flattering tolerance that is often sincere but unjustifiable, and a sense of civility that insults human virtue, intelligence, potential, and both human strength and resiliency—even as they are to be found in the young.

Such schools and classrooms—their climate profoundly affected by the agendas of special interest and advocacy factions, themselves given muscle by pandering legislators and educationist bureaucrats— are not fit places for habitation by the young. Not if education is supposed to cultivate intellectual powers and moral sensibilities, including, over time, intellectual honesty and discriminating tolerance, along with the clear awareness that the well-mannered exposure of error is neither uncivil nor intolerant.

In my view, the condition of schooling has not befallen us as a people. We have brought it on ourselves, in part by diminishing the definition of education. No reforms can rescue the education of the public without including dramatic transformation of teacher education and of current laws that gut the authority of school officials to terminate the contracts of incompetent teachers and to prevent egregious student disruption of schooling. All school reforms will fall short, if parents do not widely accept responsibility as their children's first teachers. Finally, for as long as a sentimental relativism pervades our institutions, we must expect cynicism within them, and opposition to intellectual and moral seriousness, self-knowledge, and wisdom.

NOTES

1. Michael Downing, *Perfect Agreement* (New York: Berkeley Books, 1997), pp. 71–72.
2. Charles Murray, "And Now for the Bad News," *Wall Street Journal*, 2 February 1999.

Civility in the Family

CARRIE DOEHRING

WHEN PEOPLE LIVE TOGETHER as partners and families, the combination of intimacy, privacy, and stress inevitably pulls family members into moments of intense conflict. This conflict is influenced in various ways by their gender, race, and social class from one moment to the next. Family members may use civility to cope with conflict. *Civility* is commonly understood to refer to an act or expression of politeness, as opposed to acts of rudeness and disrespect. In this essay, I will distinguish politeness based upon respect from "cold" politeness based on disrespect. Civility that fosters respect and courtesy can increase empathy in families and justice in families and society. Civility that comes out as cold politeness and underlying disrespect can increase emotional disengagement within families and oppression within families and society.

DESCRIBING
SOCIAL IDENTITY

In order to describe how civility is linked to justice and oppression in family conflict, a full description of social identity is needed. Social identity is formed from one moment to the next as family members experience more or less privilege because they are a man or woman, white or nonwhite, straight or gay, and so on. Many cultures use binary categories to describe people in biased ways. Here are examples of binary social categories used in many Western societies:

168

Binary opposites describing aspects of social identity		More privilege or disadvantage in a particular experience
Male	Female	+ 3 +2 +1 0 –1 –2 –3
White	Non-white	+ 3 +2 +1 0 –1 –2 –3
Young	Old	+ 3 +2 +1 0 –1 –2 –3
Straight	Gay	+ 3 +2 +1 0 –1 –2 –3
Christian	Non-Christian	+ 3 +2 +1 0 –1 –2 –3
Professional Status	Lack of professional status	+ 3 +2 +1 0 –1 –2 –3
Financially Secure	Financially Insecure	+ 3 +2 +1 0 –1 –2 –3
(many other aspects of social identity could be described)		

There is considerable argument in sociological, feminist, and cultural studies about how much society defines what it means, for example, to be a man or a woman. The "social constructivist" point of view represented here argues that communities, families, and individuals also shape aspects of identity. Initially these identities may be more based upon rebellion against the dominant culture. Over time, these identities can become more authentic and integral to communities, families, or individuals in their own right (that is, differentiated, not simply different from the dominant culture).

In saying that social identities are constructed *from one moment to the next* by individual, family, community, and cultural systems of meaning, many social constructivists take a poststructural or non-essentialist position. Poststructural, or nonessentialist, or nonfoundational, positions emphasize context. Meanings become provisional when they are based upon context and not essential or core qualities. Some argue that such relative meanings cannot become the basis for values or ethical imperatives. Elaine Graham, a poststructuralist practical theologian, argues that:

Principles of truth and value are not to be conceived as transcendent eternal realities, but as provisional—yet binding—strategies of normative action and community within which shared commitments might be negotiated and put to work.[1]

Within this social constructivist ethical perspective, all meaning is constructed within particular contexts, for the purpose of truthful and value-laden practices. In an ideal situation, these practices are assessed by faith communities. This assessment ought to be ongoing, critical, comparative, and available in some way to the public, so that meanings are not secret or parochial.

From a social constructivist position, essentialist categories of gender, race, and age are based upon biological indicators. For example, many cultures assign meanings to biological differences between men and women (penis = male, vagina = female) that create two categories for gender. Many societies do not have a third category for transgendered persons. They must be either male or female. Infants born with a penis and a vagina, for example, are usually surgically and biochemically altered so that their biology conforms to how society identifies men and women. There are some cultures that have a gender category for people born with both a penis and a vagina. Often this gender category carries multiple meanings, for example, being set apart for some special purpose such as a religious role in the community.

Similarly, ethnic and age identities use biological indicators in more nebulous ways to assign people to categories. In the United States the most basic historical categories for race are white and nonwhite. Biological indicators like skin tone and facial features are used to decide at a glance who is culturally defined as "white" and "of color." Just as penises and vaginas are biological indicators for the categories male and female, so, too, are "big" lips, "fuzzy" hair, and "dark" skin biological indicators of African descent.

Biological indicators for age identity are even more malleable than gender and race, and easily reconstructed in many Euro-American cultures. New categories for describing people as "old" have been created recently. The category "young old" is defined in terms of chronological age (sixty to seventy-five years old), graying/balding hair, and "high" levels of physical activities. The category "frail elderly" is defined in terms of age (often eighty-five years and older), excessive skin wrinkling, bone deterioration, and limited physical activities. Some literature on aging uses the category of "young old" to dismantle negative stereotypes about aging, while unwittingly supporting media images of the young old that are classist, objectify the young old, and foster negative biases against the frail elderly.[2]

The other categories of social identity in the chart are not linked to biological indicators, and hence may be less readily discerned and more changeable. For example, a gay person can easily "pass" for a straight person by his or her appearance (at great cost, though, to their personal health, and the health of their familial and communal systems). The way one dresses often is an indicator of financial and professional status. Someone who is financially stressed and does not have professional status can easily pass for the opposite by dressing and acting in ways associated with well-off professionals.

The experience of being "mistaken" for someone of a different sexual orientation or social status can reveal the full effects of positive and negative biases. For example, persons of African descent dressing in worn-out casual clothes instead of professional clothes are treated with suspicion in predominantly white, middle-class suburbs and stores. Such persons are seen as dangerous or untrustworthy because of the interaction of racial and social class identities. Those who dress and speak in ways that conform to their dominant culture's definitions of attractive, upper-class men and women usually have an advantage in social settings. If they were to change their appearance by wearing punk clothes, dying their hair bright pink, and having numerous visible body piercings and tattoos, they would be disadvantaged in many social settings. The experience of being between social categories used in the dominant culture can also reveal and even provoke negative attention, for example, the negative attention received by those who dress in gender-ambiguous ways. Being engaged or being pregnant can, at moments, evoke positive or negative attention that makes the pregnant or engaged person acutely aware of stereotypes associated with parenthood and marriage. Margaret Atwood, in her novel *The Edible Woman*, uses black humor to describe how a young, white, middle-class Canadian woman who becomes engaged begins to feel consumed by her impending role of wifehood. She develops a peculiar eating disorder because she sees food as alive, identifies with it, and then can't eat.[3]

Often people do not become aware of social privilege or disadvantage until they experience its opposite. White and/or Christian people may never realize their racial and religious privilege until they have an experience of being in a racial or religious minority that is devalued. This unawareness of social privilege is exacerbated in cultures where privilege is often described in terms of individual success and

achievement. For example, well-educated, professionally and financially secure white, straight men and women will often assume they
are treated respectfully because of their educational, professional, and
financial achievements. This emphasis on individual success is especially prevalent in capitalist cultures. Some white, straight, "successful" men do not experience negative bias until they are sick, retired, or
frail and elderly. When such bias is given individual and not social
meanings (such as "I am useless because I no longer work as a CEO,
lawyer, or doctor"), then social bias can lead to depression, despair,
and even suicide.

Civility can be examined in terms of its relationship with the
dominant culture, and specifically how the dominant culture defines
civilization and civilized behavior. The *Oxford English Dictionary* lists
three ways that civility is defined in terms of civilization and culture.
Civility is

1. The state of being civilized; freedom from barbarity;
2. Polite or liberal education; training in the "humanities," good
    breeding; culture, refinement;
3. Behavior proper to the intercourse of civilized people; ordinary
    courtesy or politeness, as opposed to rudeness of behavior; de-
    cent respect, consideration.

From a social constructivist position, this definition clarifies the
associations between civility and class. Civility is used to support the
dominant culture in ways that are oppressive. With sensitivity, civility
can also be used to counteract classism, sexism, racism, and hetero-
sexism.

FAMILIES, SOCIAL IDENTITY, AND CIVILITY

Families often cope with conflicts that are shaped by power
struggles occurring not only within the family but also in society. In
the home these power struggles are more intensely experienced, in
part because intimacy and privacy often reveal the "underside" of the
family and its members' public identities. Some family members actually become identified with this underside (such as the rebellious or
dysfunctional family member). For example, so-called preacher's kids

often enact the underside of the preacher and his or her family: those aspects of the preacher and the preacher's family that have to be suppressed or kept out of sight because of social expectations. Families who insist upon maintaining an image of being successful and high functioning may experience a family member's "failure" or nonconformity as threatening the whole family's identity. Some families cope with this threat by rewriting the family narrative so that it is the non-conforming member (not the family) that is sick or dysfunctional. Thus the family can maintain the cheery narratives of success told in their Christmas bulletins about how well human and animal family members are doing.

In the privacy of the home, family members may feel the pull towards deepening of appropriate intimacy and authenticity. Family members may react by becoming more emotionally disengaged or fused, jeopardizing authenticity and intimacy. When combined with power struggles, such relational dynamics can make family members cope with conflict in abusive or neglectful ways.

Some of these family conflicts are fueled by stress experienced elsewhere, for example, in work outside the home. This stress, in turn, often arises because of positive and negative biases. For example, in some social classes within the United States (particularly in the northern states) parents who do not work outside of the home are socially devalued. Such devaluation may influence conflicts with children, partners, and the extended family. For example, the parent may experience her or his authority being undermined by children, partner, family, and dominant culture. However, in some other social classes a stay-at-home parent is highly valued and given more authority in family conflicts.

Families can use civility to cope with conflicts. Civility that promotes respect and courtesy can help family members experience empathy and, with it, a deepening of appropriate intimacy and authenticity. Empathy is the capacity to step into the shoes of other family members and see the intense power struggles from their perspective, while not losing sight of one's own perspective. Such empathy counteracts the tendency to dehumanize and objectify partners and family members when conflict intensifies and an explosive interaction is triggered. As well, empathy helps family members not dehumanize each other by acting upon negative stereotypes associated with social identity. Civility can promote moments of empathy, deepening intimacy and authenticity, and, in turn, individual and social justice that subverts oppression.

Conversely, civility can be harmful when it does not promote courtesy and respect. Instead, civility can become a superficial politeness that keeps family members emotionally disengaged or fused in the midst of intense feelings, power struggles, and conflicts. When such civility is used in conjunction with oppressive stereotypes, civility promotes individual and social oppression and subverts justice.

MIKE LEIGH'S FILM *SECRETS AND LIES*

The ways in which civility can be used in family conflict to subvert or maintain social oppression are illustrated by the Purley family, portrayed in Mike Leigh's film *Secrets and Lies*. The film opens at a cemetery in London, England. Hortense is at the funeral of her mother. She is twenty-six years old, and part of a large Caribbean community. At work, she is a competent and gentle optometrist. At home, she lives alone in a peacefully uncluttered middle-class apartment. In work and personal conversations, Hortense uses power in healthy ways. At work, she demonstrates competence and empathy with a ten-year-old client. On her way out the door, she relates as a peer to a staff member. At home, she enjoys having long, relaxed, intimate talks with women friends (also Caribbean). Her authenticity comes through, as we see the continuity between how she is at work and at home, with clients, co-workers, and friends. She does not seem to carry stress home and dump it there.

After her adoptive mother dies (predeceased by Hortense's father), Hortense emotionally connects with her history of being an orphan who was given up for adoption at birth. She goes in search of her birth mother and enters the world of British bureaucracy. She moves briskly through the paperwork, encounters with a social worker, and gathering of birth certificates. She is assertive and expects to be treated with courtesy and respect. For the most part, she maintains a sense of self-possession which doesn't inhibit her from expressing sadness when she reads the name of her birth mother, determination when the social worker tries to stall her, and confusion when she reads that her birth mother is "white."

The opening scenes of the movie portray how Hortense deals with being a woman, black, middle-class, young, single, and orphaned. She copes successfully with most aspects of her social identity that can generate negative bias, particularly in her conversations with the social worker and within the British social bureaucracy. She does not allow these aspects of her social identity to intimidate her. Her Caribbean family and community have raised her in a way that has made her resilient to negative stereotypes. Mike Leigh, the film's creator, comments about how he portrays racial identity in this film:

> When I left [Manchester] in 1960, there was not one black face in school or anywhere. Manchester now has huge black and Asian populations. But that immigration is new. I wanted very much to make a film about this new generation of young black people growing up in Britain who are first generation and who are getting on with it and getting away from ghetto stereotypes. In the film, Hortense, who is a trained optometrist, is not in any way cut off from her mother's friends. She's plugged into the culture she came from.[4]

Leigh is more interested in classism than racism. He has a reputation for depicting the homes and family dynamics of working-class people. Film critic Jay Carr notes: "For twenty years, British director Mike Leigh has been making films that get inside the skin of working-class characters as nobody else's films do."[5]

Hortense's search brings her to the Purley family. Cynthia Purley, her white birth mother, is forty-two years old, lives in public housing, and makes ends meet on the meager income from her assembly-line job where she inserts pieces of cardboard into a hole-punching machine. At the age of ten when her mother died, Cynthia became responsible for looking after her father and six-year-old brother, Maurice. While she seemed to raise Maurice with great kindness and affection, she also emanated a sense of chaos and intense need that made her younger brother feel overly responsible.

Maurice has been able to get established in his own photography business and has married Monica. The business has been successful, probably because of the extraordinary skill and sensitivity Maurice brings to his wedding and family portraits. His sense of being overly responsible shapes his marriage. His denial of his own needs is apparent in the way he has had to cut out his sister (Cynthia) and niece (Roxanne) from his life for the past two years because of the conflict between his sister and his wife. This conflict was seemingly inevitable, given the intense needs of both his sister and his wife; each wanted to keep Maurice to herself.

At sixteen Cynthia became pregnant with Hortense and gave her up for adoption. She did not realize that Hortense was multiracial because she refused to look at her or hold her when she was born (a secret that comes out when Hortense confronts her). At twenty-one she became pregnant with Roxanne, and raised her as a single parent with the same smothering warmth, chaos, and intense needs that shaped her relationship with her brother. Roxanne has a permanent sneer on her face, and reacts intensely to her mother's sentimentality and neediness by yelling and slamming doors. Like her mother, Roxanne has left school and is in a dead-end job, sweeping debris around the council houses. She has a boyfriend who is almost totally silent throughout the film and seems extraordinarily shy. He twitches, involuntarily grimaces, and chokes out his words whenever anyone speaks to him.

The family conversations that go on within the Purley family illustrate how workplace stress gets suppressed and brought home, where it augments stress generated within these personalities and this family. Cynthia and Roxanne have to deal with the stress of demeaning, monotonous jobs where they talk to no one and bottle up feelings. In the privacy of their home, there is no appropriate intimacy between mother and daughter, because work and intrapsychic (within the person) and family stress make for intense anger and intense emotional needs, especially concerning the "leaving home" transition facing Roxanne and Cynthia. Cynthia wants to both hold onto and push away Roxanne. She's not sure whether she wants to be an adult-like mother of an adult-like child (a transition she has still not negotiated with Maurice). She seems to have no support system as she faces this transition. She is still cut off from Maurice, and she only talks to one person: her twenty-year-old daughter. Cynthia blurts out personal details and pries into Roxanne's privacy. She is sentimental, not realistic or honest, about being a single mother. Roxanne tries to make Cynthia ashamed, and the conversation ends in shouting, fleeing (Roxanne), and tears (Cynthia). Neither seems able to empathize. There are no healthy ways of managing the stress that is brought home from work and the social arena. The privacy of the home does not foster authenticity and deepening intimacy; rather it becomes the arena for dumping feelings and needs and furthering social oppression.

Maurice is markedly different from his sister when he has family conversations. In a memorable cinematic depiction of premenstrual syndrome and feelings about infertility, Monica tries to fight PMS physically, channeling all of her anger into frenzied vacuuming. When Maurice comes along, she acts as if he is bossing her around. He doesn't retaliate. Maurice responds with "baffled pain and fathomless dignity."[6] His kindness and affectionate humor seem to help Monica understand her complex feelings associated with PMS. This allows them to enter into an intimate conversation. Maurice does not reveal all of his feelings for Monica, only the affectionate and caring ones. He does not seem aware of the complexity of his own feelings. He just submerges them. As the actor, Timothy Spall, who played Maurice, comments:

> Every emotion was put in the bin and the lid was screwed down, tighter and tighter. . . . It was all about what he didn't say, what he was thinking, what he couldn't express, or wasn't allowed to express. . . . He was carrying with dignity a hell of a lot of discontent and sublimating what he felt for the peace of all.[7]

Perhaps Maurice, unlike Cynthia, has experienced the ways in which civility as refined polite behavior can enhance one's professional identity, and indeed be associated with professional and financial success. Such civility works well when Maurice is dealing with clients or generally, in a social arena. Maurice's strategy is to use this refined politeness at home to maintain order and avoid the chaos that would be generated if all of the secrets and lies of his marriage and family were revealed. When civility is used to keep family secrets, then two-way intimacy is stifled. In the long run, civility used for this end promotes social privilege associated with professional and financial success.

When Hortense encounters Cynthia and eventually the entire Purley family at Roxanne's twenty-first birthday party, her "just" ways of using civility contrast starkly with Cynthia's lack of civility and Maurice's unjust use of civility. In her initial encounters with her birth mother, Hortense has to be gently firm with Cynthia. Cynthia almost hangs up on her, and is intensely fearful that the secret of her first daughter's birth and adoption will come out, and she will be further shamed and judged. Hortense coaxes Cynthia each step of the way. She deals with Cynthia's astonishment that Hortense is black. Hortense wants to hear the story of her birth and understand Cynthia's astonishment and then her anguish when Cynthia realizes who Hortense's biological father must be. Cynthia cowers, whimpers, and begs for mercy. Finally she discloses that when Hortense was born, she could not look at her, much less hold her, so she didn't realize who Hortense's father was and that Hortense was multiracial. Hortense makes Cynthia be authentic, not sentimental. She endures Cynthia's chaotic eruptions of tears, self-pity, and warmth. Cynthia experiences forgiveness and a healing of shame after her confession of how she could not look at or hold her infant because of her overwhelming needs. Hortense is a stern and merciful confessor. She can easily stand in Cynthia's shoes and not be overwhelmed by Cynthia's intense needs or, indeed, the misery of her life. She teaches Cynthia to be authentic and appropriately intimate. They discover each other, as adult mother and daughter. While Hortense initially has to be the mother, Cynthia becomes more and more the adult mother who can let her daughter Roxanne leave home. Cynthia, probably for the first time in her life, becomes a rich, complex, and whole person in her conversations with Hortense. She begins to take care of herself and her appearance and she becomes a delightfully attractive woman. Her warmth and humorous expressions now convey empathy and insight. Says one critic: "[the] film is bracketed by the death of one mother and the hugely moving rebirth of another."[8]

Many viewers immensely enjoy this rebirth of Cynthia, and can probably describe it in terms of psychological transformation. Using a lens of social oppression, viewers can also see the social oppression and injustice that Cynthia experiences. Hortense uses courtesy and respect to dismantle social oppression in her conversations with Cynthia. These conversations "[loose] the bonds of wickedness, [undo] the thongs of the yoke, [let] the oppressed go free and [break] every yoke" (Isa. 48:6) that Cynthia has experienced.

The encounters between Hortense and Cynthia are the first wave of freedom with justice; the second occurs when Maurice finally breaks loose and puts words to his anger and sadness at Roxanne's twenty-first birthday party. Cynthia has, in a sense, smuggled Hortense into the party, under the pretence that she is a friend from work.

The family's racism is evidenced in Monica's immediate response as she opens the door to Hortense. Monica assumes she is selling something and condescendingly tries to send her on her way. Hortense, practiced in the ways of dealing politely with racism, interrupts to introduce herself. The family is curious about Hortense, and struck by the novelty of Cynthia actually having a friend (and a black friend). Hortense temporarily takes a break from this scrutiny to shed a few tears in the bathroom. While she is out of the room, Cynthia breaks the secret of Hortense's identity, unfortunately with wails of self-pity. All hell breaks loose. Roxanne is appalled, flees, is pursued by Maurice and her boyfriend, and coaxed into returning. The long-simmering rivalry between Cynthia and Monica comes out into the open, with nasty words (no civility here) that lead Maurice finally to lose his cool. For the first time, he declares that he can't hold the family together any more; there are too many secrets and lies; and all he wants is for the people he loves the most to love each other. The family is stunned by his words and moved to empathy, for Maurice and each other. Cynthia, Monica, and Roxanne cry about Monica's infertility (a secret that is finally revealed), what a true father and brother Maurice is, what a nice man Roxanne's father was (a secret Cynthia discloses), and the inferred despicability of Hortense's father. Maurice comforts Hortense, one caretaker reaching out to another.

The transformation of this family could be described, using the clinically bland terms of family systems theory, as a dramatic move from a dysfunctional to a functional family system. Using a lens of social oppression, the family's transformation can be described in the poetic imagery of Isaiah as a movement from oppression to freedom with justice: loosing the bonds of wickedness, undoing the thongs of the yoke, letting the oppressed go free, breaking every yoke. In this transformation the Purley family becomes different from the social systems in which they move. In their final conversations at the party they become a family that can use civility in a way that induces empathy, authenticity, and deepening intimacy, all of which subvert social oppression and make the family a place where justice is enacted.

In the closing scene of the movie, Cynthia presides as a delightful and delighted mother over her two daughters, who make plans to surprise Roxanne's friends with the news of the banished daughter, now returned to the fold. Roxanne is proud to introduce Hortense as her sister. The conversations that will ensue from this introduction will no doubt subvert racial stereotypes and challenge others to act with a civility that promotes racial justice. The Purley family is becoming a family of prophets who use civility to induce empathy, authenticity, and, in the end, justice.

CONCLUSION

Several further comments can be made about my argument for using civility in the family as a means of promoting social justice. My first comment is about using an artistic rendering of life experience (the film *Secrets and Lies*) as an engaging way to talk about civility in the family. The major advantage of using a film rather than a clinical case study is that readers have equal access to the whole cinematic portrait of this family, with all of its multiple meanings. In addition, the data that is available in a film is conveyed through an artistic medium that may be more likely to induce moments of empathy and may make hearing about family conflict more bearable.

There is a special advantage to using a Mike Leigh film as a case study. Mike Leigh works without a script. He "builds texts and characters during a long brainstorming period with the actors. They sit and talk, for hours, sometimes days, fleshing out the characters' life stories."[9]

Next, the characters begin to improvise scenes. Sometimes Leigh gives them surprise plot developments to work with. In making *Secrets and Lies* the actors spent five months moving through this process before they started shooting footage.[10] Here is how actor Timothy Spall, who played the photographer Maurice Purley, describes the process:

[Mike Leigh's] got the chemistry set and we're the organisms growing like fungi, and all of a sudden he just whacks it together. We had hours of conversations about Maurice keeping his lid on. Every emotion was put in the bin and the lid was screwed down, tighter and tighter. . . . Having the ability to create with Mike somebody like that [Maurice] was great. And also frightening, because I didn't know whether it would just look like nothing. It was all about what he didn't say, what he was thinking, what he couldn't express, or wasn't allowed to express.[11]

Leigh's portrait of a dysfunctional family is extraordinarily real because every actor has created his or her own character, and together they've created and started living the story of a family. As reviewer Tom Shone writes, "His films offer us the closest thing to real people you are likely to see at the cinema, short of craning your neck and peering at the audience."[12] Leigh and his actors can unabashedly let viewers into this family's dysfunction, because it is not a matter of invading a real family's privacy.

Commenting on this family's dysfunction, film critic Howie Movshovitz notes, "Almost everyone in *Secrets and Lies* has something hidden that has festered over the years. By the time Hortense shows up—her presence shakes the rest of the family to the bones—you can see how everyone has been dragged down by the emotional energy it takes to conceal and pretend."[13]

My second comment concerns literature on civility. When privileged people advocate civility, they may not see the ways in which civility may support social categories that, in their worst moments, are sexist, heterosexist, classist, ageist, racist. Religious traditions can also be used to promote civility that in turn maintains systems of privilege.

This unawareness of social oppression breaks through occasionally in Stephen Carter's book *Civility: Manners, Morals, and the Etiquette of Democracy*, when he speaks about sacrifice: "Civility, I shall argue, is the sum of the many sacrifices we are called to make for the sake of living together."[14] For the most part, Carter presents a complex, nuanced understanding of civility and the role of religion in supporting civility. However, there are moments when he makes bald statements, like "civility is sacrifice." He goes on to describe our society as highly individualistic, with people equating their desires with their rights. He links many aspects of contemporary life, like high divorce rates, with selfishness and an unwillingness to make sacrifices. Carter describes a society full of "takers." He advocates giving. He advocates disciplining our desires for the sake of others.[15]

I argue that giving, such as accommodating the needs of others, has to be balanced with taking and making our own needs plain. Cynthia is an example of a working-class woman who has had to make many sacrifices in her life in order to look after her father, brother, and daughter. It seems as though these sacrifices have not done her any good. In many ways, we might argue that she did not make these sacrifices willingly; hence they are not sacrifices that are freely chosen.

These obligations were forced upon her. Carter doesn't distinguish between chosen sacrifices and sacrifices that are forced upon people. Maurice, as the family peacemaker, has made sacrifices (albeit with unconscious fears about the power of secrets and lies). For years he tried to meet his sister's and his wife's needs. He ends up holding the family secrets, suppressing his own needs, and in the end, suppressing intimacy and authenticity. He sacrifices his own needs and feelings.

Unlike Carter, I argue that civility in the family is not about sacrifice; it is about an appropriate give and take in relationships. Sacrifice, when it is not balanced with experiences of self-seeking, is not civility. In reference to children, it can be problematic for parents to be too self-sacrificial, because they inevitably offer their sacrifices up to their symbol of the ideal child. The symbol of the ideal child is idolatrous, in that it becomes like a god, or a core metaphor upon which the whole family narrative depends.[16] When the symbol is broken by the child being him- or herself (if this is allowed) then the family narrative collapses and ignites parental rage over the "sacrifices" (revealed now as bribes).

Christine Gudorf elaborates "many of the ways in which parenthood gifts us, thus making parenthood an exercise in mutuality, not sacrifice."[17] She makes connections between parental self-sacrifice and patriarchy.

> In the first place, this portrayal of parenthood as sacrificial serves as an ideological support for patriarchy. Sacrificial understandings of parenthood are part of the romanticization of the family in modern Western life. This romanticization of the family serves to disguise the location and use of power in the family by pedestalizing women and children as innocent and good and therefore in need of protection by husbands/fathers. This assumption that parental power is used in the interests of children serves to undermine attacks on parental (specifically paternal) monopolization of power, and disguises the extent to which parental power is used in the interests of parents rather than children.[18]

I suggest a hermeneutic of suspicion regarding how religion can be used to support oppressive social systems of meaning. Carter brings a similar perspective, for the most part, to his study of civility. However, in the discussions about sacrifice, he is uncritical of the implicit patriarchy in many cultural and religious teachings about sacrifice.

A final comment can be made about the family, civility, and religion. As a practical theologian, I also use theological perspectives in understanding civility in the family. Religious sources and norms of authority can be used to promote oppression or justice. When a hermeneutic of suspicion is used as a norm for interpreting religious sources then one is less likely to use religious sources to promote oppression. However, oppression is often promoted unconsciously, particularly by those with social privilege.

In *Secrets and Lies*, a religious tradition is depicted in the opening scene of Hortense's mother's funeral. Religious traditions are also in the background of Maurice's work: his wedding and engagement photographs. Maurice has his own ritualized ways of coaxing smiles out of fiancés, brides, and grooms. He does this in a way that momentarily transfigures many people who seem distracted by a transition like getting married or becoming engaged. In some ways, this picture taking becomes a moment of judgment. There are aspects of religion implicit in what Maurice does, but he seems unaware of this. Maurice's use of civility to care for others but not himself could well be supported by many of the religious traditions enacted at the weddings he attends.

In examining the role of civility in the family, it can be helpful to look for the implicit or explicit role of religion, as Stephen Carter does in a caveat to his argument on the importance of religion for promoting civility. Elaine Graham puts it this way:

> If the "causes" of gender are constituted in, and enacted through, material, embodied and symbolic praxis, then the role of religious practices and ideologies in the creation and maintenance of gendered systems becomes a crucial area of study. How do religious practices, institutions and symbolic practices serve to reflect, reinforce and create particular dynamics of gender identity, gender roles and representations?[19]

One of the tasks of parents is to raise civil children. Many parents use religion to promote civility within their children. It is incumbent upon families and communities of faith to consider carefully what kind of civility is promoted, and how religion is used to support or confront social oppression.

NOTES

1. Elaine Graham, *Transforming Practice: Pastoral Theology in an Age of Uncertainty* (London: Mowbray, 1996), p. 6.

2. See Carrie Doehring, "A Method of Feminist Pastoral Theology," in *Feminist and Womanist Pastoral Theology,* ed. Brita Gill-Austern and Bonnie Miller-McLemore (Nashville: Abingdon, 1999); and Mike Featherstone and Mike Hepworth, "Introduction: Images of Positive Aging: A Case Study of *Retirement Choice* Magazine," in *Images of Aging: Cultural Representations of Later Life,* ed. Mike Featherstone and Andrew Wernick (London: Routledge, 1995) pp. 1–15, 29–47.

3. Margaret Atwood, *The Edible Woman* (Toronto: McClelland and Stewart, 1969).

4. Leigh, quoted by Jay Carr, review of *Secrets and Lies* by Mike Leigh, *Boston Globe,* 13 October 1996.

5. Carr, review of *Secrets and Lies.*

6. Mick Brown, review of *Secrets and Lies* by Mike Leigh, *London Daily Telegraph,* 21 February 1998.

7. Timothy Spall, quoted in Brown, review of *Secrets and Lies.*

8. Janet Maslin, review of *Secrets and Lies* by Mike Leigh, *Denver Post,* 27 September 1996.

9. Rick Lyman, review of *Secrets and Lies* by Mike Leigh, New York Times, 14 December 1997.

10. Mike Leigh, quoted by Howie Movshovitz, review of *Secrets and Lies* by Mike Leigh, *Denver Post,* 3 November 1996.

11. Timothy Spall, quoted in Brown, review of *Secrets and Lies.*

12. Tom Shone, review of *Secrets and Lies* by Mike Leigh, *London Sunday Times,* 26 May 1996.

13. Movshovitz, review of *Secrets and Lies.*

14. Stephen L. Carter, *Civility: Manners, Morals, and the Etiquette of Democracy* (New York: Basic Books, 1998), p. 103.

15. Ibid., p. 164.

16. Peter VanKatwyk, "Parental Loss and Marital Grief: A Pastoral and Narrative Perspective," *Journal of Pastoral Care* 52 (1998): 369–76.

17. Christine E. Gudorf, "Sacrificial and Parental Spiritualities," in *Religion, Feminism and the Family,* ed. Anne Carr and Mary Stewart Van Leeuwen (Louisville, Ky.: Westminster John Knox, 1996), p. 300.

18. Ibid., p. 300.

19. Elaine Graham, *Making the Difference: Gender, Personhood and Theology* (Minneapolis: Fortress, 1996), p. 227.

PART III

Civility in Various Cultures

On Confucian Civility[1]

HENRY ROSEMONT, JR.

THERE IS GENERAL AGREEMENT among Western political theorists today that civil society is an important component of a democratic state. But agreement does not extend much beyond this bare generalization, with liberals, libertarians, conservatives, and communitarians all having different notions of what civil society is, and what it ought to be.[2]

As I will use the term, *civil society* refers to a set of organizations in a society intermediary between the family and the state. The family encompasses the "private sphere" of life, and the state, the "public sphere." Some organizations will be nearer the former (such as a stamp collectors' club) and others much closer to the latter, such as the League of Women Voters. No hard and fast lines can be drawn between them, however—at least in practice—because the great majority of organizations have both a private and a public interest dimension to them: the American Medical Association, the National Organization for Women, the National Rifle Association, Greenpeace, and the Veterans of Foreign Wars are all examples of organizations that exist both to further the private interests and goals of their members and to attempt to influence legislation, court decisions, and elections, ostensibly in the public interest, as well.

Clearly such organizations are essential in a representative democratic state, because it is a defining characteristic of such states that its members do not share a substantive conception of the good life for human beings, or how such lives should be led. Hence like-minded individuals must have opportunities to band together to advance the concept of the good they share, be it the value of stamp collecting, sexual equality, or wildlife preservation.

Because differing substantive conceptions of the good are often in conflict—increasing production for consumption in order to maximize employment vs. protecting the natural environment, for example—the good in a representative democracy must be formal and procedural. Individuals and organizations are free to pursue their own substantive conceptions of the good so long as they do not interfere with anyone else's pursuit of a different good, and when conflicts arise they are to be resolved by democratic mechanisms such as legislation or litigation. In some form or another, then, civil society is essential for a representative democracy. (A defining characteristic of Stalinist and fascist forms of government is that they do not allow any organizations to exist independently of Party authority and jurisdiction.)

In this all-too-hurried sketch of the nature and functions of civil society, the ideal society of classical Confucianism has no place, and consequently, if civility is defined as pertaining to civil society, Confucians have nothing to say about it.

But there is another sense of *civility*, one that approximates "polite," "mannerly," "courteous," in meaning. The imperative to "be civil" is not equivalent to "join an organization" but rather to "be respectful of the other's humanity." Most contemporary Western political theorists, excepting a few feminists, tend to either gloss over this sense of civility, or dismiss it altogether.[3] For classical Confucians, on the other hand, formal politeness was central to their vision of the ideal society and the good life for human beings, and by describing how and why this is so, I hope to simultaneously show how all Western moral and political theories which neglect civility in this latter sense are impoverished thereby.

The doctrines gathered under the heading of "classical Confucianism" were set down in four texts written and edited roughly between 450 and 150 BCE: *The Analects of Confucius*, the *Mencius*, the *Xun Zi*, and the *Records of Ritual*. These works are by no means in full agreement on all points, and there are several tensions within each work itself; nevertheless, in conjunction with a few other texts that came to be classics—the Books of *Changes*, *Poetry*, and *History*— these texts do present an overall coherent view of the good life for human beings. This good life is an altogether social one, and central to understanding it is to see that Confucian sociality has aesthetic, moral, and spiritual no less than political and economic dimensions, and politeness is the way sociality is effected in all these areas, and is the means of their integration.

None of the early texts addresses the question of the meaning of life, but they do put forward a vision and a discipline in which everyone can find a meaning *in* life. This meaning will become increasingly apparent to us as we pursue the ultimate goal of being human; namely, developing ourselves most fully as human beings to become *jun zi,* an "exemplary person," or, at the pinnacle of development, a *sheng,* or sage. And for Confucians we can only do this through our interactions with other human beings. Treading this human path (*ren dao*) must be ultimately understood basically as a religious quest, even though the canon speaks not of God, nor of creation, salvation, an immortal soul, or a transcendental realm of being; and no prophecies will be found in its pages either. It is nevertheless a truly religious path; Confucius definitely does not instruct us about the Way (*dao*) strictly for the pragmatic political consequences of following his guidance.

For Confucius we are irreducibly social, as he makes clear in the *Analects*:[4]

> I cannot run with the birds and beasts.
> Am I not one among the people of this world?
> If not them, with whom should I associate? (18:6)

Thus the Confucian self is not a free, autonomous individual, but is to be seen relationally: I am a son, husband, father, teacher, student, friend, colleague, neighbor, and more. I *live*, rather than "play" these roles, and when all of them have been specified, and their interrelationships made manifest, then I have been fairly thoroughly individuated, but with very little left over with which to piece together a free, autonomous individual.

While this view may seem initially strange, it is actually straightforward. In order to *be* a friend, neighbor, or lover, for example, I must *have* a friend, neighbor, or lover. Other persons are not merely accidental or incidental to my goal of fully developing as a human being; they are essential to it. Indeed, they confer unique personhood on me, for to the extent that I define myself as a teacher, students are necessary to my life, not incidental to it. Note in this regard also that while Confucianism should be seen as fundamentally religious, there are no solitary monks, nuns, anchorites, or hermits to be found in the tradition.

Our first and most basic role, one that significantly defines us in part throughout our lives, is as children. Filial piety is one of the highest excellences in Confucianism. We owe unswerving loyalty to our parents, and our obligations to them do not cease at their death. On unswerving loyalty:

The Governor of She in conversation with Confucius said, "In our village there is someone called 'True Person.' When his father took a sheep on the sly, he reported him to the authorities."

Confucius replied, "Those who are true in my village conduct themselves differently. A father covers for his son, and a son covers for his father. And being true lies in this." (13:18)

On constancy:

The Master said: "A person who for three years refrains from reforming the ways of his late father can be called a filial son." (4:20)

And the demands of filial piety are lifelong:

While [the parents] are alive, serve them according to the observances of ritual propriety; when they are dead, bury them and sacrifice to them according to the observances of ritual propriety. (2.5)

From our beginning roles as children—and as siblings, playmates, and pupils—we mature to become parents ourselves, and become as well spouses or lovers, neighbors, subjects, colleagues, friends, and more. All of these are reciprocal relationships, best generalized as holding between benefactors and beneficiaries. The roles are thus clearly hierarchical, but each of us moves regularly from benefactor to beneficiary and back again, depending on the other(s) with whom we are interacting, when, and under what conditions. When young, I am largely beneficiary of my parents; when they are aged and infirm, I become their benefactor, and the converse holds for my children. I am benefactor to my friend when she needs my help, beneficiary when I need hers. I am a student of my teachers, teacher of my students. Taken together, the manifold roles we live define us as persons. And the ways in which we live these relational roles are the means whereby we achieve dignity, satisfaction, and meaning in life.

The difference between Western autonomous individuals and Confucian relational persons must be emphasized if we are to appreciate the different ways we may be said to live civilly. In the first place, while individuals have general moral obligations which they must meet in accordance with some set of universal principles, they have no *specific* moral obligations save those they have freely chosen to accept toward spouses or lovers, their children, friends. But we have not chosen our parents, nor our siblings and other relatives, yet Confucius insists that we have many and deep obligations to them, and they to us. That is to say, unlike individual selves, relational selves must accept responsibilities and ends they have not freely chosen. There is a good for human beings independent of individual conceptions of it.

From this emphasis on filial piety it should be clear that at the heart of Confucian society is the family, the locus of where, how, and why we develop into full human beings. A central government is also essential to the good society, because there are necessary ingredients of human flourishing—especially economic—which the family and local community cannot secure on their own: repairing dikes, ditches, and roads, distributing grain from bumper harvest to famine areas, establishing academies, etc. The early Confucians thus saw the state not as in any way in opposition to the family, but rather saw both as complementary. Indeed, families collectively, together with the state, were usually portrayed as a family writ large, with titles for the emperors ranging from "Heaven's Son" to "Father and Mother of the People."

As an aside, we may note that if the goal of human life is to develop one's humanity to the utmost, then we have a clear criterion for measuring the worth and quality of our interactions with others in the groups (family, clan, village, school, state) to which each of us belongs; we are not merely to accept them as unalterable givens. Rather must we consistently ask, to what extent do these groups, and interactions, conduce to everyone's efforts to realize their potential? That is to say, while deference—a key component of civility—had to be learned and practiced, remonstrance was obligatory when things were not going well.[5] As the Master said, "To see what it is appropriate to do, and not do it, is cowardice" (2:24).

As a second aside, we may also note that if it is free autonomous individuals with differing conceptions of the good life who came together in voluntary civic associations—thus collectively forming civil society—it follows that there would be no need for such associations in the Confucian vision of the good society; which is why, if civility is defined only in terms of civil society, Confucians have nothing to contribute to the concept.

The ideal Confucian society is civil in the other sense, however, with custom, tradition, and ritual serving as the binding force of and between our many relationships. The rituals described in the early

classics and basic Confucian texts were largely based on archaic super-
natural beliefs which were being questioned during the rationalist
period in which Confucius lived, and a part of the genius of the Master and his followers lies in their giving those ritual practices an aesthetic, moral, political, and spiritual foundation which was independent of their original inspiration. To understand this point, we must
construe the term *li*, translated as "ritual propriety," not simply as
referring to weddings, bar and bat mitzvahs, funerals, and so on, but
equally as referring to the simple customs and courtesies given and received in greetings, sharing food, leave-takings, and much more. To be
fully civil, then, a Confucian must at all times be polite and mannerly,
following closely the customs and rituals governing these and numerous other interpersonal activities. To do so was to follow the "human
way" (*ren dao*).

The authors and editors of the canonical texts all lived over two
millennia ago, and were thus monocultural in their outlook. Consequently, they were regularly highly specific about the ways in which
we should be civil—polite, mannerly, decent, courteous—to others,
but we may nevertheless interpret them more generally, and come
to appreciate what was foundational to them: interacting with others
as benefactors and beneficiaries in an intergenerational context. Confucius himself was absolutely clear on this point, for when a disciple
asked him what he would most like to do, he said:

> I would like to bring peace and contentment to the aged, to
> share relationships of trust and confidence with friends, and to
> love and protect the young. (5:26)

Both within the family, and in the larger society beyond it, custom,
tradition, manners, and rituals—civility in the highest sense—are the
glue of our intergenerational, interpersonal relationships. Even civility
at a low level—performed perfunctorily, "going through the motions"—
is obligatory and politically essential to resolving conflict by nonviolent
means: two parties to a dispute who thoroughly dislike each other can
be brought together at a negotiating table only if each is assured that
the other will treat them civilly. Politeness matters.

But for the early Confucians, rituals, customs, and traditions
served other political functions as well. They did not believe laws or
regulations were the proper way to govern society.

The Master said: "Lead the people with administrative injunctions and keep them orderly with penal law, and they will avoid punishments but will be without a sense of shame. Lead them with excellence and keep them orderly through observing ritual propriety and they will develop a sense of shame, and moreover, will order themselves." (2:3)

Even more strongly put:

The Master said: "If rulers are able to effect order in the state through the combination of observing ritual propriety and deferring to others, what more is needed? But if they are unable to accomplish this, what have they to do with ritual propriety?" (4:73)

Thus the Confucians did not believe that society should be governed by monarchical fiat; the good ruler was to reign:

The Master said: "Governing with excellence can be compared to being the North Star: The North Star dwells in its place, and the multitude of stars pay it tribute." (2:1)

If customs and traditions—"ritual propriety"—can perform the same function in the political realm as laws and regulations, they can also serve in place of universal principles in the moral sphere. Confucian morality is particularistic, in that it insists that at all times we do what is appropriate, depending on whom we are interacting with, and when. This particularism is normally seen in Western moral philosophy as decidedly inferior to universalism (Kant thought Confucius knew nothing of morality).[6] But we may nevertheless make generalizations from the canon that are no less important today than two thousand years ago: when interacting with the elderly, be reverent, caring, obedient; when dealing with peers, treat them as you would be treated; with the young, be nurturing, selfless, loving, exemplary.

Of course we do not learn these generalizations as moral principles when we are young. But it is on the basis of many and varied loving interactions with my grandmother that I learned to interact appropriately with other grandmothers. Now compared to most issues in contemporary Western moral philosophy—abortion, suicide, genetic engineering, and so forth—the importance of making birthday cards for our grandmother seems incredibly trivial, not even deserving, probably, of consideration as a moral issue, (and classical Chinese has no close semantic correlate for the English *moral*).

But as the early Confucian canon reveals with surety, these homely little activities are the basic "stuff" of our human interactions, and Confucius is telling us that if we learn to get the little things right on a day-in and day-out basis, the "big" things will take care of themselves. And in addition to grandmothers and other elders, the "little things" involve our deep interactions with peers, and those younger than ourselves, and in this way begin to bring home to each of us our common humanity. Hence early Confucianism is not liable to the accusation of, say, countenancing racism even if it has been customary in one's family to do so. Such upbringing does not conduce to our fullest development as human beings, and hence must be condemned. I can only fully realize my potential when I have learned from my interactions with my own grandmother that grandmothers share qualities, live roles, and interact with others such that, in one sense, when you've seen one grandmother, you've learned to see them all, despite differences in skin color, ethnicity, or other characteristics.

Put another way, if our task is to meet our obligations to elders, peers, and the young in ways that are both efficacious and satisfying, then the specific customs, manners, and rituals we employ in our interactions must contribute to these ends; if not, they must be changed:

> The Master said: "the use of a hemp cap is prescribed in the observance of ritual propriety. Nowadays, that a silk cap is used instead is a matter of frugality. I would follow the newer accepted practice in this." (9:3)

This argument will undoubtedly still seem forced to those who would be justifiably skeptical that learning to be polite (civil) when young—absorbing customs and traditions, participating in rituals—could overcome racism, sexism, or any other form of oppressive behavior that has been all too customary and traditional in far too many families and communities. It is for this reason that I have insisted that the efficacy of ritual propriety for the early Confucians is not simply to be seen for its social, political, or moral effects, but rather must be understood spiritually. The rituals, even if only followed formally, are essential for social harmony, as noted earlier. But unless they are made one's own and have become productive and satisfying, we can never realize our potential to be fully human.

Consider another statement on filial piety:

As for the young contributing their energies when there is work to be done, and deferring to their elders when there is wine and food to be had—how can merely doing this be considered being filial? (2:8)

And relatedly, on rituals:

The Master said: "In referring time and again to following ritual propriety, how could I just be talking about gifts of jade and silk?" (17:11)

As we mature, then, we cannot simply "go through the motions" of following custom, tradition, and ritual, nor should we fulfill our obligations civilly mainly because we have been made to feel obliged to fulfill them, else we cannot continue to develop our humanity. Rather must we make them our own, and modify them as needed. Remember that for Confucius, many of our obligations are not, cannot be, freely chosen. But he would insist, I believe, that we can only become truly "free"[7] when we *want* to fulfill our obligations, when we want to help others (be benefactors), and enjoy being helped by others (as beneficiaries).

We must also remember, again, that we are first and foremost social beings, relational selves, not autonomous individuals. Being thus altogether bound to and with others, it must follow that the more I contribute to their flourishing, the more I, too, flourish. Conversely, the more my behaviors diminish others—by being racist, sexist, homophobic, and so on—the more I am diminished thereby. In saying this, I must insist that I am *not* proffering here the Confucian view of selfless or altruistic behavior, for this would imply that I have a (free, autonomous, individual) self to surrender. But this of course would beg the question against the Confucians, whose views clearly show the supposed dichotomy between selfishness and altruism as a Western conceit, as well as the equally Manichaean split on which it is based: the individual vs. the collective. Overcoming these deeply rooted dichotomies in Western thought is not at all easy, but when it can be done, very different possibilities for envisioning the human condition present themselves.

In summary, civility is essential to leading a meaningful Confucian life. By constantly being civil, we can come to see ourselves as

essentially, not accidentally, intergenerationally bound to our ancestors, contemporaries, and descendants. All of our interactive relations,
with the dead as well as the living, are to be mediated by the customs,
traditions, and rituals we all come to share as our inextricably linked
personal histories unfold, and by fulfilling the obligations defined by
these relationships we are following the Confucian Way.

Civility thus becomes personal, and not merely social, and by following custom, tradition, and ritual we mature psychologically and
religiously.[8] This is what the Master meant when he said:

> What could I see in a person who in holding a position of in-
> fluence is not tolerant, who in observing ritual propriety is not
> respectful, and who in overseeing the mourning rites does not
> grieve? (3:26)

Some, perhaps, will not grieve at funerals. Going through the
rituals merely to "keep up appearances" is socially superior to flaunt-
ing them, but such persons are lacking some essential human quality.
Confucius believed such people were few in number, however:

> Master Zeng said: "I have heard the Master say 'Even those who
> have yet to give of themselves utterly are sure to do so in the
> mourning of their parents.'" (19:17)

Confucian civility must thus be seen as comprehensive. In addition to the aesthetic, social, moral, and political features attendant on
following this Way—meeting our obligations to our elders and ancestors on the one hand, and to our fellows and succeeding generations
on the other—the Confucian vision displays an uncommon yet religiously authentic sense of transcendence, a human capacity to rise
above the concrete conditions of our existence, enabling us to form
a union with all those who have gone before, and all those who will
come after.

This sense of feeling a oneness with all of humanity is not guar-
anteed to us if we follow the Confucian path. It is a gift of the spirit,
which is why sages are relatively rare. But we can get a little clearer
about what this feeling might be like if we adopt Wittgenstein's summary account of *Das Mystiche:* the sense that we are completely safe.[9]

If the Confucian vision still seems blurred, perhaps it is due
to the Western lenses through which we attempt to see it, as free autonomous individuals, individuals who are strongly inclined to agree
with Aldous Huxley that

we live together, we act on, and react to, one another; but always and in all circumstances we are by ourselves. The martyrs go hand in hand into the arena; they are crucified alone.[10]

Everyone with eyes to see is aware of the manifold problems attendant on an altogether individualistic conception of the self, but we do not yet take those problems as seriously as we should, evidenced clearly by the fact that barren notions of freedom and autonomy remain foundational for virtually all contemporary, social, moral, and political theorizing.[11] Ever since the Enlightenment at least, individualism has been deeply rooted in Western culture and philosophy, especially in the United States, and in my opinion is significantly responsible for much of the malaise increasingly infecting it.

But there are other conceptions of human beings, and the human condition; it is not of our essence to live "lives of quiet desperation." The early Confucians offer one such alternative conception, and consequently, though they were neither citizens, civilians, nor "civic-minded," they were always civil, and consequently may have much to teach us about civility.

NOTES

1. I am grateful to the Editor of this volume, Leroy Rouner, for inviting me to contribute to it and for his great patience when I missed three deadlines for submitting the contribution. With very good reason, he was less generous with length allowances, and as a consequence a number of controversial claims made in these pages are accompanied by only minimal evidence and argumentation. It is for this reason that I have had to make an embarrassing number of references to other of my own writings in the notes below, writings which take up in greater detail what is discussed only briefly herein. For once again helping me to turn a scrawled handwritten paper into a manuscript presentable for publication I am deeply grateful to Ms. Mary Bloomer of St. Mary's College of Maryland.

2. To affix names to these labels, I take John Rawls as paradigmatic of the liberal position, in works ranging from *A Theory of Justice* (Cambridge, Mass., 1971) to *Political Liberalism* (New York, 1993). His Harvard colleague Michael Sandel well represents the modern communitarian position, especially in his recent *Democracy's Discontent: America in Search of a Public Philosophy* (Cambridge, Mass., 1996). A recent libertarian work is *A Life of One's Own* by David Kelley (Washington, D.C., 1998). My favorite conservative

remains Michael Oakeshott, whose writings include the most incisive arguments of which I am aware for positions I cannot endorse.

3. In a recent paper on civility, for example, Will Kymlicka displays an
altogether wooden—and highly misleading—understanding of what it is to
be polite. He says:

> For a disadvantaged group 'to make a scene' is often seen as in bad
> taste. This sort of exaggerated emphasis on good manners can be used
> to promote servility. True civility does not mean smiling at others no
> matter how badly they treat you, as if oppressed groups should be nice
> to their oppressors. Rather it means treating others as equals on the
> condition that they extend the same recognition to you. While there is
> some overlap between civility and a more general politeness, they are
> nonetheless distinct. . . .

"Civil Society and Government: A Liberal Egalitarian perspective," unpub-
lished paper presented to the Ethikon Conference on Civil Society, Santa
Fe, N.M., January, 1999, p. 8. The feminist thinkers who attend more carefully to politeness—courtesy, decency, civility—than Kymlicka does include
Carol Gilligan, Nancy Chodorow, Nel Noddings, Margaret Walker, and others. For fuller discussion, and references, see my "Classical Confucianism
and Contemporary Feminist Perspectives on the Self: Some Parallels, and
their Implications," in *Culture and Self*, ed. Douglas Allen (Boulder, Colo.,
1997).

4. Here and hereafter the *Analects* will be referred to by book and
chapter number only, with all translations taken from *The Analects of Confucius: A Philosophical Translation*, trans. Roger T. Ames and Henry Rosemont, Jr. (New York, 1998).

5. Thus a Confucian would be able to criticize the present Chinese
government for its harassment and incarceration of dissidents, without ever
using the language of (first-generation) human rights based on the concept
of human beings as free, autonomous individuals. See my "Human Rights: A
Bill of Worries" in *Confucianism and Human Rights*, ed. W. T. de Bary and
Tu Wei-ming (New York, 1998).

6. For discussion and citations see Julia Ching, "Chinese Ethics and
Kant," *Philosophy East and West* 28, no. 2 (April 1978).

7. To appreciate what *freedom* might mean in a Confucian context—
it has no ancient lexical equivalent in Chinese—we can follow the incisive work of Eliot Deutsch, who sees *freedom* as an achievement term. For
discussion and references, see my contribution to the *Festschrift* honoring
Deutsch, *The Aesthetic Turn*, ed. Roger T. Ames (Chicago and LaSalle, Ill.,
1999).

8. A striking example of this was reported by Beverly Gologorsky in
her review of Alix Kates Shulman's new book, *A Good Enough Daughter*, in

The Nation, 9–16 August 1999, p. 42. Speaking of Shulman, Gologorsky says: "In fact, she relished being needed. Forty years before, she had fled her parents' suburban pretensions and discovered women's liberation. Returning to help them in their last years, she discovered that in 'the scales of fulfillment, devotion may sometimes outweigh freedom.'"

9. See my "Tracing a Path of Spiritual Progress in the Confucian *Analects*," in *Confucian Spirituality*, ed. Mary Evelyn Tucker and Tu Weiming (New York, 2000).

10. Aldous Huxley, *The Doors of Perception and Heaven and Hell* (New York, 1963), p. 12.

11. Again, some patterns of feminist thought are the exception. In addition to the thinkers cited in note 2, see, for example, Chilla Bulbeck, *Re-Orienting Western Feminisms* (Cambridge, 1998).

Harmony, Fragmentation, and Democratic Ritual

DAVID B. WONG

DOES A VIABLE democracy need a common moral culture, a set of widely shared moral[1] values recognized as such even by those who do not hold them? In a pluralistic society, it is not surprising that there should be attempts to explain why a viable democracy does not require a common culture. K. Anthony Appiah has claimed in reference to U.S. democracy that all we need is to "share a commitment to the organization of the state—the institutions that provide the overarching order of our common life"[2] and that these institutions need not carry the same meaning for all of us. For example, the separation of church and state can gain acceptance from some because they are religious. Similarly, the institutions of democracy—elections, public debates, and protection of minority rights—can bear different meanings for different subcultures. There is no reason to require that we all value them in the same way for the same reasons.

Appiah's argument illustrates the possibility that different groups within a pluralistic society might converge on a set of institutions without having to agree on moral values. But what, more precisely, is this possibility? John Rawls has distinguished two versions. In an "overlapping consensus," each party comes to agree on a set of normative rules to govern a specific domain of public life, but on the basis of her own distinctive conceptions of the good and her most fundamental beliefs. Rawls's hope for an overlapping consensus on a principle of religious toleration rests on the supposition that "except for certain kinds of fundamentalism, all the main historical religions" admit of "an account of free faith" such as can be found in Locke's *A Letter Concerning Toleration*, where it is argued that the understanding cannot be compelled by force to belief, that God has given no man authority over another, and that only faith and inward sincerity gain salvation and acceptance with God.[3]

Rawls distinguishes an overlapping consensus from a *modus vivendi*, in which consensus is "founded on self- or group interests, or on the outcome of political bargaining," and in which the stability of consensus "is contingent on circumstances remaining such as not to upset the fortunate convergence of interests."[4] By contrast, an overlapping consensus is based on each party's comprehensive religious, philosophical, and moral views, in such a way that none will "withdraw their support of it should the relative strength of their view in society increase and eventually become dominant."[5] Rawls has pointed out that the Quakers, as pacifists, refuse to engage in war, yet they also support the legitimacy of majority or other plurality rule in a constitutional regime. This is possible because the Quakers accept many political and nonpolitical values, and their allegiance to a just and enduring constitutional government may override the religious doctrine prohibiting their engaging in war. Their political values may motivate their upholding the constitutional system, even if they protest particular statutes and decisions through civil disobedience or conscientious refusal.

Rawls' way of distinguishing between an overlapping consensus and a *modus vivendi* implies an argument for the superiority of the former: an overlapping consensus is a more *stable* way of reaching consensus because it is derived from each party's conception of the good and most fundamental beliefs. It is not vulnerable to being upset in the way a *modus vivendi* is by change in the circumstances that have led to a fortunate convergence of interests. How compelling is this implied argument? It certainly is true that the sort of agreement Appiah describes could be upset by changes in the majority and minority status among various religions. The question, however, is whether an overlapping consensus is necessarily any *more* stable or any *more* realizable than a *modus vivendi*.

Consider the issues raised by *Wisconsin v. Yoder* (1972). Members of the Amish community in Wisconsin opposed, on the basis of their right to free exercise of religion, a law requiring children to attend school until the age of sixteen. They argued that their religion required a way of life tied to the local farming activities and shielded from the heterogeneous world of industrial and material distractions.[6]

Wisconsin defended the law on the grounds of the interests of the larger community and of the Amish children themselves, in seeking to assure that all children in the state received the same minimal amount of educational instruction. The majority opinion by Warren Burger concluded that the state's aim is consistent with the Amish parents' request for exemption because they were so successful in teaching what the majority hopes its public schools will teach: to be productive, self-sufficient, and law-abiding.

By arguing in this way, the majority opinion avoided confronting the question of parental or subcommunity power to limit the freedom of individual children. However, the case also raises issues about the nature of free faith. Does free faith require confrontation and familiarity with alternative ways of life and religious belief, or does it require that a child have the opportunity to fully experience a religious way of life that may need for its preservation to be shielded from the distractions and temptations offered by other ways of life? Let us grant Locke's point that understanding cannot be compelled by force to belief. But neither is belief in a religion simply a matter of drawing conclusions from a set of propositions. Indeed, it could be argued that a religious way of life may be experienced only by submitting to a discipline of rituals and practice, and that such freedom to meaningfully contemplate its adoption requires curtailment of freedom to expose oneself to more powerfully distracting ways of life.

I raise these considerations not to advance a conclusion about them but only to indicate the high degree of difficulty in achieving a genuine overlapping consensus. It is not at all obvious to me that all the main historical religions have an account of free faith that looks very much like Locke's, and the actual substance of such free faith can be a matter of deep and serious controversy. *Wisconsin v. Yoder*, usually taken as the "leading modern American legal hymn to pluralism,"[7] reveals the unresolved tensions within anything we could call a consensus on the meaning of free faith, religious toleration, and private freedom of choice.

Such concerns give rise to what I want to call the worry of fragmentation. If the requirement of a common democratic culture is relaxed so as to accommodate the fact of pluralism of moral belief and ultimate conceptions of the good, either a *modus vivendi* of the sort Appiah describes or a Rawlsian overlapping consensus on common democratic institutions might be too fragile and subject to erosion.

The fragmentation worry that "the center will not hold" without a common culture is more likely to appear in a nation such as the United States. The degree of our agreement on the viability of our common democratic institutions is greater than the degree of our agreement on the justification for those institutions, but many of us do worry that whatever overlapping consensus exists is unstable and perhaps eroding.

The fragmentation worry has a mirror image in a worry that arises from reflection on the Chinese tradition and the way that the value of harmony has acted as an excessively stringent constraint on freedom of speech and dissent. The Chinese tradition has not lacked articulation of the need for dissent. In the *Hsün Tzu*, for example, it is asserted that if there were four frank ministers in a state with ten thousand war-chariots, its territory was never diminished. If there were three frank ministers in a state with a thousand war-chariots, that state was never endangered (chap. 29). In the *Mencius* 1B:8 King Hsüan queries Mencius about King Wu's marching against the last king of the Shang Dynasty. Was regicide permissible? Mencius answers that a man who mutilates benevolence is a mutilator, that one who cripples righteousness is a crippler, that one who is both a mutilator and crippler is an outcast, but that he (Mencius) had not heard of the punishment of such an outcast as a regicide. The story is but one of several in which Mencius tells a king exactly what he thinks without apparent regard for the personal consequences.

This theme of upholding the independent and honest voice is carried through in the Neo-Confucian period. Julia Ching has discussed the Neo-Confucian conception of the relationship between prince and minister as one of moral equality, as between two individuals who had freely joined in taking responsibility for the way of governing. Because Neo-Confucians such as the Ch'eng brothers and Chu Hsi saw themselves as guardians and interpreters of the spiritual meaning of the Confucian canon, they could act as "moral judges of their sovereigns rather than as dutiful ministers."[8] Wm. Theodore de Bary has described the way in which this theme was developed with special reference to the idea that previous great thinkers and the Confucian canon itself could point to the Way but not deliver it and that one must find it for and within oneself.[9] This continuing defense of dissent and independence of thought is therefore deeply rooted in the Chinese philosophical tradition.

My present concern is a problem with the implementation of democratic rights in China. The problem lies in a deep-seated value of the Chinese tradition: harmony and a long-standing tendency to rely on the ruler to realize harmony from the top down. The theme that the ruler is to accomplish this through the moral rectitude of his own person and his policies is famously present in the *Analects* and the *Mencius*. The *Hsün Tzu* posits not only the need for frank ministers but for hierarchical divisions (chap. 9), without which harmony is impossible. Without hierarchical divisions, there will be quarreling, chaos, fragmentation, lack of power to conquer other beings, and in the end, no security in one's dwellings. To complete the Way and its virtue, establish the highest standards, unite the world in the fullest degree of order, and cause all men to be obedient and submissive are the duties of the heavenly king.

Thomas H. C. Lee tells an interesting story of the way that Neo-Confucians attempted to utilize private academies as an institutional mechanism outside state officialdom to promote social and political reform. Throughout the past millennium Chinese intellectuals have tried to use the academies to pressure rulers to conform to their conceptions of moral government. However, Lee points out that for thinkers such as Chu Hsi, the academies never constituted a separate realm of action distinct from state action. Though *shih jen* (intellectuals, literati) were not office-holding officials, they were official figures. In the context of the "organicist Chinese political and social thinking," says Lee, "harmony and integration (unity) took a priority position."[10] In fact, Lee observes,

> it is not far from the truth to suggest that Chinese intellectuals hardly ever questioned the proposition that there should not be any contradiction between the notion of intellectual autonomy and the notion that imperial rulership could remain omnipotent. Only an omnipotent government is capable of perfect rule.[11]

Given the priority of harmony, the institutionalization of moral autonomy—the legal guarantee of its practice—was not on the agenda for the *shih jen*. It was morally imperative to work within the parameters of officially sanctioned ideology until this ideology clearly failed. Only in times of extraordinary crisis could one decide that it was necessary to go beyond moral autonomy (one's personal decision to speak out and protest) and advocate its institutionalization in the form of legal guarantees of that autonomy. Unfortunately, times of crisis promote the mentality among state officials that social order cannot be sacrificed. The worry arising from reflection on the Chinese tradition is that an emphasis on fundamental agreement in belief, or at least deference to certain others with whom one disagrees, crushes dissent and frank speech precisely when they are most needed.

The other lesson of the Chinese experience is that the value of harmony can lead to a dangerous neglect of very real forms of fragmentation. The common good is a complex whole, made up of goods that can be mutually supporting but simultaneously in tension with one another. We can see this clearly in the Confucian tradition. If filial piety and brotherly respect are the root of *jen* or comprehensive moral virtue (*Analects* 1:2), it also may conflict with other aspects of moral virtue, such as our concern for others outside the family. If loyalty to family nurtures a respect for authority not based on coercion, and if this respect is absolutely necessary for the cultivation of public virtue,[12] it may also encourage a partiality for one's own that is damaging to public virtue. Confucian ethics, as David Hall and Roger Ames have observed, is liable to continuous crossing of the line separating a rightful loyalty to family from a socially debilitating nepotism and special privilege.

Reflection on the American and Chinese worries leaves one searching for some judicious balance that would avoid the dangers of entirely yielding to fragmentation and losing the common institutions of a democracy on the one hand, and the dangers of quashing healthy dissent and legitimate difference of perspective in the name of harmony. Ernest Gellner seems to be referring to something like this balance in expressing a degree of skepticism about the Enlightenment supposition that traditional regimes could be based on truth and consent. Reason by itself, he asserts, cannot engender the consensus that underlies social order. Theories are underdetermined by facts, and in any case, free inquiry undermines respect for any given authority structure. So any culture embodies a systematic prejudgment of issues that in the light of reason alone would remain open. The problem, he says, is how a society could emerge "in which the prejudgment was made milder and flexible, and yet order was maintained."[13]

The idea of civil society as a counterbalance to the state plays a crucial role in Gellner's conception of how this becomes possible. There must be a set of nongovernmental institutions strong enough to keep the state from dominating and atomizing the rest of society, yet not so strong as to prevent the state from keeping the peace and arbitrating between major interests. Civil society must embody enough social, political, and economic pluralism to counter the centralizing tendencies of the state. Yet Gellner points out that people must live in the same world and share the same concepts at least up to a point. A society must still have its rituals, at least a few of them. The common world does still exist in the Western democracies, but its authority is greatly diminished. Attendance at rituals is optional, and experimentation with concepts is tolerated. "Social co-operation, loyalty and solidarity do not now presuppose a shared faith," Gellner asserts. "They may in fact presuppose the absence of a wholly shared and seriously, unambiguously upheld conviction."[14]

Note the burden of hopes placed on civil society in Gellner's description: on the one hand, civil society must play the role of counterweight to the state both in terms of sheer political power and in terms of providing a plurality of viewpoints; on the other hand, it must support cooperation, loyalty, and solidarity in the absence of a shared faith. In short, it embodies the cultural prejudgment that is mild and flexible yet supports social order. Gellner's characterization is in fact more an expression of hope for a judicious balance between these competing demands than an articulation of the content of such a balance or an explanation of its possibility. As Adam Seligman has observed, this hope for reconciliation of possibly irreconcilable elements is characteristic of the notion of civil society and the role it has played in Western European and American political theory. A central concern of civil society thinkers, he observes, is the need to articulate some vision of the individual that would both uphold his autonomy and at the same time present a vision of a "public"—a group of individuals sharing core ideas, ideals, and values.[15] Yet Seligman sees these two elements pulling apart, as exemplified by a contrast between Eastern and Central Europe on the one hand and the United States on the other hand. One element of the notion of civil society—shared ideas, ideals, and values—is exemplified by the situation in Eastern and Central Europe, where the basic networks of trust are still woven around ethnic relations, local communities, shared religious faith, and the continuing saliency of given traditions. Such ethnic solidarities threaten the existence of civil society because each such solidarity represents an alternative moral universe of values or norms and hence a threat to universal citizenship. On the other hand, the United States represents the other element of civil society pulling away from the desired synthesis. Where the individual is freed from particular, communal identities, there occurs a vitiation of the mutuality and communality that fosters and sustains trust.

One worry about the prospects for Chinese democracy is that associations that could serve as channels of communication and influence between the family and local forms of community, on the one hand, and the state, on the other hand, have historically achieved very little independence from the state. As suggested by Lee's work on the academies, such associations have rarely sought independence. A matching worry about U.S. democracy concerns the possible disappearance or eroding authority of precisely such an intermediate infrastructure. From other quarters, the argument comes that the notion of civil society has always been more of an ideal than a functioning reality, and that in practice it has too infrequently provided the independence from the state, the pluralism of viewpoint, and the dispersion of power that have been its promised benefits.

Glimmers of hope appear for the desired form of civil society. The anthropologist Mayfair Mei-hui Yang[16] has pointed to the existence of an alternative Chinese civil society that has deep roots in the norm of reciprocity. In the *Li Chi* or *Book of Ritual*, it is said that "if I give a gift and nothing comes in return, that is contrary to *li* (the rites, propriety), if the thing comes to me, and I give nothing in return, that also is contrary to *li*."[17] This principle of reciprocity has its most intense application to the relationships of family and kin, but it radiates outward to all types of interpersonal relationships. The reciprocal exchange of gifts and benefits, especially as applied to the closest personal relationships, is bound up with and promotes human feelings (*jen-ch'ing*), the feelings of attachment, loyalty, and obligation that make being human a worthy thing to be.

Yang finds in contemporary China a particularly elaborate offshoot of this ancient principle of reciprocity. *Kuanhsi-hsieh*,[18] or the art of personal relations, argues Yang, is a pervasive social phenomenon in the People's Republic. By creating a web of friends and social familiars through gifts, favors, and banquets, channels of communication and influence are cut between society and state. However, Yang finds that the art of personal relations as practiced in urban centers tends to be more interested in the material payoff than it is in any feelings of attachment, loyalty, and obligation that may result. She finds that women and people in rural communities are more likely to think of *kuanhsi-hsieh* negatively for this reason. Yang has hopes for these networks fulfilling the desired function of a civil society, but only if the *jen-ch'ing*, the human feeling and ties of mutual loyalty and attachment, are restored. She is cautious about asserting that such social networks have any great power to affect the state, but she does believe they have had some effect.

Another reason she is hopeful for urban *kuanhsi-hsieh* is that they deemphasize the traditional ties of filial piety, ruler and minister, and unequal spousal gender relations. These networks retain occasional elder and younger relations, such as those between teacher and student or leader and subordinate, but most importantly, they develop the realm of friendship and social familiarity. Strikingly, Yang's hopes for new forms of association that will evolve from a life less centered on geographical proximity, on kinship, and sustained membership within the same social, political, and religious institutions for long periods of their lives. Consider Marilyn Friedman's call for a refocusing of communitarianism on what she calls "communities of choice" rather than "found communities" of origin, her paradigms being friendship and urban associations. For Friedman, as for Yang, part of the appeal of such communities is their voluntariness and their relative freedom from association with unequal gender roles.[19]

Doubts accompany these glimmers of hope. Will these new kinds of networks both in China and the United States be too thin, too focused on the instrumental exchange of benefits in a world economy that seems increasingly to encourage such a mentality, to create ties of attachment, loyalty, and human feeling?[20] Without such ties, will such networks ever possess enough cohesion and stability to influence and counterbalance the state?[21]

Li as it occurs in Confucius seems to refer to formal rules and ceremonies performed within a community, such as the various forms of sacrificial offering, capping (that is, initiation for boys), weddings, funeral rites, and other occasions for social gathering conducted according to prescribed forms. The concept of ritual seems to have later expanded considerably from formal ceremonial performances to customs, habits, and etiquette in the conduct of social relationships in everyday life. The proper performance of ritual must involve the expression of attitudes appropriate to the ritual in question. For example, Hsün Tzu asserts that sacrificial rites originate in the emotions of remembrance and longing for the dead which come to those who lose loved ones. Rites are needed to give expression to these emotions, which otherwise will be frustrated and unfulfilled (*Hsün Tzu*, chap. 19).

However, it is not as simple as saying that one must first have those attitudes before one performs the rituals. Hsün Tzu claims for ritual performance a crucial role in shaping, refining, and strengthening those attitudes. Rituals have a dramatic structure. They tell stories through words and action that constitute expression of the appropriate attitudes. Performing gestures of gratitude and reverence toward ancestors may evoke those very attitudes in oneself, and the way one performs those gestures may give those attitudes further content and definition and strengthen them as motivating attitudes in the rest of one's life. The rituals therefore play an essential role in a process of cultivating virtues of character that is akin to Aristotelian habituation.

Those virtues, especially as they bear upon one's relationship to others, support harmony. Consider the following passage from *The Analects* 1:12:

> Master You said: "When practicing the ritual, what matters most is harmony. This is what made the beauty of the way of the ancient kings; it inspired their every move, great or small. Yet they knew where to stop: harmony cannot be sought for its own sake, it must always be subordinated to the ritual; otherwise it would not do."

One reason why harmony cannot be sought for its own sake is that aiming directly at harmony lacks the power of summoning forth attitudes that may be shaped into mutual respect between the participants. At the same time that sacrifice to ancestors and the burial of parents train and focus attitudes of reverence, gratitude, and grief, they also foster a common bond between the living participants, a sense of community that is rooted in the past and stretches onward into the future.

However, I would like to propose other reasons why harmony must be sought through ritual. One reason is that harmony sought for its own sake frequently consists in trying to bring about agreement on a relatively specific set of values and normative doctrines, and such agreement turns out to be practically impossible given the plurality of differing value commitments the participants already have. Another reason is that agreement on values and normative doctrines is often not yet achievable in *practice* even when it is possible in *theory*, because the process of coming to agreement presupposes a willingness to listen, to consider, and to give weight to the other participants' views. This willingness depends on a significant degree of mutual respect that may not be possible without the ritual.

In other words, ritual has a unique power to promote the kind of harmony that exists apart from or as a precondition of agreement on specific values and doctrines. In his study of morality, politics, and power in a Chinese village during the nineteen seventies, Richard Madsen utilizes a conception of ritual in which the

> participants pour a rich variety of emotions into the performance of a series of stylized actions that are held to represent some phase of the fundamental meaning of their life together. The main symbols making up the rituals are actions rather than words. In some cases these emotionally resonant symbols express a richer meaning than can be put into any discursive verbal argument. The emotional resonance and fertile noetic ambiguity is what gives rituals everywhere their integrative power. The participants in a ritual become a community of feeling and sharers in a common experience that is drenched with meaning but cannot be expressed by any single set of discursive ideas. They often experience the ritual as expressing a common primordial understanding that is the font of subsequent discursive understandings. This does not mean that one can discursively interpret a ritual in any way one wishes. There is usually a range of orthodox interpretations of a ritual and some clear ideas about which interpretations would be unorthodox. But often the range of orthodox interpretations is fairly wide, so that a ritual can unite a broad group of people with different approaches toward life. Thus regular participants in certain rituals can within limits argue about their common moral responsibilities to their community and yet recognize that they are united by a shared moral understanding that transcends their words.[22]

What is especially morally valuable in this species of ritual, as Madsen describes it, is the openness and ambiguity of meaning which allows harmony to be something different from agreement on a set of doctrines.

There is, however, a bounded range of orthodox interpretations for a ritual, even if the width of that range is significant. A wedding, the burial and mourning of deceased parents, and a village feast are rituals that embody and foster certain notions of proper human relationships. To advance the aim of harmony, participants must have some significant degree of agreement on what it is these rituals embody and foster. Yet the degree of agreement needed remains open and ambiguous, partly because, as Madsen puts it so well, much of the meaning of ritual is carried by actions. Even when the meaning is carried by words, reconciliation can be achieved by regulating the degree of specificity of meaning. The effectiveness of ritual in reconciling harmony and fragmentation gives fresh meaning to the homily that what is *not* said is every bit as important as what *is* said. As D. C. Lau remarks, one Confucian rationale for study of the *Book of Odes* is that it provides one with a store of quotations for delicate situations such as diplomatic exchanges and within which one can couch one's meanings in a sufficiently indirect and somewhat ambiguous way.[23]

This fragmentation of value is normal and healthy. All complex and vital cultures contain values that exist in unresolved tension with one another. For example, values of individual autonomy and of community are in tension with one another.[24] Autonomy and community, when they coexist within a culture, often function as counterpoints *to each other*, in that one value is asserted against the other value because it is seen as addressing the liabilities of asserting the other value strongly. Autonomy gets asserted against the sort of collective responsiveness to individual need that can be a great benefit of community when that responsiveness turns into the liability of oppressive suffocation or an alienating exclusion of those who fall from good standing. On the other side, community gets asserted against the barriers to intervention afforded by autonomy when this benefit blocks responsiveness to need. The U.S. moral tradition exhibits this kind of dynamic between autonomy and community.

In the Chinese tradition, Confucianism is a repository of values of community. Taoism and Buddhism have supplied counterpoint values, but these values have served as counterpoints in ways that are different from the ways the value of individual autonomy has served as a counterpoint to community. In a Taoist philosopher such as Chuang Tzu, for instance, one finds a plea for accepting persons who do not conform to accepted standards of the good, the beautiful, and the noble. In one of his stories, a man missing a foot is refused an audience with Confucius because of his criminal history. "No-Toes" scolds Confucius for this moralistic condemnation, declaring, "There is nothing that heaven doesn't cover, nothing that earth doesn't bear up. I supposed, Master, that you would be like heaven and earth. How did I know you would act like this?" (*Chuang Tzu*, chap. 5).[25] Chuang Tzu is asserting here an ethic of inclusiveness. Underlying this ethic is a view of the world as simply too fluid and too complex to be captured by any single theory, including theories of value and right action. Established standards inevitably dismiss as bad, ugly, and mean those persons and things that have worth from other points of view. No larger theory could capture all that is of value, including what is of value in people dismissed, rejected, or condemned. These themes constitute a defense of the value of the individual voice against standards that inevitably miss that value in some voices. This defense should certainly seem familiar to us in the West, and here it serves a similar function. Yet it does not take much reflection on such advice as can be found in the *Chuang Tzu* to "leap into the boundless and make it your home"[26] to conclude that defense of the individual voice serves as a counterpoint to community in a way significantly different from Western autonomy. The solace and protection it offers to the individual suffocated or excluded by the community ultimately lies in identification with a world much larger than the human social world. Heaven cannot fail to cover all and earth cannot fail to bear up all, even if the human community does fail.

A "common culture" includes dynamic configurations of such values. The values that serve as counterpoints to each other are widely shared and recognized as such *even by those who do not hold them*. The identity of a culture is in part defined by which values are the most salient and which ones serve as counterpoints to others. The common culture is this dynamic configuration, but what is common leaves a significant degree of openness and ambiguity in how conflicts between values are to be resolved. This is the space where harmony meets fragmentation. In the U.S. tradition, the meaning of individual autonomy and the manner of its coexistence with the value of community are ongoing questions given partial and tentative answers, but these questions should never be fully and finally settled if that tradition is to remain a healthy one.

The argument for leaving the resolution of conflicts between fundamental values open and ambiguous in this way can be made from a number of different metaphysical and epistemological perspectives on moral truth. If there is a final and single truth as to how conflicts between these values in general should be resolved, it is not at all obvious to all reasonable and informed people of good will what that truth is. From the perspective assuming the truth of such a possibility, there is a strong case that a tradition must remain open to continued attempts to deepen understanding of whatever the truth is. From the different perspective that there is no final and single truth as to how these conflicts *in general* should be resolved, because there are only final and single truths about the way these conflicts should be resolved *in certain contexts* (i.e., resolution of conflicts is context-dependent), there likewise is a strong case that a tradition must allow for openness and ambiguity. The way conflicts ought to be resolved in the future cannot be fixed even if it is informed by principled precedent. And from the perspective that there simply is no final and single truth as to how at least some of these conflicts should be resolved, either in general or in certain contexts, a tradition acknowledges this state of affairs by leaving it open as to how such conflicts are to be resolved.

A striking feature of Rawls's strategy of overlapping consensus is the degree to which it is compatible with the insulation of different moral communities from each other. A somewhat more interactive possibility compatible with Rawls's strategy is that one community recommends to another community an interpretation of that community's comprehensive conception, making it possible for the two communities to agree on a set of political institutions. An atheistic liberal, for example, might recommend to Quakers an interpretation of their comprehensive conception that would result in consensus between her community and theirs on religious toleration and separation of church and state.

The conception of value fragmentation advocated here suggests another possible strategy for arriving at consensus, one that arises from greater mutual understanding of the other moral community. The more one understands fragmentation in terms of the contrapuntal conception, the more one is able to understand the other community as embodying a conception of value that is a substantial rival to one's own, its strengths mirroring the weaknesses of one's own, its weaknesses mirroring the strengths of one's own. One may hold that one's own conception is, after all is said and done, the right one, but one can see that other community playing a positive role in the search for fuller truth, if indeed its strengths mirror the weaknesses in one's own conception.

A common democratic culture need not be anything so simple as widespread agreement on values and their ordering, any more than a coherent musical piece must be everyone singing the same notes. A common culture may rather include rival moral conceptions derived from a common universe of values that are sometimes mutually supporting and sometimes in contrapuntal tension with one another. They are rivals precisely because they emphasize different values in these various relations of compatibility and antagonism. Though different moral communities may have their own conceptions of how these values are to be ordered, there exists the possibility for a significant degree of mutual respect between these communities, especially if they recognize that the different orderings may be related as point and counterpoint orderings.

This is the alternative to both Rawlsian overlapping consensus, in which alternative universes of values and belief converge only on a set of institutions, on the one hand, and on the other hand, conceptions of a common democratic culture in which the ideal harmony predominates and in which agreement is far more extensive and deep than disagreement. Mutual respect is possible between adherents to different comprehensive moral, religious, and metaphysical conceptions that overlap significantly yet are by no means the same conception.

The value of ritual lies in its power to make salient what is already shared, while not forcing specific and divisive interpretations of the way shared values are to be ordered in conflicts. This dual effect is made possible by the fact that much of the meaning is carried by the dramatic structure rather than the statement of specific doctrine. Ritual in this sense plays a crucial role in the reconciliation of harmony and fragmentation. The constructive role of ritual depends on there being significantly shared values in the first place. That is why I first sketched a conception of the fragmentation of value that is consistent with such shared values. Rituals can have the effect of making salient and reinforcing dispositions to act on what is shared rather than on the possible areas of divergence. It is a necessary condition for a viable democracy that there be widely shared values, but that is hardly a sufficient condition. Freud used the memorable phrase "the narcissism of minor differences"[27] to indicate that groups predisposed to contend with each other will magnify apparently small points of disagreement into contests between Good and Evil. On the other hand, a viable democracy is consistent with robust disagreement over how widely shared values are to be interpreted and ordered as long as the areas of agreement seem more important than the areas of disagreement. Rituals can help in the task of making these areas of agreement more important. The sort of common democratic culture that is necessary partly rests on sufficient agreement on values, but it cannot rest solely on such agreement. It is as much an achievement as a discovery of agreement. It is an achievement in which members of a common culture actively seek to understand one another well enough so that they do indeed discover the points of agreement.

Let me conclude with some suggestions as to what sort of moral and political rituals might be in accord with both the aim of reconciling harmony and fragmentation and the underlying conception of culture as a dynamic and open configuration of values often in contrapuntal tension with one another. *Voting* in an election is the quintessential democratic institution, and I think that something is learnt about its importance and role in a democracy by viewing it as ritual. Why should we vote? Most of us have probably heard urgings to vote because "you never know when it might be your vote that makes the difference." From the standpoint of the individual deliberating as to whether there is sufficient reason for her to go to the polls, the proffered justification will in most cases be unpersuasive. One knows that in all likelihood, one's vote will *not* make any difference to the outcome. Another kind of justification for voting is that failing to vote is a morally objectionable form of free-riding. A democracy works only if enough people vote, and therefore the ones who yield to convenience or apathy and fail to vote are benefiting from the acts of those who do not so yield. This argument certainly has more force than the first, but can be circumvented by the argument that if something is owed to those who vote, then the payment need not take the form of someone else voting. Why not just issue voters a payment voucher? Given the desperately low participation in elections in this country, it is difficult to reject that suggestion out of hand, but the reasoning behind it fails to explain why it is important for each individual citizen to vote. It is not just that those who choose not to vote would be free-riding on those who do vote. Even if those who voted were literally repaid precisely by the people who chose not to vote, it would still be a bad thing that those people chose not to vote. But why would it be a bad thing?

My suggestion is that voting needs to be renewed as the central political *ritual* it is. It is not because one's vote might possibly decide an election, though there will be unusual occasions where they might indeed do that. It is not because one should avoid being a free-rider (even though one should avoid that), because there are ways to avoid free-riding that do not capture the importance of voting. It is because voting is a ritual that can foster and promote the reconciliation between fragmentation and harmony that one has a civic duty to participate. The way that voting represents fragmentation, of course, should be familiar. Consider, however, familiar actions that are part of the voting ritual: going to a common place to cast one's vote alongside others and walking past campaign workers who must assume in their actions that one is still open to their candidate or cause. Moreover, there is the ritual act of courteous response to their actions—taking the literature, stopping to listen for a short time, or simply to nod and smile, even if one has absolutely no intention of voting according to their wishes. Consider the related ritual acts of the candidates on election night: the speech of the victor verbally extending a hand in reconciliation; the loser extending congratulations to the victor and, yes, calling for unity. Of course, there are mechanical and insincere performances of these ritual acts, but the more hopeful lesson is that we should insist on candidates with the character and perspective on their place in the scheme of things that would enable them to perform these rituals in genuine fashion.

John Stuart Mill at one time advocated the idea of the open ballot. The rationale was to promote a conception of voting as the deliverance of one's considered judgment on what would best promote the general welfare.[28] By making one's judgment public, and therefore having to be prepared to defend it, one is prompted to enact a certain conception of citizenship. The rituals of declaring and defending one's position would be important not just because of what they might contribute to a useful debate on the issues, but because one is acting as if one's vote is based on a judgment that needs to be defensible to other citizens. And acting in this way is a way of strengthening the general disposition to do so. I agree with the aim of Mill's proposal, but am reluctant to sacrifice the protections afforded by the secret ballot against various forms of coercive attempts to force a harmony among individuals that does not exist. Of course, there are contexts in which coercion is less of a factor: tenured professors voting on university policy might reasonably be required to publicize and defend their votes. In such contexts, the open ballot is a reasonable option.

Where coercion is a reasonable danger, however, an alternative practice is to make it compulsory. Australia has achieved very high turnout rates with relatively modest fines for failure to vote. Requiring people to vote combats the idea that it is no one's business but one's own whether one votes or not. One may keep one's vote and one's views secret, but one must contribute to the process of collective decision. The ritual of voting, the way it brings citizens together for a decision, matters too much to make it purely optional. If voting is made compulsory, then a necessary second step in reform is to allow voters to express a sentiment they currently express by declining to vote: the opportunity to check a box labeled "none of the above." Disillusionment and alienation from dominant political agents, forces, and institutions should have a channel of expression in the most central of democratic political rituals.

This proposal draws attention to the ceremonial *dimensions* of the activity without denying its other dimensions. Marriage and burial rites, two paradigms of ceremonial rituals, also have very practical functions. The Confucian perspective on ritual notes the difference between these different expressive and practical dimensions. Hsün Tzu (chap. 19) holds that the various dimensions of ritual must be kept in balance. When the dimensions of form and meaning are emphasized to the point of slighting their emotion and practical use, rituals become florid. When their emotion and practical use is emphasized to the point of slighting their form and meaning, rituals become lean. The mean between these extremes is the thing to aim for.

Practices that simultaneously have ceremonial, emotionally expressive, and practical functions, such as voting, can be especially potent in moral and civic education. Pure ceremonies, unconstrained by practical purpose and unexpressive of civic feelings, may become stultifying and meaningless or insufferably pedantic. Ceremonies expressive of civic feelings but devoid of practical purpose may become merely entertaining displays. Purely practical activities, on the other hand, lack the recurrent dramatic structure of ceremonial rituals that enables them to evoke and express value and feeling. They therefore can have far less of a role in the evocation, training, shaping, and strengthening of attitudes and dispositions of character. When the ceremonial, expressive, and practical functions are all present and have intrinsic connections to one another, as they can in the case of voting, they may be the most potent instruments of moral and civic education.

There are other examples of such practices that weave together the ceremonial, expressive, and practical. The *Mencius* puts forward a proposal for the *ching*-field system, commonly translated as the "well-field" system. A *ching* is a piece of land divided into nine parts.

> If those who own land within each *ching* befriend one another both at home and abroad, help each other to keep watch, and succor each other in illness, they will live in love and harmony. A *ching* is a piece of land measure one *li* square, and each *ching* consists of 900 *mu*. Of these the central plot of 100 *mu* belongs to the state, while the other eight plots of 100 *mu* each are held by eight families who share the duty of caring for the plot owned by the state. Only when they have done this duty dare they turn to their own affairs. (*Mencius* 3A:3)[29]

The proposed practice has a very practical point, of course. But it also expresses the reconciliation of harmony and fragmentation. The shared labor on the state-owned land represents harmony. The family-owned plots represent a kind of fragmentation. The *ching*-field system can be taken to represent their reconciliation. The practice of first sharing labor and of then turning to one's family affairs can become a ceremony for the participants. It can tell a story in words and actions that carries the meaning of that reconciliation in symbolic and expressive ways. The meaning goes beyond the concrete practical function of fairly dividing the burdens of taxation, but note that that concrete practical function does instantiate the broader meaning.

In a modern democracy, an analogy to Mencius's proposal might be some form of community or national service: not just the purely optional and underfunded gestures recently implemented, but at the least a serious call to service to a wide range of citizens that can only be set aside by an individual for good reasons, as in the American jury system. In fact, one of the possible ideas for service is calling on citizens to serve on juries or panels charged with making recommendations on initiatives, referendums, or policy issues. Experiments along these lines have shown that citizens have taken their responsibilities seriously and have striven to formulate recommendations that transcend partisan interests.[30] As in the case of voting, one of the important functions of such service may lie in its ceremonial and expressive dimensions, and not just the practical recommendations that may result from the process. Participation on such panels might be a one-time event for individuals, but public knowledge of the general practice of drafting citizens can have a broader educative effect. Another idea along these lines is a component of service learning in our schools, with the added advantage of catching future or young citizens at developing stages.

Perhaps the proposals I have made amount to no more than a few glimmers of hope for the reconciliation of harmony with fragmentation. I believe there is enough promise in these suggestions to recommend the work of discovering how much we share with one another to my fellow philosophers and to all of us who are hopeful for democracy. Indeed, I believe hopefulness to be a central democratic virtue, and one that must be cultivated through our rituals.[31]

NOTES

1. In this context I use *moral* in a broad sense to include what are usually termed "civic" and "political" values, such as equality and freedom of expression.

2. Anthony Appiah, "Culture, Subculture, Multiculturalism: Educational Options," in *Public Education in a Multicultural Society: Policy, Theory, Critique,* ed. Robert K. Fullinwider (Cambridge: Cambridge University Press, 1996), p. 86.

3. See John Rawls, *Political Liberalism* (New York: Columbia University Press, 1993), pp. 145, 170; John Locke, *Two Treatises of Government with A Letter on Toleration,* ed. J. W. Gough (Oxford: Basil Blackwell, 1956), pp. 129, 143.

4. Ibid., p. 147.

5. Ibid., p. 148.

6. My discussion of this case is in great part based on Martha Minow's, in *Not Only for Myself: Identity, Politics & the Law* (New York: The New Press, 1997), pp. 111–12.

7. Minow, *Not Only for Myself,* p. 111.

8. Julia Ching, "The Goose Lake Monastery Debate," *Journal of Chinese Philosophy* 1, no. 2 (1974): 175.

9. Wm. Theodore de Bary, *The Liberal Tradition in China* (Hong Kong: Chinese University Press, and New York: Columbia University Press, 1983), p. 73.

10. Thomas H. C. Lee, "Academies: Official Sponsorship and Suppression," in *Imperial Rulership and Cultural Change*, ed. Frederick P. Brandauer and Chun-Chieh Huang (Seattle: University of Washington Press, 1994), p. 128.

11. Ibid., p. 118.

12. Benjamin Schwartz, *The World of Thought in Ancient China* (Cambridge: Belknap Press, 1985), p. 70.

13. Ernest Gellner, *Conditions of Liberty: Civil Society and Its Rivals* (New York: Penguin Press, 1994), p. 32.

14. Ibid., p. 96.

15. Adam B. Seligman, *The Idea of Civil Society* (New York: Free Press, 1992), p. 60.

16. Mayfair Mei-hui Yang, *Gifts, Favors, and Banquets: The Art of Social Relationships in China* (Ithaca, N.Y.: Cornell University Press, 1994).

17. *Li Chi*, "Ch'u Li." See James Legge, *The Li Ki (Book of Rites)*, vols. 27–28 of *The Sacred Books of the East*, ed. Max Muller (Oxford: Clarendon Press, 1885), p. 65.

18. Yang uses the pinxin rendering, *guanxixue*, but I have used Wade-Giles for the sake of consistency with other romanizations in this essay.

19. Marilyn Friedman, "Feminism and Modern Friendship: Dislocating the Community," in *Social and Political Philosophy: Classical Western Texts in Feminist and Multicultural Perspectives*, ed. James P. Sterba (Belmont, Calif.: Wadsworth, 1995).

20. It does not inspire confidence, for example, that many of the *kuanhsi* in urban settings consist in utilizing contacts with government officials to obtain official approvals and permissions that are necessary for travel and entry into beneficial organizations.

21. See John Flower and Pamela Leonard, "Community Values and State Cooptation," in *Civil Society: Challenging Western Models*, ed. Chris Hann and Elizabeth Dunn (London: Routledge, 1996): pp. 199–221.

22. Richard Madsen, *Morality and Power in a Chinese Village* (Berkeley: University of California Press, 1984), pp. 21–22. Madsen acknowledges his debt in conceptualizing this type of ritual to Victor Turner, *The Forest of Symbols: Aspects of Ndembu Ritual* (Ithaca, N.Y.: Cornell University Press, 1967), pp. 19–20.

23. D. C. Lau, Introduction to *The Analects* (London: Penguin Books , 1979), p. 42.

24. More precisely, *aspects* of these values come into conflict, since each of these values are complex configurations of more particular values.

25. Burton Watson's translation used, *Chuang Tzu: Basic Writings* (Columbia University Press, 1964), p. 67.

26. Ibid., p. 44.

27. See Sigmund Freud, *Civilization and Its Discontents*, trans. James Strachey (New York: W. W. Norton & Company, 1961), essay 5, p. 61.

28. I owe my awareness of this fact to my colleague at Brandeis, Andreas Teuber. See John Stuart Mill, "Thoughts on Parliamentary Reform," in *J. S. Mill: Collected Works*, ed. J. M. Robson (Toronto: University of Toronto Press, 1977), vol. 68, pp. 331–38; and "Considerations on Representative Government," vol. 18, pp. 488–95.

29. Translation adapted from D. C. Lau, *Mencius* (London: Penguin Books, 1970), pp. 99–100.

30. I first encountered this idea in Robert Kane, *Through the Moral Maze: Searching for Absolute Values in a Pluralistic World* (New York: Paragon House, 1994).

31. I wish to thank a number of people who have given me very helpful comments and suggestions on previous versions of this essay: the audience for the reading of this essay as part of the Boston University Institute for Philosophy and Religion series on civility; the audience at Duke University, Martha Minow, David Wilkins, and especially Lawrence Blum for detailed comments and suggestions.

Sacred Civilities

NINIAN SMART

WE HAVE A fairly narrow conception of what counts as a moral issue or a moral rule in Western society. Killing a person or committing adultery is usually considered morally wrong; yet there is a wide area adjoining morality which counts as civility. And that shades off into etiquette. Perhaps virtues extend further in scope than moral behavior, but they again fade into other aspects of character.

Civility covers certain dispositions in humans such as gentleness, which is not precisely listed among the virtues but seems to be adjacent to humility, which is more obviously counted as one. But a gentle disposition is seen as a generally good thing to possess. And what about cheerfulness? Or humorousness? These are desirable. But are they virtues?

Civility is important partly because it includes treating other individuals in a way which regards them as persons. From one point of view the rights of a person can be seen in the manner in which they are to be treated. Many traditional religions seem not to have an explicit concept of human rights, but still demand toward human beings and animal life a certain kind of ritual behavior.

Religions tend to treat morals by examples—saints, heroes, and so on. Thus in Islam the *hadith* provides a fountain of stories which paint a rounded picture of the Prophet, and he then becomes a model to follow in life. It is peculiarly detailed, and there probably is not elsewhere so dense a collection of tales. The Buddha has many stories gathered about him, but generally he does not furnish us with so many clear human examples. (The *Jatakas*, of course, give us numerous examples, but chiefly of animals; so the examples do not have the warm human detail as provided by the Prophet.) There is the call in Christianity to imitate Christ, but it is often by analogy and rather abstract; consequently we have many detailed stories of the saints. Some are dear to Christians, such as Saint Francis, and provide a source of in-

222

spiration. In the days of the Great Proletarian Revolution especially, Chairman Mao was held as an ideal, and many of his pattern-forming exploits were recorded, as were those of others who caught his attention and were commended by him.

It is also noteworthy that ethics in religious contexts overlaps with the ritual demands of the faith. But ritual contains in it many forms of politeness and proper human interaction. In the original Confucian tradition this was valued as part of education, both as a proper aspect of it and as a way of molding it. *Li* or propriety was a vital part of Confucian training. It incorporates respect for others as part of its practice. It therefore overlaps seriously with what we would regard as morality.

Consider the various aspects of ritual and polite behavior which enter into a wedding occasion in modern times, in a Christian church. Not all of the customs enshrined come under moral rules, though they relate to them. The ritual contains a promise to be faithful sexually for the two partners. The clothing of the couple is related to this (especially because the bride's unusual gown, if worn, symbolizes such purity and faithfulness). The whole ceremony, including the banquet, involves a cheerfulness and a politeness which imply great good wishes and friendship which help to send the couple on their way. Maybe here and there some hypocrisy is present. But it has to be concealed; it is something for after and doubtless in private. Publicly it would mar the occasion: it would disrupt and render partly ineffective the ritual. Togetherness of the congregation and the families is reinforced by the touches of bawdiness that may come into the speeches. A joking relation is not to be fostered by overt enemies but by friends (or at least pretended friends). All the proper moves have to be made in the auspicious service and its aftermath. It is seen as a duty to perform the occasion properly, but it is not laid down in a commandment. Maybe Orthodox Jews or Hindus might have a religious handbook. But the detail of the religious law may not quite rate the depth of morality that their more serious elements warrant.

Of course a piously Christian person may see her actions as occurring in praise of God. This is where praise is superimposed upon moral, civil, or polite action to give it a deeper sense. But this does not subtract from its other meanings.

Consider by contrast what may be done to a person to humiliate him, for instance through prison and torture. He is deprived of his dignity, by having exiguous clothes, a filthy lavatory, a bad cell, revolting food, little drink. The warders who come in contact with him use foul language, calling him all sorts of names, swearing at him. And then they torture him. They love to kick his private parts, and in other ways to cause him excruciating pain. In all these ways they help to lower his self-esteem and make him look belittled in the eyes of others. Apart from the actual pain that they may cause him, much of the other acts are ritual in character and have a symbolic character. What can he do to counter them?

Well, if he is a pious Christian he can see himself as identifying with the suffering of Christ. He can dedicate his pain to God. This imports into it a new meaning, positive in its way. And so he does not seek delicacies or luxuries. He does not hate the guards. Indeed, he loves them or tries to. He is sorry for them; they must need to be cruel out of some obscure lack of self-esteem. And if he has to die he will thank his Lord who has clasped him to his eternal Self. That is how he will try to behave in his great misery and privation, which he sees only as an opportunity to follow his God. Once again we see an individual superimposing meaning on his actions, to perceive them as following Christ. It does not subtract from the pain, but it gives it a different meaning.

And so in all this there is something which goes well beyond the rules of morality as usually laid out. The ritual and symbolic character of action takes us into the realm of civility and incivility.

Perhaps it is in the Confucian tradition that we have the most vital fusing of the notions of the ethical and civility. This is through the ideas of *jen* and *li*. The idea of virtue in a human being is summed up in the former character; it was translated as benevolence by the famous translator of Chinese, James Legge. The reason is that morality is at root framed in relation to other people. The person who has *jen* is other-regarding. It also has a natural manifestation, in the way in which we respond to others. On the other hand, *li* originates, as the character implies, from ritual used in a religious act. But it spreads far beyond its narrower use, even extending to etiquette. The rules of propriety are the condition of a well-ordered society. Confucius' emphasis on education was intended to produce a harmonious social life, a kind of paradise on earth. It was a vision born of much strife and chaos in existing social relations. By the time and example of Hsun-tzu (Third Century BCE) it had become more or less secularized. But it might still have had a sacred aura—much as politicians nowadays may refer to sacrifices as sacred, especially in war.

To approach the topic from a different direction: why did Confucius think music was so vital in education? First, of course, we need to rid ourselves of the modern tendency to treat education almost wholly in terms of knowledge and technical skills. His education was conceived more as spiritual, but with strong ethical concerns. So it was a question of "how to bring up" a good offspring. But again, the West looks on education as a thing chiefly for the young, while for Confucius it should last all a person's life. I think, by the way, that both forms of education are important, and should complement one another. We now return to the question of: why music? Clearly because music plays so strongly upon the emotions. How does something so complex in genesis come to have this impact? The assumption is that some forms of music can encourage good feelings (and others by contrast bad feelings), and presumably this wells from deep springs in our nature. A similar appeal to the power of music and its *ethos* was found in Plato. I think he would be distressed by much of our popular music, some of which expresses hatred, rebellion, violence, and aspects of vulgar sexuality.

For the Confucian tradition a knowledge both of music and of sacred *li* could nurture good and just behavior in society. Again, however, we must look on knowledge as more than book knowledge, or laboratory knowledge. It is more that existential, in-experience knowledge which I like to call *gnowledge*. The word *gnowing* descends as it were from the Greek *gnosis*. It is knowing what love is, or genuine loving conduct. It is part of what existential education teaches. It does not despise factual or theoretical knowledge; and in the arts and literature it overlaps with it. The aesthetic is not even absent in scientific and mathematical discoveries.

But we live in a different world from that of Confucius or Mencius or Hsun-tzu. For one thing, the nisus of our world is towards democracy. Even our tyrannies claim to work for the people. For another thing, it is capitalist and often in a rather harsh market form. But old China was somewhat hierarchical, with an elite on top. Admittedly the elite was not a crude, powerful one but somewhat refined. The moral and political system depended on a ruler and an oligarchy. The emperor could, if necessary, of course call on armed force. But he was surrounded by dense rituals, which were much more effective, day in and day out, in controlling the country. Behind the ritual, notably in the relations between the scholarly elite and the lesser orders, there were a philosophical attitude and relevant forms of "gnowing."

We have vestiges of an elitism even in the modern world, but the more important forces are driven by the market. Our civil service and system of administering things is driven by a mass of bureaucrats, who are not especially admired or rated for moral or spiritual excellence. Nor are politicians greatly admired for their moral standing. But there is nevertheless in our society a large role played by politeness and civility to one another, largely because of the democratization of the elite. Let me expand on this.

Having an elite can encourage positive virtues. The elite can be used to elevate manners. The fact that a member of a certain class can be counted a gentleman (and in effect created as such by a certain ritual, namely, a kind of address) can lead to a transformation of the social order by democratization. After certain phases of social revolution, everyone becomes a gentleman or a lady. All are addressed as "Sir" or "Madam," and so on, in various languages and societies. And so manners spread out from the elite and become entrenched in social relations. The waiter who addresses the customer as "Sir" exchanges his uniform for other clothes and dresses for a dinner in a restaurant where a waiter addresses *him* as "Sir." And in this way everyone is equally respected, at least as a person and a human being. Courtesy becomes the way a person gains human dignity.

In the Confucian ethos there are different relations appropriate between different sorts of people, but generally these differing classes of folk are treated without the superimposition of religious meanings. The sage and the ruler are described as such. Similarly, in Theravadin Buddhism there are straight descriptions of social entities, such as the wife or the farmer. But something else occurs to titles sometimes in religious contexts. For a person is not just a person, for example, in Christianity, but also a son or daughter of God and a brother or sister in Christ. Here a way of looking on people gives them in principle a deeper social dignity, and one more deeply egalitarian. Accordingly, it may be held alongside social class distinctions. Naturally this situation lends itself to hypocrisy, but where a religious meaning is superimposed, it produces a kind of sacred civility.

Civility is related to human rights because of the secular ritual involved in treating other persons with dignity. There has sometimes been a somewhat negative reaction to a Western insistence on human rights, as though this vocabulary is the only one to use. From a Confucian perspective the individual has an obligation to *jen* and with it the associated proper behavior. From a Buddhist viewpoint there is the unfortunate aspect of rights as a possession. We may sometimes admire a person for standing up for her rights, but it is more admirable when others out of benevolence and compassion can stand up for them on her behalf. Even though the language of rights has emerged out of a Christian civilization, there is an uneasiness as to how we can square the demand for our rights with unselfishness and humility, which are Christian virtues in the path of following Christ. But Christians nevertheless have no difficulty with the idea that the person is sacred, which means in effect that the concept of a person is a performative one.

Consider the following example. If I were walking in a wood and found various logs lying there, I might hop on them in walking across them happily enough. But suppose I found two or three people lying there. I would normally carefully avoid stepping on them. If I did trample on their faces, it would be a deliberate and heartlessly cruel act. In civilized behavior I would avoid them so as not to cause pain. But even if perchance they were anesthetized I still think I would avoid stepping on them, out of respect. A person is something toward which certain kinds of behavior are to be avoided. This is what I mean by calling it a partly performative concept. And in calling a person sacred, say, in a theistic context, I am linking the appropriate behavior to that of worship. She is seen to reflect the divine nature. It is as though a person has a sort of charisma, as part of her basic endowments. The adjective *charismatic* implies that the person to whom it is applied exudes a kind of power and attraction, for whom deference is the appropriate reaction. It may be noted that my performative analysis here differs from Buber's "I-Thou" account, though it is compatible with it. It also calls on the behavior of others, rather than making the person in herself the bearer of rights. The concept of rights is a social construct. But in a theistic framework, we note that the society is comprised of persons, not just humans. For it includes the supreme Person, who has conferred personhood on individuals.

But in a nontheistic framework such as in Buddhism, does the performative aspect of the person have the same force—especially in view of the *anatta* doctrine? It is true that in Mahayana Buddhism the notion of the Buddha-nature evolved, which assigned a quasi-transcendent nature—a capacity for liberation—to each individual. Therefore Buddhahood became a sort of substitute for the eternal soul and carried with it the idea of a resemblance in each individual to the Buddha. Still, Theravada Buddhism scarcely included this notion, or only dimly. The rights of the individual could only spring from the suffering which might attract the compassion of others. In addition, perhaps, there was the demand for *mudita* or joy in the joy of others, which could be an invitation to courtesy.

We may note that there is some emphasis on courtesy in the depiction of people's responsibilities. For instance, in order to honor teachers a person should rise in salutation at their coming, should attend upon them in various ways, and so on. Students should show an eagerness to learn, which boosts the morale of teachers. Again, a husband should respect his wife and be courteous toward her. He should supply her with adornments, and so forth. In such advice (notably in the *Sigalovada Sutta*) we notice how there is a duty to adhere to good manners. This stems from the *brahmaviharas* or holy virtues. One would suppose that if people adhered to the Buddhist ethic, human rights would be respected, but the emphasis upon them is stronger elsewhere.

My brief survey of some traditions and some aspects of civility would conclude that civil behavior is continuous with ethics and is part of education. The Confucian ethos of continuing that education through life is important. Self-improvement should have a continuous place in the spiritual life. The Christian concept of the sacred person who reflects the nature of God helps us to see how performatively the person may induce proper behavior in others. Buddhism does not give much sacred significance to the individual, but in its practical advice emphasizes courtesy and respect for persons.

Making Peace:
International Civility and the
Question of Culture

VIRGINIA STRAUS

THE CONCEPT OF CIVIL SOCIETY

Civility derives from the Latin word *civitas,* meaning "city." In human history, the use of the term arose when people moved from agrarian to city life and found themselves living at close quarters with strangers speaking different languages and observing different customs. As they traded together and conducted other activities necessary to city life, they needed to develop workable strategies to communicate across barriers of language and custom. Civility, therefore, was a set of behaviors, involving polite speech, good manners, and respect for the other person, that allowed a community of strangers to live together peaceably.

In political theory, civility is a quality exhibited in the broad social context of civil society. Civil society as a philosophical concept dates back to antiquity, when it was used to refer to the entire society, the whole "polis" as Aristotle put it. However, as the idea was further developed by European political thinkers during the eighteenth and nineteenth centuries, it gradually took on a narrower meaning. Its parameters delineated only that part of a democratic society which is separate from the state. During this period in Europe, as state governments began to assume greater responsibility for military, policing, legal, administrative, and other functions, the pluralistic realm of society that was governed by the state but operated independently from it was dubbed civil society. Among its many parts are the partially autonomous spheres of the economy, religion, culture, intellectual life, and politics.

229

As Tocqueville observed in touring America during the nineteenth century, a vibrant set of civic associations that lie beyond the control of state institutions serves to keep a popularly elected government from becoming oppressive. He noticed the lively relational networks in American society at that time, consisting of a multitude of active voluntary citizen associations busily pursuing various joint purposes and projects. He saw such networks as helping to maintain democratic equality and to prevent tyranny of the minority by the majority in a democracy.[1]

Civic associations also were training grounds, he observed, for the cultivation of good citizenship—a quality of civility—because in these associations individuals could direct their attention to common aims greater than the selfish, conflictual, and narrowly private goals that might otherwise shape the character of public life. In doing so, citizens could experience the satisfaction of cooperation with fellow citizens, and see that they are not independent from their fellows.[2] Because this spirit of willing civic participation has animated no small portion of the American population during its history, America has been presented in political theory as a model of civil society.

Interestingly, during the 1970s and 1980s in the Communist countries of central and eastern Europe, nonviolent revolutions led by political dissidents were fueled by civic associations created initially to provide a refuge from state power. As democracies were established in these countries, the dissidents—now holding political office—defined their first task as one of expanding these emergent civil societies as guarantors against state tyranny. Thus, they went about rebuilding such networks as the unions, churches, political parties, cooperatives, neighborhoods, and the various brands of civic associations so admired by Tocqueville for their ability to sustain a continual "democratic revolution."

CIVILITY WITHIN A CIVIL SOCIETY

One of the writers on this subject who has reflected on the quality of civility and its relationship to a civil society is Edward Shils.[3] Civility and civil society, he says, both postulate a minimal dignity for all citizens. Civility in civil society means regarding others as members of the same inclusive collectivity and respecting them as such. Even one's enemies must be included in this same moral universe. In addition, civility describes the conduct of a person who has a concern for the good of the whole society. In Shils's words, this is a person "whose individual self-consciousness has been partly superseded by his or her collective self-consciousness."

Key features of civility, he says, involve two capacities: the capacity to regard one's fellow citizens with good will and accord them dignified treatment and the capacity, when necessary, to give precedence to the common good over individual self-interest. He also regards civility as an attachment to the institutions of a civil society, a willingness to participate in them and otherwise support and even hold affection for these institutions, since they embody and sustain the civility of the whole society.

Adam Seligman, another writer on this subject, also lays particular stress on the ethical component of civil society. Like Shils, he sees civil society, by virtue of the civil qualities of its citizens, as a crucial arena where the conflicting demands of individual interest and social good can be harmonized, where a balancing of private interest and public responsibility can occur.[4]

In other words, these two writers both point to a quality of respect, care, and concern among fellow citizens—a kind of social solidarity—as one key component of civility and, as the other key feature, a willingness to put the common good above private interest. They see civility as interdependent with the state, serving to cultivate respect, regard, and participation in the institutions of the state, especially as these institutions are led by individuals exhibiting civility in good measure themselves.

Of course, there are lower forms of civility. Sometimes, civility connotes a certain hypocrisy. It is taken to be the outward show of good manners that acts as a smokescreen for self-interested behavior. Benjamin DeMott comments on this kind of civility when, in *Nation* magazine, he sends up the "leader class," who he claims are basically motivated by power and profit these days but are busily criticizing ordinary citizens for the decline in the civility of *their* behavior. DeMott regards the widespread "incivility" among the ordinary masses of people as a justified cynicism toward a morally bankrupt leader class that has no true regard for democratic values.[5] The kind of insincere civility appropriated by an amoral leader class is not at issue here.

Neither is the kind of civility defined in the *Oxford Unabridged Dictionary* as a recent usage of the term. Civility, says Oxford, has sunk in recent use to mean a bare minimum of courtesy, or being not actually rude, as implied in the phrase, keep a "civil" tongue. The civility I would like to discuss is civility in the sense that has become commonly understood among political philosophers and other writers on the subject of civil society, of whom Shils and Seligman are representative. This civility involves respect and care for fellow citizens and a capacity to put the common good over private interest.

INTERNATIONAL CIVILITY AND THE STATE SYSTEM

How can we think about this kind of civility in an international context? There are two social orders we must deal with at the international level: the state system and a far-flung nongovernmental sector. The nation-states that compose the state system are jealous of their sovereignty and competitive with one another. Hard power politics is the prevailing mode of interaction in this society of nation-states. This reflects the workings of *realpolitik* under the dominant "Westphalian Model" of international relations, which traces its origin to the Peace of Westphalia in 1648.

This treaty established a system of territorial states asserting total sovereignty and independence from each other. Were we to imagine these states, for the purposes of our discussion here, as citizens in some larger social order, we can easily see how a society promoting the independence and territoriality of its subjects would prove inhospitable to civil behavior and discourage any displays of such "soft" sentiments as good will and neighborliness. There is not much room for civility here.

This Westphalian order also bears no resemblance to the single moral universe into which civility draws even one's enemies. Instead, the Westphalian model is informed by moral skepticism. Recognizing the state as the basic unit of international society and the sole standard for measuring international conduct, this agreement permits, in fact encourages, a state within the system to see its primary responsibility to be one of pursuing the national interest. Moral principles take a distant second place to a state's immediate interests, whatever they may be.[6]

In practice, the society of nation-states is not much of a society at all. It is a disorganized association of governments that alternately compete for political and economic power and cooperate for mutual benefit. Various regional and international institutions have grown up around their cooperative efforts, from NATO in the military realm to the World Bank and the International Monetary Fund in the economic, from ASEAN to the Big Seven. The workings of these institutions reflect the uneven distribution of power, resources, and military strength among the participating nations, as well as shifting alliances between them.

THE UNITED NATIONS: A SINGULAR HOPE

The one international body with multiple functions that includes all nation-states and does have a moral foundation is the United Nations and the agencies making up the UN system. The United Nations was founded in a rare instance of international unity after the Second World War, based on a profound revulsion against war and a commitment to peace. There are traces of the birth of a true international civility here. The UN's agenda reflects an ethical vision of a world at peace—giving precedence to human rights, disarmament, the elimination of poverty, human development, and, more recently, environmental protection.

In practice, the UN's effectiveness in pursuing these goals has been limited by the reluctance of nation-states to cede any degree of their sovereignty to the UN by giving it the necessary powers of enforcement. It has also been hampered by an undemocratic structure that accords greater power to the five countries that are permanent members of the Security Council. In crucial matters before the UN, the Security Council has greater authority than the General Assembly of all nations.

Therefore, the UN, the one institution with the purpose and potential for putting the good of the whole world over individual state interests—a quality of civility—and for establishing a minimal degree of neighborliness within the world community—another quality of civility—is prevented from doing so by the undemocratic character of its organizational structure and by the sovereignty claims of states represented within this body.

Today the UN, this singular hope, is floundering. It has been subjected to increasing pressure and criticism in the face of mounting
evidence that the global problems the UN is now expected to address
are worsening daily and vastly exceed the reach of its limited powers.
The problems the UN must address are well known. They include:
increasing incidence of ethnic violence, rising levels of poverty as income gaps between and within nations widen, and the dangerous deterioration of ecological systems throughout the world.

OTHER LIMITS ON CIVILITY WITHIN THE STATE SYSTEM

There are other fundamental behaviors of the state system that
militate against civility. Civil discourse among states suffers a fatal
blow when the use of force is employed to resolve disputes. The
UN Charter actually outlaws the use of military force except for self-
defense. It also contains a provision for states to establish a collective security system that would multilaterally enforce this prohibition
against the offensive use of force by a single state. Collective security
did not gain support among the states for obvious reasons during the
Cold War. The end of the Cold War, however, opens the door to revisit
this question, but this is unlikely to happen if the Westphalian model
of international relations prevails.

Another deterrent to civility within the state system is the rudi-
mentary nature of international law. An uneven hodgepodge of treaties on various issues of mutual concern dot the inter-state landscape.
Yet consensus on stronger statutes has been prevented by state sovereignty concerns, and compliance is weak at best. This almost complete
absence of the rule of law at the international level compromises the
foundations on which international civility otherwise might be built
within the state system.

INTERNATIONAL CIVILITY BEYOND THE STATE SYSTEM

As we have seen, civility among nation-states today is practically
a contradiction in terms. Is there any hope for the emergence of international civility anywhere—say, from outside of this inhospitable array
of sovereign states? Does hope lie with the civic associations commonly known as international nongovernmental organizations, NGOs?

NGOs are the primary actors in the second realm of social order at the international level. Since many of these NGOs object to a term that defines them in the negative sense, by reference to what they are not, I will use the preferred term, civil society organizations, or CSOs for short.

Peace scholar Elise Boulding has called the emergence of international CSOs one of the most important developments of the twentieth century. In 1909, there were only 176 international CSOs.[7] Today there are more than thirty thousand. They have come into existence because of a shared concern for human well-being across national boundaries.

The character and scope of these people's associations is extremely varied. They pursue a wide variety of goals in all the fields in which the UN is active—from disarmament to human rights, to sustainable development, and even peacekeeping. They are much more willing than states to work with the UN on the UN's global agenda, and they want to make the UN more effective. Compared to the UN, these organizations have greater flexibility, better access to on-the-ground networks in various regions of the world, and a continuity of interest that political structures, with shifting leadership, lack.[8] Today, international CSOs serve as a training ground for global citizenship as did the civic associations Tocqueville admired in the nineteenth century.

As the problems pressing on the world for its undivided attention have increased, this people's movement has steadily gained more adherents and now presents a strong challenge to the prevailing Westphalian order of the nation-state system. The shared ethical concerns of CSO members are strong motivating and unifying forces. By definition, CSOs possess the capability to put the world public interest over national interests—a key ingredient of civility which sovereign states lack. But they sometimes display their own sovereignty concerns by focusing so exclusively on their particular missions that they miss opportunities to collaborate with one another and to strengthen the standing of the whole movement overall in relation to the state system.

A KEY BREAKTHROUGH:
THE HUMAN RIGHTS DECLARATION

How have these people's associations grown up alongside the system of all-powerful nation-states? Ironically, a key move on which the rapid growth of this movement was based came from the states shortly after the founding of the United Nations. CSOs active on human rights issues prior to the UN's founding were disappointed to see no mention of human rights in the UN Charter. This omission occurred in spite of the fact that public support for the war effort had been generated in large part by an idealistic vision of "establishing the supremacy of human rights everywhere," a phrase used by United States President Franklin D. Roosevelt and echoed by other national leaders.

So, these CSOs pushed for a statement of principles in the form of the Universal Declaration of Human Rights, which was eventually adopted in 1948 due to the leadership of a committee headed by Eleanor Roosevelt. This Declaration and the human rights regime to which it gave birth stand as the greatest legal challenge to every aspect of the Westphalian system.

As human rights specialist Winston Langley has pointed out, the Treaty of Westphalia in effect "defined states as subjects, and vested them with all rights and responsibilities under international law. Individuals, on the other hand, were objects—objects like ships, mud-islands, and boundaries—to which international law applied and had effects." The Human Rights Declaration, by contrast, defined the individual, not the state, as the basic unit of the international community and viewed "the community of individuals as morally prior to the society of states." From this perspective, the Human Rights Declaration becomes a kind of foot in the door for international civility by giving the individual human being and her "moral sentiments" standing in the international arena.[9]

UN CONFERENCES: A GATHERING MOMENTUM

More recently the movement of people's associations has gathered strength from opportunities created by the UN itself. A series of international conferences was held by the UN on various pressing issues in the 1970s, 1980s, and at frequent intervals during the 1990s. CSO forums were permitted to be staged alongside the governmental forums and became particularly active during the 1990s, developing their own agendas for action and pushing the states to make concrete commitments.

Many CSO leaders got themselves appointed to the state delegations that attended the governmental forums and worked as intermediaries between the CSO forums and the official conferees. In this way, these people's associations proved to be adept at influencing state policies and also learned to network together and share information for the sake of common interests, rising above the specialized interests that any one of them might have previously held paramount.

Women's groups proved to be particularly effective in this arena, uniting CSOs and working across their sovereignty lines on common issues. They have shown how civil society groups can unite in common cause across a number of related issues. The late Bella Abzug was a leading figure in these activities, through the worldwide association she founded, Women's Environment and Development Organization.

Partly because of these UN conferences which served to build the social solidarity (a key component of civility) among the CSOs, what Elise Boulding calls "women's culture" has begun to affect this whole movement, creating a new kind of politics. According to Boulding, the women leading international CSOs generally see patriarchy and militarism as closely linked. As they begin to participate in international affairs, the patriarchal order erodes because they refuse to maintain it.

In addition, in the collaborative participatory processes they set in motion through their customary modes of relating to others, they also begin to replace power politics with a politics of mutual aid. The politics of mutual aid is a type of human relations that is fundamentally based on civility, on good will toward one's fellow citizens.[10] Along with an agenda-setting role, the UN has also granted international CSOs on-the-ground operating roles, as the UN has found that CSOs can expand their effectiveness in the field in dealing with humanitarian emergencies, sustainable development, and peace building.

A CHALLENGE TO THE STATE SYSTEM

Most recently, another historic development has occurred in large measure because of the intensive lobbying of CSOs: the creation of an International Criminal Court. This breakthrough reflects a change in international ethics, a new conviction that crimes against humanity cannot go unpunished. The establishment of the Court works with the Human Rights Declaration to further establish the primacy of the human being and human morality in the international order. The Court's statute, by giving CSOs standing to bring complaints to the International Court, in effect recognizes CSOs as agents for the protection and advancement of the common interests of humanity and as a civilizing influence.

An upcoming event is likely to promote greater solidarity and self-organizing capacity among international civil society organizations and thus further strengthen their standing in relation to states. This is a millennial people's assembly that will meet in the year 2000 in New York at the invitation of current Secretary-General Kofi Annan. CSOs have been speaking for some time about the possibility of establishing a CSO voice at the UN, exercising the kind of policy influence they did at the series of world conferences.

There are many who, with Daisaku Ikeda, the founder of the Boston Research Center, believe that a Civil Society Forum at the UN is the way to finally make the fundamental democratic reforms in that body which the states will not make on their own. In his words, "My basic concept is that the United Nations will be properly reformed only when it succeeds in hearing and empowering the voice of the common people."[11]

The challenge being mounted by civil society organizations working alongside UN structures, I am contending, holds out the greatest hope for the emergence of civility in the international order. This people's movement has staying power and the qualities of global citizenship which embody the essential qualities of international civility: they put the common good of humanity above parochial interests and they uphold a standard of human dignity and humane behavior in the international order.

INTO THE NEXT CENTURY

If not from CSOs, the other alternative would be that civility emerges from the community of nation-states themselves. With the end of the Cold War, shouldn't the attention of those nations interested in peace for the sake of the world community turn to institution building? According to Edward Shils, one of the characteristics of a civil citizen is support for, and even love for, the institutions of a civil society.

Unfortunately, the United States is showing the opposite inclination. It is the chief scofflaw on UN dues, setting an example of nonsupport to all the other nations of the world. In addition, its national policy statements fly in the face of the UN Charter in regard to the use of force in international relations. These statements reserve the right to use military force to protect national interests in any part of the world, while the UN Charter clearly states that military force should be used by nations only in self-defense.[12]

Also, the United States, far from exerting a leadership role on peace and disarmament, human rights, environmental protection, and sustainable development—all of the pressing issues of the day—frequently takes obstructive action against international treaties that are clearly in the collective interest of all nations, but compromise in some way the wealth and power of the United States. Its recent bid to be the only nation exempted from the workings of the statute of the new International Criminal Court is just another example of this attitude of incivility on the part of the United States.

To some, it may seem absurd to apply these standards of civility in the present world order. Yet such standards ought to be applicable in a changed world order. In fact, some nation-states are standing up on their own to meet this challenge, in spite of United States leadership in the opposite direction. For example, Spain is seeking to bring Chile's Pinochet to trial in its national court for crimes against Chilean residents even as Pinochet continues to serve in a legislative body of his own country. This represents the first time a state has sought to assert human rights in its own courts for its citizens as well as for citizens not its own against a foreign political leader, holding him criminally accountable for human rights violations that occurred during his rule.

This move, in effect, opens the door for other states to act in this fashion, to hold the collective good of humanity over their own national interest. Should this become the modus operandi in world politics, then the state system could be self-policing in regard to human rights violations. A powerful new enforcement mechanism would be created and the UN, Amnesty International, and the many human rights CSOs throughout the world would find potential partners toward their goals among the most powerful units of the current international order. With human rights fully established in the world, the level of international civility would be greatly improved.

However, because of the prevailing Westphalian model, it is extremely unlikely that other states will rush to follow Spain's example.

And the obverse may be true. Many are already seeking to discourage Spain from its stated goal.

NEXT STEPS: BROADER ETHICAL MOVEMENTS
WITH RELIGIOUS SUPPORT

The key development the world needs now is the evolution of a better organized international civil society, that can more effectively challenge the disordered state system. This is starting to occur through a strengthening of the shared ethical foundations of the CSO movement. What threatens to divide CSOs, however, is interest lines. CSOs specializing in sustainable development and environmental protection work together on their interests. On a somewhat separate track, human rights groups work on theirs.

Only recently have some human rights organizations in the West considered expanding their scope to include development groups as they begin to seek a larger vision of human rights that emphasizes not just civil and political rights but also economic and social rights. In another field, disarmament groups are working together in a broad-based movement, Abolition 2000, to eliminate nuclear weapons and are beginning to develop an even more far-reaching strategy for abolishing war, leading up to the Hague Conference in 1999.

A more integrated ethical vision, with the capacity to inspire the allegiance and understanding of a broader world public, is beginning to take shape in several areas. In these areas, it is developing through an alliance between CSOs and broader cultural resources, most particularly religions. In my view, religions are taking on a role here, seeking in part to atone for past involvement in fomenting war, but also to express the spiritual yearnings of their adherents for world peace.

A brief history is in order. German theologian Hans Küng, working with a group of religious scholars, developed a shared ethical statement for the Parliament of the World's Religions held in Chicago in 1993. This statement sought to build on versions of the golden rule found in almost every world religion to create a larger spiritual vision for a peaceful world. Unable to reach a consensus on exact language, the Parliament nevertheless agreed to give its approval to this document as a stimulus to further public dialogue and named it "Toward a Global Ethic."

In another move, the Interaction Council, a CSO founded by former Prime Minister of Japan Takeo Fukuda, has submitted to the General Assembly for its adoption a draft Universal Declaration of Human Responsibilities to complement the Human Rights Declaration. Hans Küng has also been involved in this initiative. The focus on duties reflects the greater influence in the international order now enjoyed by those religious and cultural traditions, especially Eastern ones, that give weightier emphasis to responsibilities than do the rights-minded traditions of the West.

A project in the environmental area with a strong religious grounding promises to bring new cultural resources and support to what has been a primarily secular environmental movement. The "emerging alliance of religion and ecology," an unprecedented series of conferences and published volumes, has been undertaken during the last three years by Bucknell University professors Mary Evelyn Tucker and John Grim at Harvard's Center for the Study of World Religions. At the project's culminating UN conference, Maurice Strong, senior adviser to UN Secretary General Kofi Annan, took into account these and similar religiously motivated international initiatives when he observed, "I do not believe that our civilization will in fact make it through the next century unless . . . our economic and security and political life is driven by, motivated by, and in the service of our highest moral and spiritual instincts and values."[13]

Today, various ethical strands are being gathered together in a new worldwide social movement launched by the Earth Council and the Earth Charter Commission, of which Maurice Strong and Michael Gorbachev are co-chairs, working with Steven Rockefeller, a religion professor at Middlebury College. The Earth Charter seeks not just to elaborate a new set of ethical principles to guide human-earth relations but also, more broadly, to serve as a people's treaty, providing an integrated vision of the ecological, economic, and social values needed to address the full range of interrelated problems facing humanity.

This Charter challenges the anthropomorphism that has permitted so much destruction of the world's ecosystems. For the first time, the Earth Charter would expand the human community's moral universe to include nonhuman living beings. The religion and ecology project and the Earth Charter are harbingers of hope, promising to draw in new cultural resources and grassroots participation to support the objectives of the CSO movement.

Richard Falk, a scholar of international law, in commenting on the religious dimension of these global movements, has observed that "time partially displaces space as the essence of what the experience of global citizenship means; citizenship thereby becomes an essentially religious and normative undertaking, based on faith in a world to come—not in heaven, but on earth—guided by convictions, beliefs, and values."[14]

THE QUESTION OF CULTURE

These broader global movements indicate that a larger and deeper process than simply the further growth of international civil society is going on here. Peace scholars are beginning to speak in terms of an evolving culture of peace, replacing the dominant culture of violence and war. Or rather, to avoid hegemonic constructions, this evolutionary process might be better conceived as the emergence of numerous cultures of peace. These cultures are enabled to harmonize rather than clash with each other, because a shared ethical and spiritual vision is developing through respectful dialogue.

This is why, at this stage, the UN and UNESCO are beginning to seek broader support for a humane, even spiritual, vision through something called the Culture of Peace Program. UNESCO initiated this program as a peace-building effort in war-torn countries. The UN has decided to expand it by establishing the International Year of a Culture of Peace as the theme during the year 2000.

In addition, peace scholars, who have been working with UNESCO on its culture of peace program, have begun to write and think about peace in terms of culture. Their conviction is that war itself is a cultural invention. Therefore, it can be replaced by another set of cultural inventions that will make it possible for humans to live in dynamic peace with other humans and the earth.[15] Similarly, UNESCO sees the goal of its culture of peace program as nonviolent relations not only between states but also between states and their citizens and between human beings and their environment.[16]

I find this concept of cultures of peace to be an extremely promising one. As a way to think about peace, it has several advantages over the concept of international civility. By progressing from a political idea to a cultural one, we leave behind some cumbersome baggage.

For instance, there's a more inclusive sense to the notion of a culture of peace. Everyone's participation is needed, not just that significant and growing vanguard of international CSOs. Further, this conception of peace cultures does not have the historical connection to city life that the idea of civility does. Therefore, it has a more personal, familial ring to it. The term *culture* holds out the prospect of balancing and integrating modern lifestyles with the lifeways of indigenous, preindustrial, and agrarian societies, implying a recovery of intimacy with the earth. The cultural approach even seems to strike a better balance between the feminine and masculine, since women have historically participated much more fully in the shaping of cultures than they have in the shaping of the public space of city life.

The root word from which culture derives is *cult*, which at least linguistically brings religion back into the picture of peacemaking. The inclusion of religion raises possibilities for drawing on a deeper well of inspirational feeling than mere civility offers. Culture is also tied more closely to education, as its chief means of transmission. Civility, on the other hand, implies training—a learning that is not as deeply rooted and fundamental as education.

MAKING PEACE

Denise Levertov was a lifelong peace activist and a poet, who during her long writing career served as poetry editor of *Nation* magazine. Her poem "Making Peace" suits our topic well. Peace researchers have pointed out that though war can be used as a verb, as in "to war against evil," peace cannot.[17] To activate peace, we must combine it with another word. Also, when Denise Levertov refers to poets, she is addressing all of us, not just people who make poems. All of our imaginative potential and good will is needed to accomplish the cultural change involved in peace making.

> A voice from the dark called out,
> "The poets must give us
> imagination of peace, to oust the intense, familiar
> imagination of disaster. Peace, not only
> the absence of war." . . .
> A feeling towards it,

dimly sensing a rhythm, is all we have
until we begin to utter its metaphors,
learning them as we speak.
A line of peace might appear if we restructured the sentence
     our lives are making,
revoked its reaffirmation of profit and power,
questioned our needs, allowed
long pauses. . . .[18]

It is for all of us to become a voice from the dark, for all of us to carry out the work that derives from imagining peace.

NOTES

1. John Keane, ed., *Civil Society and the State: New European Perspectives* (London: Verso, 1988), pp. 55–62.

2. Ibid.

3. Edward Shils, "The Virtue of Civil Society," *Government and Opposition* 26, no. 2 (Winter 1991): 3–20.

4. Adam Seligman, *The Idea of Civil Society* (New York: Free Press, 1992).

5. Benjamin DeMott, "Seduced by Civility," *Nation* 263 (1996): 11ff.

6. Winston Langley, "The Significance of the Universal Declaration of Human Rights," *Institute of Oriental Philosophy Journal*, forthcoming.

7. Elise Boulding, *Building a Global Civic Culture: Education for an Interdependent World* (Syracuse: Syracuse University Press, 1988), p. 35.

8. Ibid., pp. 35–55.

9. Langley, "Significance of the Universal Declaration of Human Rights."

10. Boulding, *Building a Global Civic Culture*, p. 46.

11. Daisaku Ikeda, "Light of the Global Spirit: A New Dawn in Human History," annual peace proposal (Soka Gakkai International, 26 January 1994), p. 10.

12. Randall Forsberg, *Abolishing War: Dialogue between Peace Scholars Elise Boulding and Randall Forsberg* (Cambridge, Mass.: Boston Research Center for the 21st Century, 1998), p. 57.

13. Edith M. Lederer, "Religious Findings Released by UN," AOL-News @aol.com Press Release, 21 October 1998.

14. Richard Falk, "*Global Visions: Beyond the New World Order*," ed. Jeremy Brecher, John Brown Childs and Jill Cutler (Boston: South End Press, 1993), p. 49.

15. Elise Boulding, "Peace Culture," *Encyclopedia of Violence, Peace, and Conflict* (San Diego: Academic Press, 1999).

16. David Adams and Michael True, "UNESCO's Culture of Peace Programme: An Introduction," in *International Peace Research Newsletter* 35, no. 1 (March 1997): 15–18.

17. Boulding, *Building a Global Civic Culture*, p. 141.

18. Denise Levertov, "Making Peace," in *Breathing the Water* (New York: New Directions, 1983).

Author Index

Subject Index